Talking Politics

Talking Politics

Political Discussion Networks and the New American Electorate

TAYLOR N. CARLSON, MARISA ABRAJANO, AND LISA GARCÍA BEDOLLA

Oxford University Press is a department of the University of Oxford. It furthers the University's objective of excellence in research, scholarship, and education by publishing worldwide. Oxford is a registered trade mark of Oxford University Press in the UK and certain other countries.

Published in the United States of America by Oxford University Press
198 Madison Avenue, New York, NY 10016, United States of America.

CIP data is on file at the Library of Congress
ISBN 978-0-19-008212-3 (pbk.)
ISBN 978-0-19-008211-6 (hbk.)

Lisa and Marisa would like to dedicate this book to APEN, CoCo, SCOPE, and WPUSA, and all the grassroots organizations that work tirelessly every day to make the U.S. political system more equitable, just, and inclusive.

Taylor would also like to dedicate this book to her loving and growing family who first exposed her to politics through conversation.

Contents

Acknowledgments

First and foremost, this research would not have been possible without the generous support and funding of The James Irvine Foundation. We would like to thank Connie Malloy and Virginia Mosqueda for their dedication to these efforts and their unwavering commitment to changing the electorate.

We would like to thank our fantastic editor, Angela Chnapko at Oxford, who was so enthusiastic and supportive of the project. We would also like to thank the anonymous reviewers whose comments improved the content of the book considerably.

Taylor would like to thank her family for all of their support during the data analysis and book-writing process. Without their love and support, this book would not have been possible. She would especially like to thank Baby Boy Carlson for delaying his arrival until after this book was completed and for constantly motivating her. She is also grateful for helpful feedback she received from conversations at the Political Networks Conference (PolNet), thoughtful discussants and fellow panelists from presentations at APSA 2016, 2017, and 2018, as well as conversations with and written feedback on early drafts from Jan Leighley, Tetsuya Matsubayashi, and Sergio Wals. She is also grateful for the patience and support from her coauthors on other projects, especially Jaime Settle, Seth Hill, and Nazita Lajevardi. Finally, she is deeply grateful for the mentorship she received from Lisa and Marisa during this book-writing process. Lisa and Marisa were incredible mentors and collaborators on this project, and it was truly inspiring to work with and learn from such a brilliant team of women.

Marisa would like to thank her family for all their support and patience during the book-writing process. She is also very grateful for the feedback she received from the various talks where she presented this research: ASU, University of Michigan, University of Chicago, USC, UCSD REP (Racial and Ethnic Politics) workshop. Special thanks also go to Agustin Markarian, Cristina Mora, and Stan Oklobdzjia for their superb research assistance. Most especially, she is grateful for her two collaborators, Lisa and Taylor, who were so supportive and collaborative throughout the entire process, and it was really and truly a team effort.

Lisa would like to give thanks to her family for their support and patience as she has been working on this project. As always, she is grateful for the grounding and joy they bring to her life every day. She also wants to express her appreciation for the six community-based organizations that have been part of the broader Integrated Voter Engagement (IVE) study, of which this analysis forms a part—Alliance San Diego, the Asian Pacific Environmental Network (APEN), Communities for a New California (CNC), Community Coalition, SCOPE (Strategic Concepts in Organizing and Policy Education), and Working Partnerships USA. She is humbled by their willingness to engage deeply in coconstructing research and their dedication to improving their own practice and the field. Their staff and volunteers work hard every day to try to make California better. It is a privilege to get to partner with and learn from them. Finally, Marisa and Taylor have been incredible collaborators; Lisa has appreciated their thoughtfulness, commitment, and good humor, all of which made it a pleasure to be a part of this project.

1
Introduction

> I have friends that like go to college and take political science as a major, you know, like and I'm actually able to learn from them as they learn from me because they're learning from textbooks. I'm learning from first-hand experience. You know, like I'd rather speak to someone who actually is in my situation and my shoes, than someone who just is going off of what they read from a book, because it's two completely different things. I mean, I'm not knocking it, because it does give you a better, helps you grasp things a little better . . . But still, that has nothing to do with first-hand accounts.
>
> Male Latino canvasser, Community Coalition

Conversation theory tells us that individuals arrive at meaning through conversation (Pask 1980). Conversation is defined as "the kind of speech that happens informally, symmetrically, and for the purposes of establishing and maintaining social ties" (Thornbury and Slade 2006: 25). In this book we explore the importance of engaging in *political* conversation and talk within political discussion networks for developing connections that foster political engagement. Importantly, this refers to informal discussion "of politics and current events that occurs within a social network of peers: friends, colleagues, family members, and other individuals who are present in our social environment" (Klosftad 2011: 9). We understand intuitively that people might find themselves in conversations about politics or current events. We discuss what is happening in the world with friends. We discuss the latest news with colleagues in the workplace. Growing up, we depend upon our family members, teachers, and others to educate us, through conversation, about how the political system works and what our role is within it. What is so critical about these informal conversations, and one of the reasons why they are so powerful, is that they are casual and impromptu—they are typically the

Talking Politics. Taylor N. Carlson, Marisa Abrajano, and Lisa García Bedolla, Oxford University Press (2020).
DOI: 10.1093/oso/9780190082116.001.0001

byproducts of people going about their daily activities and routines (Downs 1957; Walsh 2004; Klofstad, McClurg, and Rolfe 2009).

Yet we also know that these conversations are happening within very different community contexts; people's social environments are not all the same, particularly along the lines of ethnorace,[1] gender, and partisanship. As the opening quote from a formerly incarcerated Latino male canvasser from the South Los Angeles organization Community Coalition indicates, the types of conversations he has with his community members, and the knowledge he gains from them, matter and are mediated by his life experiences and those of his community. It is important to remember that the political opportunity structures that exist within those social environments vary in important ways (Meyer and Minkoff 2004). This is especially true in areas with high levels of ethnoracial segregation, which has increased in the United States, particularly among Whites (Frey 2015). This ethnoracial segregation may be correlated with partisan segregation. Because White racial identity is highly associated with Republican party identification (Jardina 2019), predominantly White communities are also likely to be predominantly Republican. Similarly, African Americans almost exclusively identify with the Democratic Party (Frymer 2010), meaning that African American communities are likely to be strongly Democratic. Thus, community composition can exert political consequences based on the types of individuals with whom a person may be in conversation (e.g., Huckfeldt and Sprague 1988: 470; Djupe and Sokhey 2014).

Beyond potential geographic homogeneity based on the correlation between ethnorace and partisanship, we know that *political discussion networks* are largely homogeneous in terms of partisanship (Huckfeldt, Johnson, and Sprague 2004; Mutz 2006). Political discussion networks are a subset of one's broader social network, which includes the people with whom one discusses politics (Sinclair 2012). While we know that in general Democrats tend to talk about politics with other Democrats and Republicans tend to discuss politics with other Republicans, we know less about the ethnoracial makeup of these political discussion networks. Because few studies exploring political discussion networks include diverse samples, we know even less about how the partisan composition of political discussion networks varies across non-white groups, with the exception of some pioneering work by Leighley and Matsubayashi (2009).

It is important to consider whether the presumed benefits of political discussion networks are afforded to all groups in the same ways. For instance, research has found that one of the main benefits of political discussion networks is that individuals are exposed to information about politics. When discussion networks are homogeneous, however, individuals are likely to be exposed to information from only one perspective. Being embedded in a political echo chamber can affect how individuals interpret political information. Studies have shown that party identification influences individuals' willingness to believe certain claims, what Bolsen, Lomax, and Cook (2014) call partisan-motivated reasoning.[2] Research suggests that social media may be exacerbating these trends, with the result that people tend to be connected to, and receive information from, those who share their interests (Bisgin et al. 2010; but see Settle 2018; Garrett 2009a, 2009b; Stroud 2008).

Ethnoracial segregation may intensify this tendency to discuss politics with individuals who share the same life experiences and/or worldview. The term *racial segregation* tends to bring to mind concentrations of people of color in particular areas, but it is important to point out that Whites are the most segregated group in U.S. society in the current moment (see Figure 1.1). That is true of their neighborhoods and their

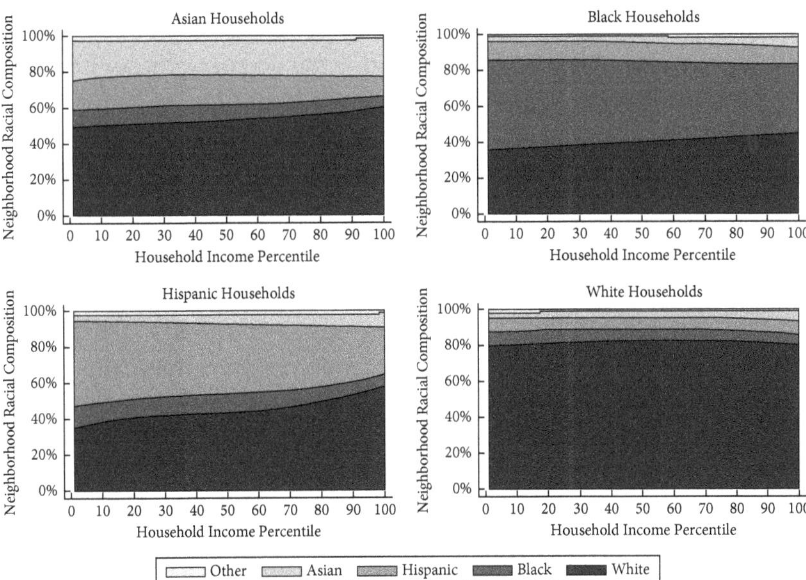

Figure 1.1. Average neighborhood racial composition, by household income and race 2007–2011.

Source: Reardon, Fox, and Townsend 2015.

Note: Figure 5 presents four panels, each of which shows the average neighborhood racial composition by household income, for households of a specific racial/ethnic group for the years 2007–2011. The x-axis is household income, on the national scale, in percentiles and dollars. The y-axis is proportion. Panel 1 presents neighborhood composition for Asian households, panel 2 for black households, panel 3 Hispanic households, and panel 4 white households. As an example of how to read the figure, consider households at the 40th percentile of the household income distribution in panel 1. The typical racial composition in the neighborhoods of Asian households at this income level is close to 50% white, 10% black, 18% Hispanic, 20% Asian, and 2% other.

networks, regardless of income. Yet, the burgeoning literature on political discussion networks has, by and large, been based on majority White samples. That means that what we know about how political discussion networks operate really is what we know about how highly segregated *White* networks operate. Given the high levels of residential segregation among Whites and the particular patterns of participation and partisanship situated among them, we cannot assume that what their political discussion networks look like, and their effects on civic and political outcomes, will be the same for the rest of the electorate.[3]

The goal of this book is to help gain a more comprehensive understanding of the effects of political discussion networks by ethnorace, nativity, and gender. We use an original data set of nearly 4,000 White-, Black-, Latino-, and Asian-American identified respondents, whose nativity also varies. Our data set includes information from both the respondents and their discussion partners to gain a deeper understanding of their political discussion networks. We then merged our original survey data with public voting records to obtain a wealth of additional demographic and political engagement information about each respondent. In addition to this survey, we also conducted more than a dozen qualitative interviews with community organizers to assess how their experiences with political conversations affected their orientations toward politics and their political discussion networks.[4] Taken together, this information provides a rich, detailed portrait of what political discussion networks look like across diverse groups within the electorate and how their impact varies according to voters' relative social positions within U.S. society.

The richness and breadth of our data allow us to explore the political discussion network characteristics across ethnorace, nativity, and gender and to begin to consider the intersections of all these categories. With whom do Blacks primarily discuss politics, relative to Latinos and Asians? Are they mostly family members, coworkers, or friends? Do gender differences arise in Asian Americans' political discussion networks? What role does nativity play for the structure and impact of naturalized voters' discussion networks? Our original data set enables us to address these questions and to provide an important comparative analysis that has largely been missing in the existing research. We are also able to examine the inter- and intraethnoracial, nativity, and gender differences in political discussion network size, partisan composition, and discussion frequency. Additionally, we examine the extent to which these networks are homophilous in terms of policy and political attitudes, political knowledge, and political and civic engagement. The book, therefore, makes three key contributions:

- Expanding the scope of the political discussion network literature by providing a detailed comparative analysis of differences in political discussion network characteristics across and within ethnoracial and nativity groups;
- Demonstrating how historical differences in partisanship, policy attitudes, and engagement are reflected within groups' social networks; and
- Revealing how the social position of our respondents affects the impact that networks can have on their trust and efficacy in government, political knowledge, policy attitudes, and political and civic engagement patterns.

We argue that: (1) most individuals have a limited, closely connected set of people with whom they discuss "important matters," including politics; (2) the makeup of those discussion networks is associated with their relative social positioning, including ethnoracial group membership, nativity, and gender; and (3) given the important relationship that exists between partisan attachments and ethnoracial group membership, political discussion network analysis needs to consider the ethnoracial composition of these networks in order to understand how they affect network members' political attitudes and activity. The empirical analysis that we provide is novel, given that no existing studies have examined comprehensively and comparatively whether political discussion networks are positively associated with political engagement, turnout, efficacy and levels of political knowledge across ethnorace and nativity, and, to a much more limited extent, along the lines of gender.[5] Given the importance that political discussion networks have been found to play in explaining nearly all aspects of political behavior in the United States, it is important to know whether those findings hold for groups of individuals with varying social positions.

In so doing, we are answering Hall and Lamont's (2013: 49) call for political scientists to bring "richer conceptions of social relations" into our analyses, seeing social actors as "relational entities embedded in social and cultural structures that connect them to others in multifaceted ways." They define social relations as "the multiple ways in which people are connected to one another in society" (50). In particular, we are looking at political discussion networks, which comprise one aspect of social relations. We see political discussion networks as empirical phenomena, not observational tools, and as the "agents of change" that decades of research have shown to have "an independent effect on many crucial social processes" (Erickson and Occhiuto 2017: 230; see also Mouw 2006).

Our main innovation is our focus on the inter- and intragroup differences within and among these networks, particularly in relation to ethnorace, nativity, and gender. Although a wealth of political discussion network research examines homophily within networks (Chiang 2007; McPherson, Smith-Lovin, and Cook 2001), very few studies have focused specifically on how political discussion networks might vary by ethnorace and nativity, and there is still work to be done on how discussion networks vary by gender. No studies, to date, have explored how these informal discussions affect non-whites' levels of political engagement and activity, feelings of political efficacy and trust, or levels of political knowledge and attitudes on important policies such as criminal justice and climate change. Thus, one of the main goals of this book is to test whether political discussion networks, as has been shown for White Americans, have a great amount of influence on non-whites' political behaviors and attitudes.

Political Discussion Networks

Our analysis speaks to the broader literature in political science that focuses on the political effects of political discussion networks. Political scientists have long been interested in the influence of social networks on political attitudes and behavior. The seminal work by Berelson, Lazarsfeld, and McPhee (1944) made a strong argument for how influential social networks can be for our political behavior. This research clearly demonstrates that the informal political conversations that occur in our networks can influence our civic and political behaviors, and collective action overall (Abrams, Iversen, and Soskice 2010; Baldasarri and Diani 2007; Bursztyn and Jensen 2017; Centola and Macy 2007; Chwe 1999). Since then, research on political discussion networks in particular has exploded, positing that politics is inherently social and that the more connected we are to other people, the more likely we are to engage in politics (e.g., Zuckerman 2005; Putnam 2000; Huckfeldt and Sprague 1995; Klofstad 2011). When we talk about politics, we are explicitly recruiting our friends and family to become politically involved and engaged (Klofstad 2011).

It is important to note that these informal political conversations, or what Klofstad (2011) refers to as "civic talk," differ in important ways from public dialogue or deliberation (Walsh 2007). The primary difference rests on the fact that public dialogue and deliberations are not casual or informal, and that the social aspect may be less of an influence. As Walsh's (2007) pioneering study of dialogues on the issue of race in midsized cities in the United States reveals, these conversations require a great deal of planning and strategizing among government officials, community leaders, and social justice organizations. Given the deliberate nature of these conversations, they are not the kind that take place unintentionally or as part of one's daily routine. The types of informal conversations captured in Walsh's insightful work (2004) are more in line with our interests here. While we do not take the impressive deep qualitative dive that she does, we hope to capture the composition and impact of political conversations in the everyday lives of Americans from diverse backgrounds.

Why Ethnorace: The Importance of Social Position

In focusing on the role that ethnoracial group membership may play in the structure and function of social networks, we are not arguing in favor of what some have called "identity politics." That formulation of ethnoracial politics in the United States is focused at the individual level, arguing implicitly that differences across groups are simply the product of particular identity choices made by individuals. That is not the claim we are making here. Instead, we argue that ethnoracial group membership in the United States is important because of the impact it exerts on one's social position within U.S. society. That positioning is not under the person's individual-level control. In addition, we are not making an essentialist argument that all group members are "naturally" the same (Beltrán 2013). Rather, we contend that the contexts within which people are situated and the social, economic, and political opportunity structures attached to those contexts affect their political attitudes and engagement. Those contexts, in turn, are shaped by an individual's social position, which, for political and historical reasons, is strongly affected by their ethnoracial group membership. Thus, if we find that Latinos in our study hold similar attitudes, those similarities should be interpreted as a product of U.S. history and politics, not anything "natural" or "essential" about being Latino.

We therefore define a social group as "a collective of persons differentiated from others by cultural forms, practices, special needs or capacities, structure of power, or privilege" (Young 1990). According to Young (1990), what makes a collection of people into a group is "less some set of attributes its members share than the relation in which they stand to others." In other words, defining a particular population as a social group does not mean that we need to assume that all group members are the same, share the same experiences, or have the same goals or aspirations. What is similar (but not necessarily always the same) about the ethnoracial group members is where they are placed in the U.S. racial hierarchy and how that placement has affected their social, political, and economic opportunity structures. As Eveland and Kleinman point out, "political discussion networks are heavily influenced by the opportunity structure of the social settings in which we are embedded" (2013: 84). We would add that those opportunity structures also are influenced by a particular person's social position. Thus, it is important to explore the ways in which political discussion networks vary across groups who hold different social positions—this is a key focus of this book.

These opportunity structures, and the constraints they may place on political behavior, are especially important when considering the target voters in this study—mostly low-income non-white voters. These target voters belong to social groups that historically have been excluded from the polity, which has extended to the present day. Numerous scholars, including Rogers Smith (1997, 2003), have shown how citizenship and inclusion in the U.S. polity was defined ascriptively in terms of both race and gender classifications (see also Jacobson 1998; King 2000; Goldberg 2002; Ngai 2004; Gardner 2005). These studies demonstrate the many ways that discourses of political inclusion and exclusion were the product of explicit public policies, particularly U.S. immigration policies, which were designed to maintain the United States as a White Protestant nation and to materially privilege the White population (Haney-López 1996; Lipsitz 1998; King 2000). These ascriptive understandings, in turn, have been found to affect the development of political thought within non-white communities, as well as approaches to and engagement with political and collective action (Tate 1993; Gutiérrez 1995; Jones-Correa 1998; Cohen 1999; Dawson 2001; Kim 2000; García Bedolla 2005, 2014; Parker 2009). All these factors derive from individuals' social position and play an important role in the structure and function of their political discussion networks.

We therefore reject the formulation that lower levels of engagement among ethnoracial (or any) voters is the result of some sort of individual-level pathology such as apathy or a lack of concern about what is happening in society. Instead, we would frame disengagement in this context as a logical product of having experienced a marginalized social position and the lack of internal political efficacy that can arise as a result. We see political discussion networks as holding the potential to mediate the negative impact of marginalization. Their transformative potential is one of the factors that draws us to study how they vary in terms of composition and impact. But it is important to keep in mind the many ways that these networks reflect and intersect with an individual's social position, be it marginal or privileged.

Social position also carries numerous implications for an individual's ability to exercise individual-level agency. As Masuoka and Junn (2013: 25) point out, "the notion that there is uniformity in political agency—in one's ability to participate, to be mobilized by political parties and elites, to consider political alternatives, to seek and consume political information, to form positions on political phenomena" is widely held by public opinion scholars, but "agency at the individual level is constrained by relative group position." They ably demonstrate that what results is a systematic variation on a vast array of public opinions and topics. This seems to be a simple and obvious point, but the fact of the matter is that scholars often interpret group-level differences as a reflection of individual identification with an ethnoracial group rather than a product of their structural position (as a group member) within U.S. society. As Hancock (2016: 33) explains, "relational power structures lived experiences, the shape of social locations within which people function and interact, and the discursive norms that shape how they understand and interpret the stimuli they encounter." Therefore, an approach to political discussion network analysis that overlooks the role of ethnoracial group membership and social position in those networks, we contend, is incomplete.

Nativity and Political Discussion Networks

Studies examining the impact of nativity, or foreign-born status, on political engagement have found mixed effects. Much of the earlier work focusing on the behavior of Latino and Asian-origin naturalized voters suggested that the foreign born voted at lower rates than those born in the United States (DeSipio 1996; Cho 1999). More recent work, however, particularly studies conducted in California after the anti-immigrant wave of the 1990s, suggests that naturalized citizens voted at higher rates than the U.S. born (Pantoja, Ramirez, and Segura 2001; Ramakrishnan and Espenshade 2001; Ramakrishnan 2005; Michelson and García Bedolla 2014). Explanations for these variations include the context of racial threat (Pantoja et al. 2001), the presence of mobilizing agents, including Spanish language television (Michelson and García Bedolla 2014), and differences in the "group context of participation." The latter explanation draws upon the work of Logan et al. (2012: 994), who see it as a variant of Portes and Rumbaut's (2014) idea of the "context of reception," applied to all Americans instead of just to immigrants. They find that group-level representation among elected officials, local voting regulations, and state-level immigration policies all affect political engagement among naturalized voters. Their context-based findings suggest that the character of individuals' neighborhoods and their institutional contexts, particularly as it pertains to electoral institutions, affect participation patterns.

To our knowledge, no study has comprehensively explored the role that political discussion networks play in fostering or hampering political integration and engagement among naturalized voters. Yet we know that social networks play a central role in integrating immigrants into society more broadly. This vast literature, only some of which we reference here, demonstrates the importance of social networks to immigrants' socioeconomic mobility (DiMaggio and Garip 2012; Lin 1999), employment (Hellerstein, McInerney, and Neumark 2010), health outcomes (Abraído-Lanza, Echeverría, and Flórez 2016; Castañeda et al. 2015; Donato and Duncan 2011), mental health (Almeida et al. 2011; Fu and VanLandinham 2012), ethnoracial identity and assimilation patterns (Balogun 2011; Brown 2006; Mouw et al. 2014; Smith 2010), and migration flows (Curran and Rivero-Fuentes 2003; Davis, Stecklov, and Winters 2002; Erel 2010; Hunter, Luna, and Norton 2015; Jewell and Molina 2009; Liu 2013; McKenzie and Rapoport 2010; for a critique see Krissman 2005). Given the important role that social networks play in numerous aspects of the immigrant integration process, it stands to reason that social networks in general, and political discussion networks in particular, also serve a key function in integrating immigrants politically. Yet very little scholarly research has focused on the ways that political discussion networks can help or hurt how immigrants get integrated into host country politics (for studies looking at immigrant civic integration more generally, see Ebert and Okamoto 2013; Jones-Correa 1998; Stoll and Wong 2007; Ramakrishnan 2005; Ramakrishnan and Bloemraad 2008; Wong 2006). We address this gap in the literature by analyzing the composition and impact of political discussion networks by nativity.

Gender and Political Discussion Networks

Similar to thinking about social position relative to ethnoracial group attachments, it is important to take a nonessentialist view on gender.[6] Iris Marion Young (2005: 493) argued that our society exhibits "multiple logics of gender" that may "have loose or contradictory relationships to the comportments of actual men and women." As such, "gender is better thought of as a set of ideational and social structural relationships that people move through, rather than attributes they have attached to their persons." Like Young, we believe that ethnorace and gender are sociological phenomena that affect people's lived experiences, and therefore how they see and interpret the political world, in a way that is fundamentally different from, for example, age, union membership, or ideology (Omi and Winant 1994).

This approach is similar to Virginia Sapiro and Pamela Conover's (1997) distinction between positional and structural approaches to the study of gender and political behavior. They argue that the positional view assumes that women's and men's political beliefs, values, or issue positions differ, leading them to make different electoral choices. The structural explanation posits that gender will gain political significance through the structure of relationships among political attitudes, values, and judgments. In other words, even if men and women hold exactly the same policy positions, the value and weight they place on each issue, because of their life experiences, will vary, making it possible for men and women to vote similarly, but for very different reasons (Sapiro and Conover 1997: 498).

Thus, if women's political discussion networks look qualitatively different from those of men, it should not be construed to mean that essential differences exist between women and men. Rather, these differences can be understood in terms of political socialization and women's particular social position within U.S. society, and how those two factors affect women's political opportunity structures and worldviews. As Huckfeldt and Sprague (1995: 191–192) point out,

> [g]ender is important because it is a primary element in the structure of social interaction, and processes of social interaction are central to political life . . . Gender is important not simply because being a woman or a man leads individuals to different assessments of political issues or appeals. Gender is important because it is an important structural element imposed on politically relevant social interaction.

In their analysis of the role that gender played in political discussion networks during the 1984 presidential election, Huckfeldt and Sprague (1995) argue that understanding the role of gender within politics requires that we not simply explore whether women's attitudes or behaviors differ significantly from those of men (who are treated as the default category). Instead, they argue that even if there are no differences in the structure of networks among male- and female-identified respondents, the impact and function of those networks could be quite different. Similarly, Morehouse Mendez and Osborn (2010: 278) argue that political discussion, particularly in relation to political knowledge, is affected in important ways by social dynamics, including differences in power and perception between men and women.

With respect to gender effects on political discussion, Huckfeldt and Sprague (1995: 195) find that political discussion is largely "sex segregated." Among the men in their sample, 84 percent named only male conversation partners beyond their family members; among the women, 64 percent named only women as nonfamily discussion partners. In order to tease out the effect of gender segregation in political discussion, they focus on the spousal dyads, seeing if they shed light on the intersection of gender dynamics and political conversation. Their analysis suggests important gender effects. First, although 76 percent of female respondents named their spouse as a discussion partner, only 55 percent of men did (Huckfeldt and Sprague 1995: 198). Second, even when men named their wives as discussion partners, they tended to devalue their wives' political competence. Thus, "[e]ven when men do discuss politics with women, they tend to downgrade the political capacities of women" (203). They conclude that "gender has a pronounced effect on the choice (and evaluation) of discussion partners by men and women" (203).

However, Huckfeldt and Sprague's (1995) analysis was based on a survey conducted in 1984. It is possible that gender norms have shifted during the intervening 35 years, leading to different gender patterns within political discussion networks. Using the 1996 Political Network Election Study, Morehouse Mendez and Osborn (2010) provided an update, at least with regard to the intersection between gender and political knowledge within social networks. They found that both women and men perceive women to have lower levels of political knowledge than they actually do, yet those differences do not affect discussion frequency. In other words, both male and female respondents may perceive that their female discussants are less knowledgeable, but that does not affect how often they engage in political discussion with them (277). Morehouse Mendez and Osborn suggested that these perceptions may help to explain differences in political engagement between men and women.

These perceptions may also affect how women and men engage (or not) in these political discussions. Scholars exploring the role of gender in deliberative democracy arrived at similar results (Karpowitz, Mendelberg, and Shaker 2012; Karpowitz and Mendelberg 2014; Mendelberg and Karpowitz 2007; Mendelberg, Karpowitz, and Oliphant 2014; Mendelberg, Karpowitz, and Goedert 2014). In their analysis of participants' actions in deliberative spaces, Conover, Searing and Crewe (2002: 56) find that "women in particular, do not participate in political discussions because they are systematically discouraged from doing so . . . And, those who do choose to participate often find that men do not accord them mutual respect and that their opinions are not taken very seriously."

The research on gender and social networks would lead us to expect that women's political discussion networks may look and operate differently than men's. What we know less about is how we would expect these gender dynamics to vary by ethnorace and nativity. The political behavior literature has demonstrated that gender also interacts with ethnoracial categories in a variety of ways that affect political engagement (García Bedolla 2005; Wong et al. 2011; Hardy-Fanta et al. 2016; Dittmar, Sanbonmatsu, and Carroll 2018). Seeing intersectionality—the idea that human beings possess multiple identifications simultaneously and that the intersection of those identities exerts important implications for their beliefs, attitudes, and experiences—is important for understanding political engagement among women and men (García Bedolla 2007; Hancock 2016). Among all groups except for Asian Americans, women register and vote at higher rates than men (Carroll and Fox 2018). Women within each ethnoracial group, relative to men within their ethnoracial groups, also tend to identify with the Democratic Party and more frequently vote Democratic (Fraga et al. 2006; Wong et al. 2011). It stands to reason that these differences would affect the composition and influence of their political discussion networks.

We do have some understanding of the way in which gender and nativity intersect within political discussion networks. Gidengil and Stolle (2009) used survey data to explore how women's political discussion partners differed in terms of strong or weak ties and how that affected political incorporation patterns among immigrant women in Canada. Their foreign-born respondents were less politically engaged across all types of activity and were less likely to know about the availability of government services and other public programs (741). They conceptualized homophily among discussion partners as the presence of bonding (homophilous) or bridging (heterogeneous) conversations, hypothesizing that bridging leads to greater political incorporation by exposing the discussion partners to a broader range of information. They found that their foreign-born female respondents' networks included more bridging than those of the Canadian born.

Theoretical Expectations

Existing research has found that three aspects of political discussion networks—network size, discussion frequency, and partisan homogeneity—are the most influential in determining networks' influence on policy attitudes and engagement. In the subsequent chapters, we frame our analysis around these three key network attributes. Based on our analysis of existing research, next we lay out our theoretical expectations regarding how these network attributes will vary by ethnorace, nativity, and gender.

Network Size. There is some empirical evidence that Whites' political discussion networks contain about three to four people on average (Klofstad et al. 2009), but it is difficult to determine what the actual network size is in the real world. Perhaps more important than the average discussion network size, there is a general consensus that the size of political discussion networks matters. In particular, those in larger networks, with more political discussants, are expected to be exposed to more political information, especially when those networks include individuals who have greater levels of political knowledge (Lake and Huckfeldt 1998). Also, individuals in larger discussion networks are expected to be more politically engaged (Knoke 1990; Lake and Huckfeldt 1998; Mutz 2006).

In one of the few social network studies that includes a diverse sample, Leighley and Matsubayashi (2009) found that Whites tend to be in larger networks than are Blacks, Latinos and Asians, with Latinos and Asians having particularly small networks. The authors argued that much of this variation pertains to the supply of possible political discussants being constrained by socioeconomic factors, and the fact that people prefer discussants who are similar to them. Ethnoracial group members, for instance, may prefer to discuss politics with coethnics, but socioeconomic features that can lead some members to be less politically engaged constrain the number of people with whom other members can discuss politics. Their study, however, only examined the effects of networks on policy preferences toward affirmative action and aid to Blacks. As such, there is still much to learn about the role of political discussion networks in explaining the political behavior, knowledge, and attitudes of Latinos, Blacks, and Asians, and how it compares with that of White Americans.

Based on their findings, our expectation is that Black, Latino, and Asian American social networks will be smaller than Whites'. The proportion of individuals' political discussion networks that is made up of coethnics will depend on the size of the coethnic population and the levels of ethnoracial segregation in their neighborhood. This would lead us to assume that White and Latino networks should contain the highest percentage of coethnics, simply due to the relative size of those populations and levels of ethnoracial neighborhood segregation in California. Blacks should be next in terms of proportion of coethnics in their networks because their high levels of residential segregation are mediated by the relatively small size of the Black population in California. Asian American networks should contain the smallest number of coethnics given the relatively small size of the Asian American population and their lower levels of residential segregation.

Considering nativity, the extensive research on immigration and networks has consistently found that migration patterns and employment among immigrants once they have arrived in the United States is heavily dependent on networks. Immigrants tend to settle in places where they have established network contacts, and they thrive more in places where those networks are well connected within the labor market. That would lead us to expect that naturalized voters might have larger networks than the U.S. born. However, the one study we found that considered the relationship between nativity and political discussion networks in Canada, at least among female respondents, found that immigrant women had smaller networks than those born in Canada (Gidengil and Stolle 2009). Within the U.S. context, it is reasonable to assume that time is related to network development and that, therefore, naturalized voters may have simply had less time in the United States to develop their networks.

For nativity, then, we would assume that migration affects network size and composition. Because they may have had less time to develop their networks, we would expect those of naturalized voters' to be smaller than those of the U.S. born. Given the importance of immigrant networks to migration and subsequent employment, we hypothesize that the networks of naturalized voters will include a larger number of foreign-born members than the networks of our U.S.-born respondents.

With regards to our expectations as it relates to gender, we theorize that political discussion networks will be approximately the same size among men and women, but the composition of those networks will likely differ, with women more likely to name family members as discussion partners than men.

Discussion Frequency. Given that Whites tend to say that they are more interested and engaged in politics, compared with Latinos, Asians, and Blacks, we expect that Whites will report discussing politics most frequently. With larger discussion networks, as we anticipate Whites to have, comes the opportunity for more frequent discussion. Similarly, when it comes to nativity, we expect U.S.-born respondents to discuss politics more frequently than their foreign-born counterparts. In addition, discussion frequency may have less of an impact on political engagement given that it is likely that naturalized voters discuss home country politics within their networks, as opposed to U.S. politics. Looking at gender, given the consistent finding that women and their command of politics tend to be undervalued within political discussion but that their discussion frequency remains the same, we would not expect discussion frequency to differ significantly between men and women. However, similar to Huckfeldt and colleagues, we hypothesize that, even when men's and women's networks look the same, their composition and impacts may differ in important ways. Thus, we expect that discussion frequency might have different effects for men than women, even if the overall levels of discussion remain the same.

Partisan Homogeneity. As discussed previously, social networks, broadly speaking, are generally composed of people who are more similar to each other than they are different (McPherson et al. 2001). The primary explanation for this is homophily—the idea that individuals self-select into social relationships with people who are similar to them (Knoke 1990; McPherson et al. 2001). When it comes to politics, this means that we should expect political discussion networks to be largely homogeneous, which we define here as partisan heterogeneity. However, substantial debate continues to persist in the literature about the level of disagreement within political discussion networks (Klofstad, Sokhey, and McClurg 2013). On one hand, Huckfeldt et al. (2004) argue that a surprisingly large amount of disagreement exists in political discussion networks. On the other hand, Mutz (2006) argues the levels of disagreement reported by Huckfeldt and colleagues are largely overstated. Klofstad and colleagues (2013) argue that the core of this debate is methodological in nature, and depending on the way scholars measure disagreement, the statistical results will vary considerably.

These studies, however, are based on largely White samples and fail to differentiate among network members by ethnorace. We expect the partisan composition of ethnoracial minority political discussion networks to differ from those of Whites for several reasons. First, we know that partisan allegiances vary across ethnoracial groups. For example, Blacks tend to overwhelmingly support the Democratic Party (Frymer 2010; Dawson 1994), whereas the partisan allegiances of Latinos and Asian Americans are not as firmly rooted with one political party (Alvarez and García Bedolla 2003; Abrajano and Alvarez 2012). To the extent that individuals of the same ethnorace tend to find themselves sorted—intentionally or otherwise—into ethnoracially homogeneous communities (Leighley and Matsubayashi 2009), we should expect Blacks' political discussion networks to be more Democratic when compared with Latinos' and Asian Americans' discussion networks. Given that a large proportion of Asian and Latino immigrants do not identify with a political party (Hajnal and Lee 2011), it could also be that there will be more partisan diversity, meaning the presence of nonpartisans, in their political discussion networks than in those of Blacks.

Similar to the disagreement over the amount of dissention present in discussion networks, considerable debate exists over the influence of political diversity on political behavior. On the one hand, Mutz (2002, 2006) argues that exposure to alternative political views can make people more tolerant of those on the other side of the aisle at the cost of making individuals politically apathetic. Mutz argues that individuals who are exposed to multiple, disagreeable points of view are more likely to feel "cross-pressured," second-guess their initial views, and ultimately opt out of political participation. On the other hand, Scheufele and colleagues (2004) argue that individuals in heterogeneous political discussion networks are *more* likely to participate. The authors suggest that exposure to different views increases knowledge and political interest and inspires information-seeking behavior that can be politically mobilizing. Thus, there is an ongoing debate about both (1) how much political disagreement exists in political discussion networks and (2) how disagreement impacts political behavior.

Considering the relationship between disagreement and partisanship, individuals could be deliberately sorting into political discussion networks based on (dis)agreement (e.g., Bello and Rolfe 2014), instead of another reason, like ethnorace (Knoke 1990). Yet, the race and politics literature within the American politics subfield has made it clear that the political behavior of ethnoracial minorities is often distinct from that of U.S.-born White Americans (for African Americans, see Dawson 1994, 2001; Pinderhughes 1990; for Latinos, see Abrajano and Alvarez 2012 and García Bedolla 2005, 2014; for Asian Americans, see Wong et al. 2011 and Hajnal and Lee 2011). In particular, Hajnal and Lee (2011) find that individual-level attachments to the two main U.S. political parties vary significantly by nativity. This distinctiveness in political behavior and party identification suggests that naturalized voters' social networks may look different than they do for U.S.-born White Americans, particularly in terms of partisan composition. At a minimum, whether or not this is the case is an open empirical question, one that has not been addressed adequately in the existing literature (for an exception see Leighley and Matsubayashi 2009).

Part of this omission may be due to data limitations, since most of the existing research uses data with very small samples of ethnoracial group members or of those born outside of the United States (e.g., Huckfeldt and Sprague 1995; Huckfeldt et al. 2004; Mutz 2006; Berelson et al. 1944; but see Leighley and Matsubayashi 2009). Yet, it nonetheless leaves a significant gap in the political discussion literature. With our analysis, we hypothesize that partisan homophily within political discussion networks among ethnoracial group members will follow the same patterns we see in partisan identification overall: Black networks will be strongly Democratic, White networks will lean more Republican but contain more variation, and Latino and Asian American discussion networks will be the least partisan. Similarly, we would predict that our foreign-born respondents' networks will be less partisan than those of the U.S. born, simply due to the fact that most are Latino and Asian origin—the two groups found to have the least strong partisan attachments—and that party identification can be expected to get stronger over time in the United States.

Finally, because of the strong social norm to avoid conflict in conversation, particularly among women, we would expect women's, relative to men's, political discussion networks to be more homophilous in terms of partisanship (Tannen 1991). When it comes to attitude formation, we expect network composition to be more influential among women than men because women tend to be more likely to conform in political discussion contexts (Settle and Carlson n.d.). It is difficult to develop strong expectations about how network characteristics might affect political knowledge differently among men and women, given that knowledge measures can exaggerate gender gaps (Kraft n.d.).

In light of the rapid demographic changes over the past fifty years in the United States, understanding the ways in which political discussion networks are formed and how they affect the political behavior of non-whites and the foreign born is of even greater import. More importantly, the potential benefits of political discussion networks—distributing political information and mobilizing individuals to action—might not operate in the same ways, if at all, for non-whites whose experiences and relationships to U.S. politics may vary significantly from those who have been the primary focus of study in most existing research.

Networked Politics: Situating Discussion Networks in Context

Bringing together these varied strings of literature leads us to a different way of thinking about the structure and function of political discussion networks. In particular, we argue that network scholars need to situate their political discussion network analyses within contextual and historical space. Decades of research have shown the important differences across groups in terms of their neighborhood contexts, their opportunity structures, and their basic civil rights. Given that most of the network analysis to date has included majority White samples and that Whites tend to be the most racially segregated of any group in U.S. politics, perhaps the finding that social networks tend to be politically homophilous is simply an artifact of the lack of diverse individuals available to most Whites to become network members. Similarly, one can imagine that the role that networks played in Black politics during the civil rights movement is quite different from the role they play in Black politics today. It logically follows, then, that these types of factors influence the network contexts within which these group members are situated.

We also must take more seriously the integrating role that political discussion networks can potentially play in U.S. politics. In 2017, 44.5 million immigrants lived in the United States, making up 13.5 percent of the population.[7] Although these individuals come to the United States with some sense of U.S. history, culture, and politics, it is still necessary that they be integrated into the U.S. political system once they arrive. Most immigrants arrive in the United States with established networks that facilitate their social and economic integration. Studies have shown that these networks provide migrants with important information about jobs, neighborhoods, schools, and other factors that help them to navigate a confusing landscape. Given that networks have been found to be so important to the immigrant integration process overall, it stands to reason that those same networks, if they contain political discussion and information, could play an important role in facilitating their integration into politics as well. That is one of the central questions our study attempts to shed light on.

However, these integration processes are difficult to demonstrate empirically, particularly with cross-sectional data such as the survey that forms the basis for this book. A central question is whether individuals choose networks because they contain others who agree with them or have a particular set of political characteristics, or whether the network moves the individual to adopt different attitudes and/or behaviors. Pinpointing that causal direction is an empirical challenge that several scholars aim to address (e.g., Song et al. 2016; Sinclair 2012; Bello and Rolfe 2014; Klofstad 2011). Klofstad's research, in particular, offers a novel approach to addressing the endogeneity problem by designing a quasi-experimental panel survey, known as the Collegiate Social Network Interaction Project, that randomly assigns University of Wisconsin, Madison, students to different discussion groups. Then, some of the groups are randomly assigned to talk about politics, while others are not. By doing so, Klofstad seeks to identify a causal relationship between political discussion networks and political engagement. His findings reveal that talking to people leads individuals to become civically engaged via recruitment and engagement. That is, when we talk to our friends and family about politics, we are often explicitly asking them to become politically involved.

While our research design prevents us from tackling the issue of causality head on, research by Klofstad (2011) and others provides strong evidence that our social environment influences our political behavior, and not vice versa. Additionally, 40 percent of the political discussion network relationships we analyze in this study were among relatives—a spouse, parent, child, or other relative. While it is true that we choose our partners, the other network members our respondents identified as family were not selected by choice. This suggests that it is reasonable to assume that at least some of the network effects we find are the product of being within the network itself, rather than of individuals "shopping" for a network that suits their political needs. Even without solving the endogeneity problem endemic to network analysis, we are still able to make important contributions to the literature. At a minimum, we test the degree to which political homophily exists within political discussion networks across the groups included in our sample and whether or not its impact has different effects on the respondents' reported political behavior patterns and validated voter turnout.

Our analysis shows that the individual-level differences that scholars have demonstrated in participation patterns among ethnoracial group members and naturalized voters are reflected in our respondents' political discussion networks. This may seem like an intuitive finding, but it is one that has not been subject to many rigorous empirical tests (the one exception is Leighley and Matsubayashi 2009). Our results underscore not only the degree to which individuals engage with politics in conversation, but also the view that those conversations are situated within broader opportunity structures that are demographically and attitudinally distinct from one another. Developing a better understanding of the implications of those differences should be the focus of future research.

Plan of the Book

Chapter 2 begins by providing a discussion of the challenges faced by research in studying the discussion networks of ethnoracial minorities. We then introduce our approach to overcoming some of these issues in our 2016 Political Discussion Network Survey (PDNS). Additionally, we conducted several in-depth qualitative interviews to supplement this data and offer a detailed explanation of the interview protocol in this chapter.

In Chapter 3, we provide a comprehensive analysis of political discussion network characteristics by ethnorace, nativity, and gender. We first compare the composition of discussion networks (are they family, close friends, acquaintances, or coworkers?) as well as the three network characteristics that the existing research has found to be most consequential in explaining political behavior: (1) the size of our respondents' discussion networks, (2) the frequency of political discussion within them, and (3) the degree of partisan homophily they contain. In order to understand fully the complex relationships we unpack throughout this volume, we believe it is important that our reader understand our data, particularly the descriptive characteristics of our sample. We find that the composition and character of these political discussion networks vary in important ways. For instance, naturalized and non-white individuals are embedded in smaller networks that are more politically diverse in terms of partisanship than those of the U.S. born.

We then analyze the factors that could explain the size of individuals' networks, how often they discuss politics in their networks, and the degree of partisan homogeneity that exists in their networks. After taking into account both individual-level and contextual-level factors, the findings suggest that membership in either a religious or secular group is associated with larger and more informationally rich networks, though it is important to note that these patterns are not uniform across ethnorace, nativity, and gender.

Chapter 4 explores the relationship between crucial precursors of political and civic engagement, political trust and political efficacy, and political discussion networks. The extent to which individuals feel that their voice matters in politics, and that they have faith in what the government does, is critical in determining whether individuals become politically engaged, particularly for socially marginalized groups (García Bedolla 2005). Once again, we focus on network size, discussion frequency, and partisan composition and uncover important variations by ethnorace, nativity, and gender. We find that network discussion characteristics are a much stronger predictor of political efficacy than they are of political trust.

In Chapter 5, we turn our attention to the relationship between political discussion networks and information. The goal of this chapter is to determine the role that information plays in one's discussion networks, and how it goes on to influence one's levels of political knowledge as well as policy opinions and preferences. We consider three possible ways that information flows through a network—frequency of political discussion within the network, the size of the network, and the partisan composition of the network.

Our evidence supports the conventional wisdom regarding the importance of political discussion networks in the formation of issue preferences as well as in enabling individuals to become more politically knowledgeable. However, our results also suggest that network effects are not uniform across ethnorace, nativity, and gender. Overall, we find that frequent political discussions with one's network has a positive impact only on Asian Americans levels of political knowledge. When we compared network effects between U.S.-born and foreign-born respondents, we generally found them to have more predictive power for U.S.-born respondents, who have had more time to develop their social networks. Gender differences also emerged, such that women's discussion networks aided in their gains of political knowledge to a larger extent than men's did.

The final empirical analysis, presented in Chapter 6, focuses on political and civic engagement and its relationship to network composition. Political discussion networks have long been shown to play an important role in political engagement. We analyze the ways in which political discussion network characteristics predict self-reported civic and political engagement and validated voting patterns by ethnorace, nativity, and gender. Our analysis provides some evidence that frequency of political discussion is a positive predictor of political participation. The degree and strength of copartisanship in one's networks, however, tend be less robust predictors of political participation and turnout. In our analysis of gender differences, we find that all three network attributes positively predict self-reported political engagement for both men and women.

Our final chapter summarizes our main research contributions and findings and offers some guidance and possible next steps for researchers interested in deepening our understanding of the way political discussion networks operate along the lines of ethnorace, nativity, and gender. It is our hope that our research endeavors offer just a first step in a very fruitful avenue for future efforts.

Conclusion

Individuals experience politics in community. We discuss and watch elections with our friends; we watch the news with our family; we argue and debate about policy with our coworkers. Our understanding of our social position within U.S. politics is the product of years of conversation and interaction with our community members. Yet, the dominant methods political scientists have used to understand political behavior, such as observational and experimental research, primarily use the individual as the level of analysis. The beauty of social network analysis, and political discussion networks more specifically, is that it allows us to begin to unpack the *social* aspects of the political *socialization* process in order to better ascertain how those political conversations affect our ongoing engagement with politics.

Decades of scholarship on race, politics, and political socialization make it clear that marginal groups are situated within a different set of opportunity structures than the majority. It stands to reason that those differences are reflected in their political discussion networks. Our research endeavor, therefore, gives us an important window into those differences and, perhaps, helps us to better understand the reasons underlying the variations in political engagement that exist across these groups. In the next chapter, we provide a detailed discussion of what we believe to be one of the main contributions of our research efforts, which is the designing and fielding of the 2016 PDNS survey.

2

Empirical Shortcomings

Why Do We Know So Little about Non-White Networks?

While there is a large and burgeoning literature on political discussion networks, it focuses almost exclusively on White Americans who hold a more privileged social position in U.S. society and were socialized into politics in the United States. Most political discussion network research relies on surveys that include a discussion network battery, including a name generator in which respondents list people with whom they discuss politics or important matters, and then answer a series of questions about their discussants. Large, nationally representative surveys such as the American National Election Study (ANES), General Social Survey (GSS), and Comparative National Election Project (CNEP) have occasionally included these name generators in their surveys, which have provided a wealth of information on political discussion networks from nationally representative samples (e.g., Eveland 2004; Leighley 1990; Huckfeldt, Mendez, and Osborn 2004; La Due Lake and Huckfeldt 1998; Klofstad et al. 2013). However, nationally representative samples often lack large enough samples of non-white respondents to make meaningful inferences about their discussion networks or political behaviors and attitudes. As a result, scholars have insufficiently discussed or explored variation in political discussion networks across groups by ethnorace, nativity, and/or gender.

Beyond the nationally representative surveys that occasionally include discussion network batteries, some of the seminal research on political discussion networks comes from convenience samples that are not generalizable beyond the White community. The pioneering research by Lazarsfeld, Berelson, and Gaudet (1944) relied on interviews with residents in Erie County, Ohio, in 1940. This data made a major contribution to the literature and produced *The People's Choice*, which is one of the most seminal works on political behavior.[1]

Decades later, Huckfeldt and Sprague embarked upon another impressive data collection effort in creating the Presidential Election Campaign Study (the 1984 South Bend Study)[2] and the 1996 Indianapolis—St.

Talking Politics. Taylor N. Carlson, Marisa Abrajano, and Lisa García Bedolla, Oxford University Press (2020). © Oxford University Press.
DOI: 10.1093/oso/9780190082116.001.0001

Louis (ISL) Election Study[3] data sets. In both data collection efforts, the authors interviewed a large sample of registered voters in their communities of interest, followed by a one-stage snowball sample survey of the initial respondents' named political discussants (see Huckfeldt et al. 2004: 14, for a discussion of the ISL study).[4] This impressive data collection allowed for an incredibly rich analysis of individuals' political discussion networks by providing detailed information on both the initial respondents *and* their political discussants, beyond simply their perceptions of their discussants. Both of these data sets have been invaluable in advancing research on political discussion networks. However, despite what they gain in detail, depth, and rigor, they lack generalizability beyond the White population.

Research relying on convenience samples of predominantly White communities or nationally representative samples that lack sufficiently large samples of non-whites make it difficult for researchers to understand fully how political discussion networks operate within an increasingly diverse society. Some research has shed light on this question, such as Leighley and Matsubayashi's (2009) analysis of the 1992–1994 Multi-City Study of Urban Inequality data. However, most authors continue to rely upon nationally representative surveys, without consideration for the very real possibility that discussion networks operate differently for groups within the electorate whose experiences and understanding of the U.S. political system can vary. To be sure, some existing studies do account for ethnorace, most often by using a dummy variable for whether a respondent is White or non-white. But, only including a dummy variable of this type tells us little about potential variation among different ethnoracial minority groups, who can have unique political experiences (see Tate 1993; García Bedolla 2005; Wong et al. 2011). Simply accounting for ethnorace as a White/non-white binary treats ethnoracial groups as homogenous, not allowing exploration of within-group variation. Such assumptions are particularly troublesome for Latinos and Asian Americans, both of whom are panethnic groups that include individuals from highly diverse socioeconomic and ethnoracial backgrounds, of different nativities, and countries of origin.

Ultimately, we know a great deal about political discussion networks among the White majority, but empirical limitations have prevented us from thoroughly understanding the extent to which these findings can be generalized to non-whites. The same limitations also exist for scholars interested in studying variations across nativity. And rather surprisingly, variations in the political discussion networks across gender have also received fairly limited attention (see Huckfeld and Sprague 1995 and Sokhey and Djupe 2014 as exceptions).

Our Empirical Approach

The empirical analysis for this book relies upon data from an original survey that we designed and fielded in order to understand the network characteristics of voters along the lines of ethnorace, nativity, and gender. Our 2016 Political Discussion Network Survey (PDNS) is notable for its diverse sample of respondents, coupled with a battery of discussion network questions. In addition to this survey data, we also conducted qualitative interviews of individuals who are charged with canvassing, and therefore talking about politics with their communities.

Survey

Given our theory and goals of this project, we had no intention of conducting a nationally representative survey. Just as the Midwest was an ideal case study for understanding discussion networks among White Americans (e.g., Huckfeldt and Sprague 1995), the state of California provided an ideal setting where we were able to collect a sizable number of respondents from the four major ethnoracial groups in the United States, Whites, Blacks, Latinos, and Asian Americans, given that the state's population is majority-minority (meaning that a majority of the population is non-white). California's large foreign-born population also enables us to achieve variation by nativity.

Consistent with practice within the social networks field, the survey instrument included a social network battery including a name generator in which respondents listed up to five people with whom they "discussed important matters." Respondents then answered several questions about each person they listed, followed by a host of demographic, political attitude, and political engagement questions. We then merged our survey results with the California voter file to obtain respondents' validated vote histories, party registration, and other demographic information.

To conduct the 2016 Political Discussion Network Survey, we partnered with four community groups that work primarily with voters of color.[5] Specifically, we worked with Community Coalition (CoCo), Strategic

Concepts in Organizing and Policy Education (SCOPE), Working Partnerships USA (WPUSA), and Asian Pacific Environmental Network (APEN). Both SCOPE and CoCo work in South Los Angeles. SCOPE's mission is to reduce structural barriers to economic and social opportunities for the poor and working-class African-American, Latino, and immigrant communities in South Los Angeles. CoCo was founded by Congresswoman Karen Bass, and it also works to improve the economic, social, and political conditions for South Los Angeles residents. Our other two groups are based in Northern California. WPUSA works with communities of color and immigrants in the Silicon Valley and advocates for affordable housing and living wages. Finally, APEN works primarily with Asian and Pacific Islander communities on issues of environmental, social, and economic justice. While APEN's offices are based in Oakland, California, it conducts outreach among Asians and Pacific Islanders across the state.

Our partnering community organizations provided us with the voter identification numbers of all individuals whom they had targeted for contact in the November 2016 election. Individuals' email addresses were made available by the voter file vendor that we worked with, Political Data, Inc. (PDI); in total, we acquired 250,000 email addresses. We then randomly sampled respondents, proportional to the number of contacts provided by each organization to be surveyed. We offered survey incentives in the form of a five-dollar Amazon gift card.[6] Because we have voter file information on all individuals invited to the survey, we can check to see how our survey respondents differed from those who declined to participate on several observable dimensions including age, race, income, gender, vote history, and party registration.[7] The overall response rate was approximately 3–4 percent; surveys were administered from December 1, 2016, through January 1, 2017.

As we discussed earlier, participants who completed the survey were asked to name up to five people with whom they discussed important matters. The final survey question asked participants to provide the email addresses for each person they named so that we could invite them to participate in the survey as well. We obtained 1,210 valid email addresses and invited all 1,210 individuals to complete the same survey on January 9, 2017. About 80 invitation emails bounced, and a total of 276 individuals completed the survey, yielding a response rate of about 24 percent. We had reason to believe that the response rate was higher in the snowball sample for three possible reasons. First, those who are likely to complete an online survey are probably socially connected to other people with similar traits, meaning that the friends of survey takers are more likely to also be survey takers. Second, our first survey respondents might have told their friends to expect a survey invitation and a $5.00 Amazon gift card. Third, our first survey respondents could have had more accurate or recent email addresses than those we obtained from the organizations' contact lists and PDI.

Somewhat to our surprise, the response rate across ethnoracial groups varied dramatically. Asian respondents comprised the bulk of our sample, approximately 50 percent, which left us with relatively small samples of Black, Latino, and White respondents. To address this imbalance, we conducted an oversample of Black and Latino respondents who were not randomly selected to be invited to complete the first survey. We invited about 48,378 Latino and 46,297 Black individuals to participate in the survey on April 27, 2017.[8] In total, 3,569 emails bounced from the Latino sample and 4,897 emails bounced from the Black sample.[9]

Just as in the original survey, participants in the Latino-Black oversample were asked to name people with whom they discuss important matters, and they were also asked to provide contact information for those people. Of the contact information received, we sent an email invitation to 283 individuals to participate in the survey on May 30, 2017. About 29 invitation emails bounced, and we sent reminder emails on June 2, 2017 and June 5, 2017.[10]

Survey Sample Characteristics

A total of 3,815 individuals responded to our survey. Figure 2.1 provides an overview of the basic demographic characteristics of our respondents. By design, our sample contains a much larger percentage of non-white respondents than what we would typically find in a public opinion survey. Just slightly more than 50 percent of our respondents identify as Asian American, 18.3 percent identify as Black, 22.9 percent as Latino, 6.3 percent as White, and the remaining 1.7 percent identify as "other." About 57.1 percent of our sample is female, while about 42.9 percent is male. Approximately 16.6 percent of our survey respondents reported being born in another country,[11] 57.9 percent of our respondents reported that neither of their parents were born in the United States, and about 29.5 percent reported that both of their parents were born in the United States. According to the U.S. Census Bureau, 27 percent of California's population is foreign born. Using data from the voter file, we can see that consistent with state and national trends, Asian

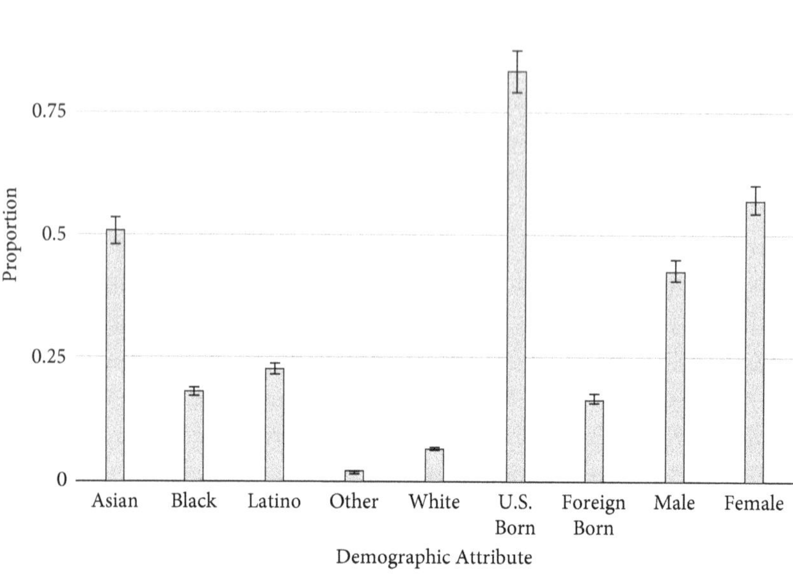

Figure 2.1. Demographic attributes of survey respondents.

respondents resided in census blocks with the highest median income of about $65,611, relative to White respondents at $53,664. Black respondents lived in census blocks with a median income of approximately $39,033, and Latino respondents at $39,433.[12]

Official party registration data suggests that our sample was composed primarily of Democrats (63.8 percent) and those who decline to state their party (28.2 percent), with only about 7.9 percent of our sample being registered Republicans. This Democratic skew is likely due to a combination of: (1) the sample being drawn in California, (2) the sample focusing on non-whites who tend to register and vote Democratic at higher rates than Whites, and (3) the sample being drawn from individuals who were previously contacted by organizations who work to engage voters in communities of color. Our sampling frame was somewhat more politically active than the California and U.S. public overall. For example, 78 percent of individuals in our initial sampling frame turned out to vote in November 2016, while 75.3 percent of registered voters and 58.4 percent of the voting eligible population in California turned out to vote in that election. Those who actually completed the survey were even more engaged, with about 84.5 percent turning out to vote in November 2016.

Again, given that our main research question and hypotheses focus on the social network characteristics of individuals from diverse backgrounds, our sample was not intended to be nationally representative in nature. Thus, we realize that these findings may not be generalizable at the national level, but we believe our results are instructive given our ability to explore these questions across and within ethnorace, nativity, and gender.

Externally Validating Our Survey

We fully recognize that our survey data is not without its limitations. First and foremost, the respondent population is restricted to just one state: California. We focused on this particular state due to its sizable percentage of both immigrants and the four major ethnoracial groups in the United States—Whites, Blacks, Latinos, and Asian Americans. Moreover, because our sample came from individuals whom community organizations had in their contact lists, it is likely that our sample varies from the average voter along the lines of ethnorace, gender and nativity. In addition, those who had valid email addresses on file, who had spam filters that did not screen out our survey invitation email, and who ultimately completed the survey are likely different from those who did not complete the survey. Finally, although the characteristics that make someone more or less willing to complete an online survey might not be related to our outcomes of interest, we cannot know that for certain.

To address the concern about the nonrepresentative nature of our respondent population, we analyzed three nationally representative surveys that include a name generator and, to the extent possible, a large enough sample size of non-white individuals for us to make comparisons.[13]

Three surveys fit these criteria: (1) the 1992–1994 Multi-City Study of Urban Inequality (MCSUI) was conducted in Atlanta, Boston, Detroit and Los Angeles,[14] used by Leighley and Matsubayashi (2009); (2) the 2004 General Social Survey, which is conducted by the National Opinion Research Center;[15] and (3) the 2008–2009 American National Election Panel Study.[16]

Table 2.1 offers a breakdown of the respondents for each of these surveys, by ethnoracial group. By far, MSCUI contained the largest number of non-white respondents; the study interviewed 1,390 Latinos, 2,179 Blacks, 2,953 Whites, and 1,128 Asian Americans. Both the GSS and ANES contain fewer non-white respondents relative to our survey. For

Table 2.1. Comparison of Surveys with Name Generators

	Latino	Black	White	Asian American
MCSUI	1390	3179	2953	1128
GSS 2004	75	374	2222	101
ANES 2008–2009	275	492	3292	90
2016 Political Discussion Network Survey (PDNS)	804	643	220	1790

instance, our survey contained 804 Latino respondents, compared with 75 Latino respondents in the GSS and 275 in the ANES. The number of Asian American respondents also vary by survey. While our survey interviewed 1,790 Asian American, only 90 Asian American respondents were in the ANES and 101 in the GSS. Thus, just in terms of sheer sample size, our survey comes closer to the respondent demographics of the MSCUI than the GSS or ANES.

It is also important to recognize that variation exists across the surveys on the exact question wording of the name generator, the types of network characteristics included in the questionnaire, and the number of discussants that respondents were asked to provide. It ranged from a minimum of three in the MCSUI to a maximum of eight in the 2008–2009 ANES; we nonetheless recognize the importance of validating our study with existing ones.

Comparisons of Network Relationships

Table 2.1 compares the network relationships in one's political discussion networks across these four surveys. Similar to the patterns that emerged in our survey, as we discuss in more detail in Chapter 3, relatives and close friends comprise the bulk of respondents' political discussion networks, irrespective of ethnorace. One might wonder why the percentage of relatives in the MCSUI survey is lower compared with the other surveys; the reason for this discrepancy is that the survey question did not permit respondents to name their spouses as discussion partners. Given that one's spouse or partner is frequently named as a discussion partner (see our detailed breakdown of network relationships in Chapter 3), it helps to explain why these percentages are markedly lower than in the other surveys. Following friends and relatives, coworkers and other acquaintances round out one's discussion network. Overall, the similarity in who comprises the majority of discussion network members across all the surveys gives us reassurance about the validity of our survey results.

Comparisons of Copartisanship. In terms of the copartisanship in one's networks, we can only compare our distributions with those from 2008–2009 ANES (which are presented in Table 2.2). Similar to the PDNS, the ANES reveals that Blacks have the largest percentage of copartisans in their

Table 2.2. Comparison of Network Characteristics across Different Surveys

MCSUI	Latino	Black	White	Asian Americans
Relative	26.0	30.6	25.6	18.5
Friend	40.4	36.5	40.1	32.6
Coworker	3.0	3.8	9.4	3.2
Other	9.2	5.5	7.3	4.1
GSS				
Relative	88.2	56.7	101.4	70.5
Friend	50.0	37.5	53.9	36.4
Coworker	17.7	10.1	18.3	18.2
Other	2.9	3.9	3.5	22.7
ANES				
Relative	72.7	39.8	77.9	46.7
Friend	NA	NA	NA	NA
Coworker	NA	NA	NA	NA
Other	NA	NA	NA	NA
2016 PDNS Survey				
Relative	42.5	42.4	45.1	36.9
Friend	33.2	35.0	36.4	40.6
Coworker	14.4	12.5	10.3	13.6
Other	9.9	10.0	8.2	8.9
Copartisanship (PDNS)	57.0	61.8	53.3	53.7
Copartisanship (ANES)	60.5	80.1	64.6	58.1

Note: All entries are percentages. In the GSS, participants could select all relationships that applied to a given discussant (e.g., a discussant could be a spouse and a coworker), so the relationship categories for the GSS are not mutually exclusive. Moreover, the "relative" category sometimes combines responses for specific familial relationships (e.g., sibling, spouse, parent). For the GSS, this results in an unusual case in which the percentage of relatives in networks exceeds 100.

discussion networks, relative to other ethnoracial groups. In our survey, 61.75 percent of Blacks had discussion networks with other copartisans, and in the ANES, it was 80.1 percent. In contrast, Asian Americans reported the lowest percentage of copartisans in the ANES: 58.1 percent. We also saw a similar pattern emerge in our survey; Asians Americans and Whites reported the lowest percentage of copartisans when compared with other ethnoracial groups. Once again, although the magnitude varies, the direction is the same between the ANES and our survey. These comparisons offer us some reassurance that the patterns we observe in our survey data are not specific to ethnoracial groups in California, nor do there appear to be any systematic biases in our data collection process and efforts.

Comparisons of Network Size. We do our best to compare the average network size across the different surveys, though we note that the number of discussants that respondents were asked to provide varied greatly from survey to survey. In the MCSUI, respondents were able to list up to three discussants, whereas GSS respondents were asked to provide up to six discussants. The ANES provides respondents with an even greater number of named discussants—up to eight. The 2016 PDNS asked respondents to provide five discussants. Despite these variations, two notable patterns emerge. First, Whites tend to have the largest networks in our survey, the MCSUI, and the GSS. Second, in both the PDNS and the ANES survey, Asians report the smallest networks, when compared with other ethnoracial groups. That being the case, the sample sizes are particularly small for Asian American respondents in the ANES survey (N = 90), thus making us cautious about the inferences we can draw from these comparisons.

Operationalization and Model Selection

We construct a variety of network variables for our analyses, primarily focusing on network size, discussion frequency, and network political homogeneity (partisan composition). We present a thorough descriptive analysis of these variables in Chapter 3 and then use them as dependent variables as we explore the determinants of discussion network characteristics. In Chapters 4–6, we use these network characteristics as independent variables to examine how these network characteristics are associated with political efficacy, trust, knowledge, and engagement.

Network Size. We measure the size of one's political discussion network by summing the number of political discussants each respondent listed on the survey. Thus, an individual's political discussion network size can range from zero to five. We recognize that one limitation of this measure is that networks are capped at a maximum of five discussants and individuals could certainly be in networks larger than that. Most respondents who completed this question listed five discussants. Of course, we are not the first to face this limitation; estimating the number of discussion partners is a challenge faced in all name generator research.

Discussion Frequency. We measure discussion frequency by asking respondents to reflect upon how often they discuss politics with each of the discussants they named. Respondents were given the following set of response options: never, rarely, occasionally, and a great deal. We created a continuous scale of these responses, from a "0" indicating that they never discuss politics to a "4" indicating that they discuss these matters a great deal with their discussion partner. We then calculated the average discussion frequency within the network by summing the scores across each discussant and dividing by the number of discussants.

Partisan Composition. We measure the partisan composition of political discussion networks by calculating the percentage of the discussion networks that have the same partisanship as the respondent. For each person named in the name generator, participants were asked to indicate how they would describe each person's political party identification. The response options were: Strong Republican, Republican, Weak Republican, Independent, Weak Democrat, Democrat, Strong Democrat, Don't Know, or Refused.

We first created a dichotomous variable for whether each named person was a copartisan with the respondent. We determined the respondent's partisanship using estimates created by PDI.[17] We used a party identification variable that accounts for party registration, political contributions, and primary ballot requests. For example, respondents might decline to state their party in their formal voter registration, but they contribute to Republican or conservative causes or request a Republican Party primary ballot. For the purposes of our analysis, this respondent would be considered a Republican. We operationalize copartisanship in two ways. In general, respondents are considered to be copartisans with their social tie if the respondent perceives the social tie to identify with the same party.

Table 2.3 presents a more inclusive conceptualization of copartisanship in line with Hajnal and Lee's (2011) operationalization; here, we consider those who decline to state their partisanship as Independents. Thus, those who decline to state their partisanship are considered copartisans with Independents. We also consider those who decline to state their partisanship to be copartisans with those discussants whose partisanship is unknown. In this book we generally use the inclusive operationalization of copartisanship, but most of our results remain robust using alternative operationalizations (see online Appendix).

After determining whether each respondent's political discussant was a copartisan, we calculated the percentage of each respondent's network that consisted of copartisans. To do so, we simply totaled the number of copartisans a respondent named and divided by the total number of people the respondent named. For example, if someone named five people with whom he or she discussed important matters, three of whom were copartisans, the percent copartisan in this respondent's political discussion network would be 60 percent (3 divided by 5). This variable captures how much partisan agreement the respondent perceives to be in his or her political discussion network.

Model Selection. In each chapter, we begin by presenting some basic descriptive statistics on the variables of interest, followed by critical tests of our hypotheses using ordinary least squares (OLS) regression. Given the structure of our data, there are multiple ways to set up our regression analyses, but we chose to present the simplest models in the text, primarily for ease of interpretation and to avoid issues of model overspecification.[18] The unit of analysis for most tests is the ego, or the survey respondent, making them *egocentric* analyses. In each of the political outcomes chapters

Table 2.3. Copartisanship Operationalization (Decline to State Included)

		Perceived alter partisanship			
		Democrat	**Republican**	**Independent**	**Don't Know**
Ego PID	**Democrat**	Copartisan	X	X	X
	Republican	X	Copartisan	X	X
	Decline to state	X	X	Copartisan	Copartisan

(Chapters 4–6), we use the network characteristics as the primary independent variables of interest (e.g., the percentage of copartisans in one's network, the size of one's network, and the frequency of discussion in one's network). The dependent variables come from well-established measures of political behavior and attitudes used by political scientists, such as an index of the number of political knowledge questions correctly answered, policy opinions, the number of political engagement activities in which one reports engaging, and validated voter turnout.

We introduce a variety of control variables in each model to help show the extent to which the network characteristics are associated with the political outcomes above and beyond the impact of other individual-level characteristics we know to be important from previous research. The individual-level controls include demographic characteristics, such as gender, age, and education. Additionally, we account for neighborhood-level factors that could help to explain political behavior and attitudes. We use information from the voter file information provided by PDI, which includes census block–level information on the median household income, the percentage of Black, Latino, and Asian Americans residents, and the percentage of high school graduates within the respondent's census block.[19]

Another way to capture the effect of contextual level factors is by using an estimation technique known as hierarchical linear modeling (HLM) regression. Since our individuals reside within neighborhoods, our HLM analyses clustered respondents at the zip code level.[20] Using this estimation process, which directly takes into account the hierarchical nature of our data, we found that the vast majority of our core results remain the same. The HLM results can be found in the online Appendix.

In estimating our OLS models, we did so by disaggregating the data by ethnoracial group and then conducting a separate analysis for each group. While this allows us to examine the variation in network characteristics and political behavior between groups, it substantially reduces our sample size. Moreover, we lose a significant amount of our data with some of our variable constructions and due to nonresponse. As a consequence, we chose to keep our core models presented in the book as simple as possible in order to avoid overfitting. In order to ensure that our analysis does not suffer from omitted variable bias, we conducted substantial robustness checks and additional model specifications, all of which are available in the online Appendix.

Qualitative Interviews

As we discussed at the onset of this chapter, the primary motivation of our survey design was to provide systematic comparisons of political discussion network characteristics along the lines of ethnorace, nativity, and gender. Yet, the survey data is limited in other ways, particularly in helping us determine the role networks play in recruiting individuals to become more engaged in politics, the content of the conversations they have with voters, what individuals learn from each other, what it is about this engagement that could spark them to become politically engaged, and whether that spark spreads within their networks. In order to gain these insights, we conducted in-depth telephone interviews with canvassers from three of the community organizations (CoCo, SCOPE, and APEN), with whom we partnered to conduct the survey.[21] We asked each organization to provide us with at least five names of individuals who have served as canvassers for them. Altogether, we conducted thirteen interviews with canvassers of various ages, demographic backgrounds, and levels of experience with the participating organizations. Given that canvassers are the ones whose job it is to discuss a variety of important political matters, whether it be on ballot initiatives that directly impact their community or an upcoming election or event, these are the ideal individuals to interview to better understand the role that political conversations play in political engagement and social network development.[22]

The composition of the canvassers by ethnorace, nativity, and gender largely reflected makeup of their respective communities. As we would expect, all five of the APEN canvassers are Asian American, and most were Chinese American. The majority of CoCo canvassers are of Latino/a background, with one identifying as Black American. In contrast, the majority of our SCOPE canvassers identified as Black, with one canvasser identifying as a Latina immigrant (this interview was also conducted in Spanish). The gender distribution among the canvassers matched that of canvassers in the field, with the overwhelming majority being women.

The primary goal of our qualitative interviews was to paint a more nuanced picture of political discussion within communities of color. In the burgeoning discussion network literature focused on Whites, we have excellent data, both quantitative (e.g., Huckfeldt and Sprague 1995; Sinclair 2012) and qualitative (e.g., Walsh 2004; Conover et al. 2002). Here, we use the qualitative data to enhance the story that the quantitative analysis shows. You will see that story unfold in the subsequent chapters.

Conclusion

All research endeavors involve choices in their analytic approach and methods. Just as with all research, our approach is far from perfect, but we believe it allows us to make important contributions to the field, despite its limitations. In the chapters moving forward, we leverage our unique survey data of a diverse sample of California residents to answer questions about how discussion networks vary across enthorace, nativity, and gender (Chapter 3), how discussion networks might differentially be associated with the precursors to political engagement—political efficacy and trust (Chapter 4), political knowledge and policy positions (Chapter 5), and civic and political engagement (Chapter 6). We complement these empirical analyses with evidence from our qualitative interviews that help enrich our picture of the way political discussion operates among groups with varying social positions in the United States.

3

The Composition and Determinants of Political Discussion Networks

> I definitely think people should talk about politics. Politics are literally, to me, the forces and conditions that are shaping our lives, and so, it doesn't make any sense to me to not talk about that.
>
> Male Asian American Canvasser

As one of our Asian American canvassers from APEN points out, at its core politics is inherently social (Zuckerman 2005; Settle, Bond, and Levitt 2011). Social networks are one of the key mechanisms that mediate between the social and the political, thus playing an important role in shaping political attitudes and behavior (Berelson et al. 1944; Sinclair 2012). Of particular importance for political behaviors are political discussion networks (Huckfeldt and Sprague 1995; Huckfeldt et al. 2004; Klofstad 2011; Mutz 2006; Walsh 2004), which include the subset of a person's social connections with whom they discuss politics. However, as discussed in Chapter 1, nearly all of the research on political discussion networks relies on samples of predominantly—if not exclusively—U.S.-born White respondents who were socialized into politics in the United States and have a relatively privileged social position. Given that individuals who have been socialized into politics differently, be that in another country or through experiences of marginalization, focusing almost entirely on Whites overlooks important variation in the influence political discussion networks can have for political behavior among the diverse U.S. populace.

In this chapter, we present a descriptive picture of how we find that key political discussion network characteristics vary by ethnorace and nativity. Specifically, we examine network size, partisan composition, and homophily based on political engagement, political knowledge, and demographic characteristics. We analyze each of these network properties by nativity, specifically whether one was born in the United States or in another country;

Talking Politics. Taylor N. Carlson, Marisa Abrajano, and Lisa García Bedolla, Oxford University Press (2020). © Oxford University Press.
DOI: 10.1093/oso/9780190082116.001.0001

ethnorace, focusing on Asian Americans, Black, Latino, and White respondents; and gender. As expected, we find important differences in political discussion networks among each of these groups. These differences suggest that there are systematic differences in the composition of political discussion networks, variation that we argue derives from individuals' social position relative to other groups and the impact that has on their socialization into politics.

With Whom Do We Discuss Politics?

We begin our analysis by describing the nature of the relationships between the survey respondents and members of their political discussion networks. We asked respondents to report the relationship they had with each of the (up to) five people they listed in the name generator. The response options were: spouse/partner, parent, child, another relative, close friend, coworker, and acquaintance. While this surely does not exhaust the universe of possible relationships, it does allow for an analysis of "strong" and "weak" ties in assessing the nature of the relationships in our respondents' political discussion networks. Even though there is a growing consensus that discussion networks are overwhelmingly comprised of strong ties, such as family members and close friends, it is important to be able to analyze the impact that weak ties (e.g., coworkers or acquaintances) also have (or not) on individuals' political discussion networks.[1]

Among our respondents, family members were the most common relationship mentioned among their network members. Combining the four family categories together (spouse/partner, 12.1 percent; parent, 10.6 percent; child 2.7, percent; and another relative, 14.7 percent), family members are truly the most dominant relationship in political discussion networks, making up just over 40 percent of reported network members. Next, we see that 37.1 percent of our respondents reported discussing important matters with close friends. Overall, our data indicates that nearly 80 percent of the political discussion network relationships were with strong ties. Of the other 20 percent of reported discussion partners, about 13.3 percent of reported relationships were among coworkers, and about 9.5 percent of the relationships were among acquaintances.

The broad patterns in terms of strong and weak social ties hold across ethnoracial groups, as shown in Figure 3.1. However, important differences do arise by ethnorace. Figure 3.1 shows the percentage of dyads

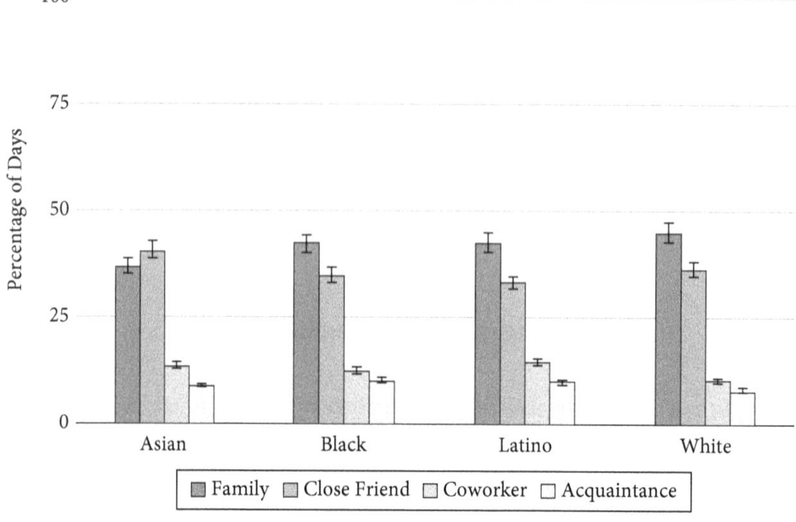

Figure 3.1. Percentage of dyads with each type of relationship by ethnorace.
Note: Error bars are at the 95% confidence interval.

(respondent–discussant pairs) that are characterized by each type of relationship within each ethnoracial group. Across all groups, close friends were the most common single type of relationship. However, if we combine the four family relationship options, then family members become the most common discussion partners. Looking at family in this way, we see that Blacks (42.4 percent), Latinos (42.6 percent), and Whites (43.8 percent) all reported more family members as network members than close friends and these differences were statistically significant. Only Asians had significantly more discussion network relationships with close friends (40.6 percent) than with family members (37 percent) ($p < .01$). Another important difference is that Latinos were far more likely to discuss important matters with other relatives beyond their immediate families, compared to respondents from the other ethnoracial groups.[2] Blacks were substantially more likely to discuss important matters with their children[3] and Whites were most likely to discuss important matters with their parents.[4] Finally, Whites were least likely to discuss important matters with their coworkers.[5]

Next, we analyze the reported relationships in discussion networks by nativity. Figure 3.2 presents the percentage of dyads with each type of relationship by nativity. Once again, most discussion network relationships

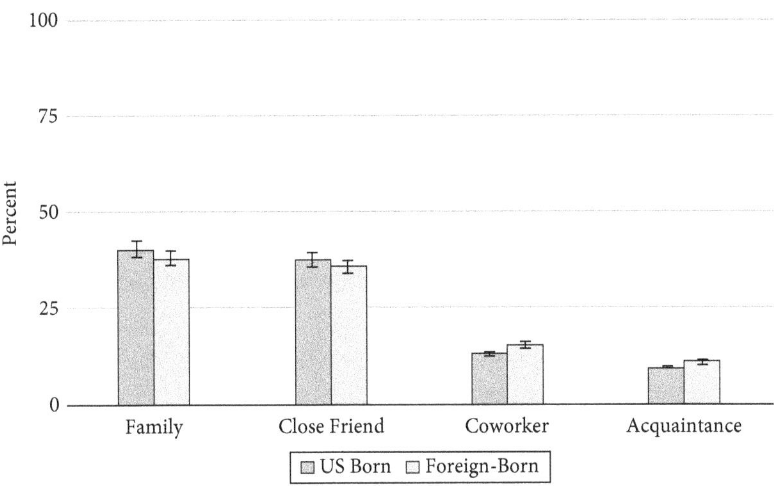

Figure 3.2. Percentage of dyads with each type of relationship by nativity.
Note: Error bars are at the 95% confidence interval.

were among close friends among both the U.S.-born and the foreign-born respondents. However, family relationships were the most dominant if we combine across the specific types of familial relationships: 40.3 percent of the discussion network relationships among the U.S.-born respondents were with family members, as were 38.3 percent of the relationships among foreign-born respondents. This difference is not statistically significant, suggesting that discussion with family was most common for everyone, regardless of nativity.[6] Foreign-born respondents were more likely to discuss important matters with coworkers (15.3 percent) than were U.S.-born respondents (12.9 percent), but this difference is not statistically significant.

In order to explore these nativity differences in even greater depth, we break down nativity by ethnoracial group, specifically for Asians and Latinos, since they are the ones with the highest percentage of foreign-born respondents. Our results suggest that U.S.-born Latinos were far more likely to discuss important matters with close friends than were foreign-born Latinos. Foreign-born Latinos were roughly equally likely to discuss important matters with another relative as they were with a close friend. In contrast, U.S.-born Latinos were nearly twice as likely to discuss important matters with a close friend than with another relative. If we look across all family relationships, foreign-born Latinos were far more likely to discuss important matters with family members (54.5 percent) than U.S.-born Latinos

(40.6 percent). Foreign-born Latinos were also more than three times as likely to discuss important matters with their children than were U.S.-born Latinos. This pattern may reflect what Tseng and Wong (2008) describe as the process of reverse socialization, whereby immigrants are likely to acquire political information from their children and therefore learn about politics from them. It could also be the case that foreign-born Latinos are limited to talking about politics with relatives as a result of language constraints, or fewer opportunities to develop friendships and acquaintances, relative to their U.S.-born counterparts.

The importance of political conversations with family members was echoed in our qualitative interviews. Almost every one of our canvassers reflected on political conversations with their families and how it facilitated political awareness, efficacy, and engagement. This seemed to be particularly important when English was not the dominant language spoken by the canvassers' family members. For example, one of our Asian American interviewees reflected on the empowering experience of discussing important issues with his relatives:

> I would say that with my friends, it's pretty much the same because I have a lot of other similarly politically active friends, but I have seen a big, big difference with how I interact with my family because a lot of my family were against the two propositions that I was advocating for. And so, I just found that canvassing definitely made me feel empowered with knowledge and then also practice of saying kind of our spiel to outline my argument to my family and to feel like I had a lot of talking points to bring up. And I think that really helped, and just also being able to speak to my family in Chinese about these topics definitely is a very new way for us to relate, and I think it's been a really powerful experience for me and for my family.

As we discuss in Chapter 1, studies have shown that Latino and Asian-origin immigrants vary in their U.S. socialization patterns in important ways and that there are significant national origin differences within these panethnic groups (García Bedolla 2009; Lee and Zhou 2015). U.S. immigration law has treated both groups quite differently, which has led to differences in immigrants' socioeconomic status, their contexts of reception, and their subsequent integration processes. Given those differences, we would expect to find differences in the structure and function of each group's political

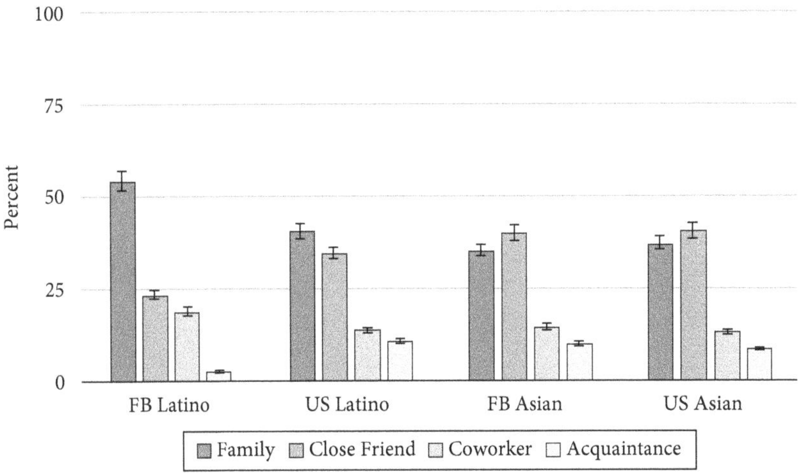

Figure 3.3. Percentage of dyads with each type of relationship by ethnorace and nativity.

Note: FB denotes foreign born, US denotes U.S. born. Error bars are at the 95% confidence interval.

discussion networks. That is what we found. As shown in Figure 3.3, regardless of nativity, our Asian American respondents were more likely to report discussing important matters with close friends than family members, the opposite of what we found for Latinos. When we collapse across the different family relationships, we find that U.S.-born Asians were slightly more likely to report discussing important matters with family members than were foreign-born Asians (37.4 percent vs. 35.3 percent), but that difference was not statistically significant. This suggests that Asian Americans have largely similar discussion networks, regardless of whether they were born in the United States or not, which stands in sharp contrast to what we find for Latinos.

Finally, Figure 3.4, provides the percentage of dyads with each type of relationship by gender. As discussed in Chapter 1, studies have found that men were less likely to include their spouses in their discussion networks than women and were more likely to talk to friends. Figure 3.4 shows that this expectation holds true in our survey, even though our male- and female-identified respondents come from much more diverse backgrounds than those normally included in social network surveys. Our male respondents were significantly less likely than our female respondents to report family members as discussion partners. Instead, they were much more likely than

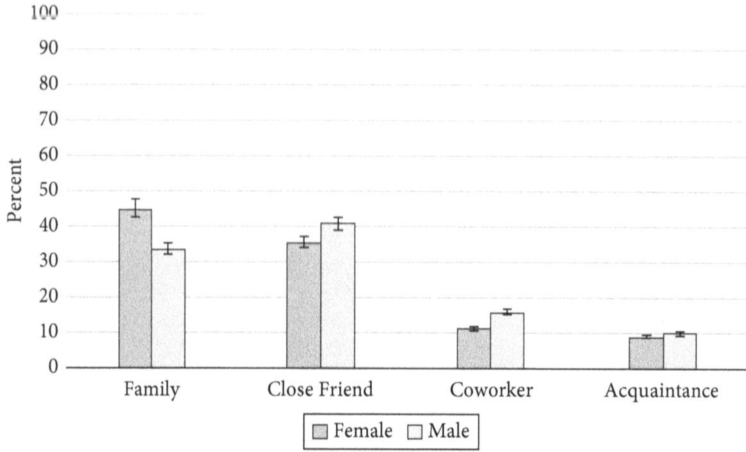

Figure 3.4. Percentage of dyads with each type of relationship by gender.
Note: Error bars are at the 95% confidence interval.

women to say that their discussion partners were close friends or coworkers. All of these differences are statistically significant.

Coethnorace in Networks

In this section, we present descriptive statistics on the degree of coethnorace in our dyads. Previous research has shown that social networks are largely sorted along the lines of ethnorace (Lewis 2013; Knoke 1990). Likewise, studies have found that individuals primarily discuss politics with those who share the same ethnoracial background (Leighley and Matsubayashi 2009). That is, Blacks tend to be in political discussion networks with other Blacks, and likewise for Latinos, Asians, and Whites. However, recent work suggests that racially diverse political discussion networks are more common among Blacks than Whites (Eveland and Appiah 2019). The reason behind the general pattern of political discussion occurring among coethnic individuals can likely be attributed to the concept of homophily—the idea that individuals prefer to connect with others who are similar to them. This phenomenon may be even more acute for our study population, given that language constraints, for example, coupled by the high rates of residential segregation by ethnorace, limit the range of individuals with whom ethnoracial group members can interact. Our data allows us to offer some insights on the role of coethnorace in political discussion networks, with the caveat that our statistical power for this analysis is limited.[7] Despite this constraint, our findings are consistent with previous research documenting the tendency for individuals to interact with and discuss important matters with those who share their ethnoracial identity.

The majority of the dyads (72 percent) consisted of respondents who shared the same ethnorace.[8] Table 3.1 presents the raw numbers of egos (initial respondents) and alters (snowball sample respondents) who identified with each ethnoracial group. Table 3.2 shows the percentage of alters from each ethnoracial group for each ego ethnorace. The results suggest that 71.7 percent of Asian respondents named Asian discussants, 91.7 percent of Black respondents named Black discussants, only 50 percent of Latino respondents named Latino discussants, and 79.3 percent of White respondents named White respondents. However, we are *extremely* cautious in analyzing these results because of the very small sample sizes. We observe that individuals were most likely to name discussants from their own ethnoracial group, but the actual percentages are subject to significant statistical uncertainty since

Table 3.1. Number of Egos and Alters in Each Ethnoracial Group

	Number of egos	Number of alters
Asian	111	86
Black	13	13
Latino	22	21
White	33	54
Other	22	22
Refused	1	5

Table 3.2. Percentage of Dyads of Each Ethnoracial Combination

		Alter ethnorace				
		Asian	Black	Latino	White	N
Ego ethnorace	Asian	71.7%	0%	6.6%	21.7%	111
	Black	0%	91.7%	0%	8.3%	13
	Latino	25%	0%	50%	25%	22
	White	6.9%	6.9%	6.9%	79.3%	33

the confidence intervals around these percentages are very large due to the small samples.

Our Black respondents were the most likely to have coethnic discussion partners, with over 90 percent of their reported discussion partners being Black. But we would note the very small sample size, suggesting the need to interpret this result with caution, especially given recent evidence suggesting that Black respondents tend to have more racially diverse networks (Eveland and Appiah 2019). Whites were the second-most ethnoracially homophilous group, with almost 80 percent of their discussion partners also being White. This is an especially surprising finding given our White respondents were, by and large, located in ethnoracially diverse neighborhoods. Yet, despite the fact that, unlike segregated Whites, they have the opportunity to have a diverse set of discussion partners, there were few people of color with whom they reported discussing important matters. Our Latino respondents were the least likely to have coethnic discussion partners, with only half of their network members also being Latino. But again, our sample size is very small. We would therefore describe our findings as suggestive and not definitive. This question of homophily among network members should be the focus of future research and definitely needs to consider the impact of ethnoracial homophily within White political discussion networks.

Network Size

A prominent advantage of discussion networks is to help facilitate political information flows, so if someone discusses politics with more people, he or she is expected to be exposed to more political information. Also, individuals in larger discussion networks are expected to be more politically engaged (Knoke 1990; Lake and Huckfeldt 1998). In turn, individuals who are more engaged in their communities are more likely to participate in politics, relative to those with low levels of engagement (e.g., Putnam 2000). To the extent that we view frequent political conversations as an important form of political engagement (e.g., Huckfeldt and Sprague 1995; Mutz 2006), individuals who are embedded in larger political discussion networks are assumed to be more politically engaged.

As we noted earlier, Leighley and Matsubayashi (2009) are one of the few researchers to conduct a comparative analysis of political discussion networks by ethnorace, with the caveat of the data limitations discussed above. They find that Whites are in larger networks than other ethnoracial group members, with Latinos and Asians having particularly small networks. Leighley and Matsubayashi (2009) attribute this variation to the supply of possible political discussants being constrained by socioeconomic factors, paired with the demand of individuals to prefer discussants who are similar to them. Ethnoracial group members, for instance, may prefer to discuss politics with coethnics, but because some groups' members are less likely to be politically engaged than Whites, that constrains the number of available people with whom they can discuss politics. This lack of available politically engaged people could lead to smaller discussion networks.

Network Size by Ethnorace. Figure 3.5 presents the distribution of network size by ethnorace. Whites had significantly larger political discussion networks than all other ethnoracial groups. Whites' networks had an average size of 3.95, followed by Asian Americans with an average size of 3.51, Blacks with an average size of 3.44, and Latinos with an average size of 3.31. There

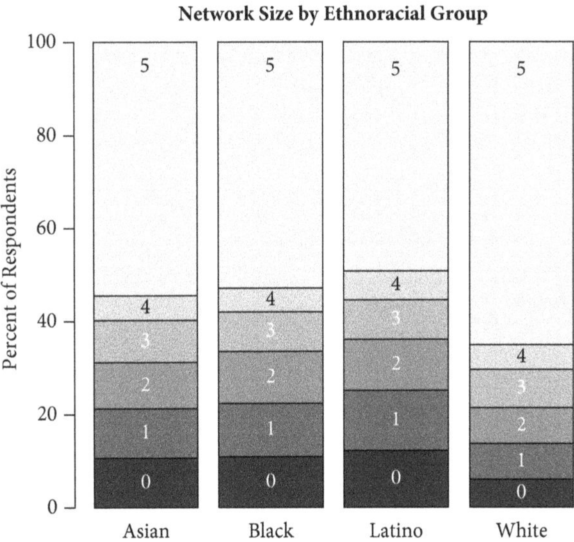

Figure 3.5. Network size by ethnorace. This figure shows the percent of respondents who had each possible network size. Network size was determined by the number of political discussants each respondent listed in the name generator on the survey.

was no statistical difference in network size between Blacks and Latinos, nor between Asians and Blacks. The starkest differences in network size is between Latinos and Whites. For instance, only 5.9 percent of Whites listed no political discussants, whereas 12.2 percent of Latinos did not list any political discussants. At the other end of the spectrum, 65 percent of Whites listed the maximum of five political discussants, but only 49.3 percent of Latinos listed five discussants.

Network Size by Nativity. Figure 3.6 presents the distribution of network size among foreign-born and U.S.-born respondents. We find that U.S.-born respondents reported being in significantly larger political discussion networks than did foreign-born respondents. The average discussion network size of a U.S.-born respondent (3.5) was significantly greater than the average discussion network size of a foreign-born respondent (3.3) ($p < .001$).

As illustrated in Figure 3.6, about 13 percent of foreign-born respondents reported no political discussants, while about 10 percent of U.S.-born respondents reported no political discussants. On the other side of the

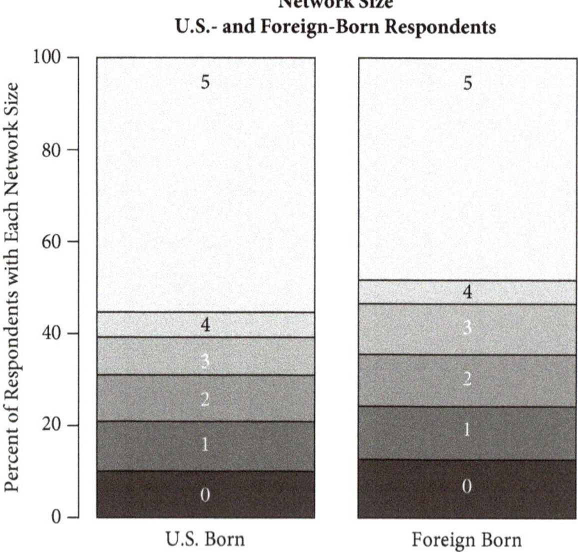

Figure 3.6. Network size by nativity. This figure shows the percent of respondents who had each possible network size. Network size was determined by the number of political discussants each respondent listed in the name generator on the survey.

spectrum, about 55 percent of U.S.-born respondents reported having five political discussants (the maximum we could measure), whereas only about 48 percent of foreign-born respondents reported having five political discussants. Given that foreign-born individuals are still acquainting themselves with and learning about the U.S. political system, we would expect the number of their codiscussants to be smaller relative to their U.S.-born counterparts. These results are aligned with those of Leighley and Matsubayashi (2009), although we are able to explore more variation in network size because our name generator was capped at five instead of three individuals.

Network size appears to increase the longer one's family has been in the United States. Specifically, first-generation Americans had significantly smaller discussion networks than those of the second- ($p < .01$) or third- ($p < .001$) generation. Fifty-four and a half percent of second-generation respondents, compared to 48.3 percent of first-generation respondents, had discussion networks of the maximum size of 5. On the opposite end of the spectrum, 12.7 percent of first-generation respondents did not list any political discussants at all, whereas only 9.3 percent of second-generation and 8.5 percent of third-generation respondents did not list any discussants. Together, this suggests that the longer one's family has been in the United States, the larger his or her political discussion networks will be.

Breaking nativity down by ethnorace, we can see that this result is largely driven by Asian Americans respondents. Foreign-born Asian Americans were in significantly smaller political discussion networks (3.2) than U.S.-born Asian Americans (3.6) ($p < .001$), while there was no statistically significant difference in network size between U.S.- and foreign-born Latinos.

Network Size by Gender. Next, we examine variation in network size by gender. Because men and women, particularly women of color, hold very different social positions within U.S. politics (e.g., Cole and Stewart 1996; Sapiro 2004; McDevitt and Chaffee 2002), we might expect men and women's political discussion networks to vary from one another. Conover and colleagues (2002) suggest that women have historically been dissuaded from participating in political activities, including discussing politics. Thus, we might expect men to have larger discussion networks than women. However, in our sample, men and women had the same average network size overall and within each ethnoracial group.[9]

Partisan Composition

Consistent with the concept of homophily (Knoke 1990; McPherson et al. 2001), we would expect political discussion networks to be largely homogeneous in terms of partisanship, vote preferences, policy preferences, and ideology. Democrats should therefore be more likely to have discussion partners who are Democrats, and we would expect Republicans' discussion partners likely to self-identify as Republican. If homophily is at work, political discussion networks should include only limited differences along these lines, what scholars broadly define as *disagreement*.

We expect the partisan composition of ethnoracial group members' discussion networks to differ for several reasons. First, we know that partisan allegiances vary across ethnoracial groups. For example, Blacks tend to overwhelmingly support the Democratic Party (Frymer 2010; Dawson 1994), whereas the partisan allegiances of Latinos and Asian Americans are not as firmly rooted with one political party (Alvarez and García Bedolla 2003; Abrajano and Alvarez 2012). To the extent that individuals of the same ethnorace tend to find themselves sorted—intentionally or otherwise—into ethnoracially homogeneous communities (Leighley and Matsubayashi 2009), we should expect Blacks' political discussion networks to be more Democratic when compared with the Latino and Asian American's discussion networks. But, Eveland and Appiah (2019) find that White discussion networks are more politically diverse than Black discussion networks, raising the possibility that the opposite may be true. Given that the concept of partisanship is still in flux for Asian-origin and Latino immigrants (Hajnal and Lee 2011), it could also mean that there would be more partisan diversity, meaning the presence of nonpartisans, in their political discussion networks than those of Blacks.

Partisan Composition by Ethnorace. Figure 3.7 offers us a glimpse of the party composition of respondents' political discussion networks by ethnorace. Here we see that irrespective of ethnoracial group, our respondents' discussion networks were composed primarily of Democrats. This pattern is generally consistent with the percentage of self-identified Democrats for each ethnoracial group among California registered voters.[10] The most striking feature of this analysis, however, is that Whites were the least likely to report not knowing the partisanship of their discussants. Only 8 percent of White respondents said they were unaware of their discussants' partisanship, relative to 15 percent among

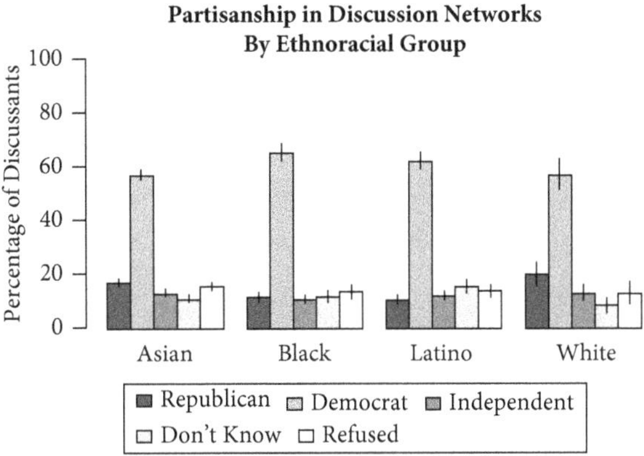

Figure 3.7. Percentage of discussion networks perceived to identify as Republicans, Democrats, or Independents, or the percentage of discussants participants reported not knowing the partisanship or refused to report it, by ethnorace. Vertical lines represent 95% confidence intervals.

Latino respondents. Among Asian Americans, 10.8 percent said they did not know their discussion partners' party affiliation, compared with 11.5 percent of Blacks. Why this is the case harks back to our argument that partisanship may not be as meaningful and relevant to Latino and Asian American respondents. Or, it may be less common practice among non-whites to ask about or know the partisanship of their discussants because it does not come up in conversation, the discussion partners may not be as politically engaged, or they could simply not think of themselves in these terms.

In Figure 3.8, we show the degree of partisan homogeneity in discussion networks by ethnorace. The left-hand panel of the figure presents the distribution of the percentage of copartisans in each respondent's discussion network by ethnorace. While there is some variation between groups, overall, they follow a similar, bimodal distribution. Most individuals are in fairly homogeneous networks with most of their discussants being copartisans; however, there was a nontrivial number of respondents with very diverse networks, having fewer copartisan discussants. The right-hand panel of Figure 3.8 shows the average percentage of copartisans in one's network for each ethnoracial group. The results suggest that overall, our respondents were in fairly homogeneous networks with more than half of their discussants being copartisans.

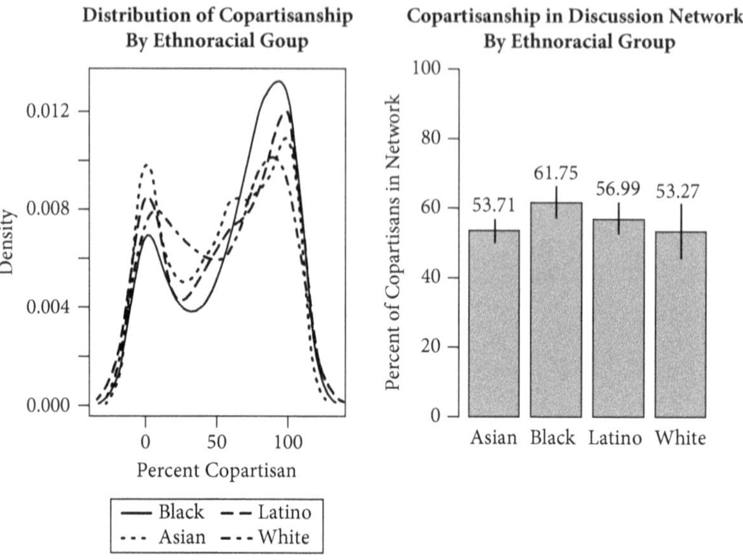

Figure 3.8. Distribution of copartisanship by ethnorace. The left panel shows the distribution of the percentage of copartisans in one's network for each ethnoracial group. The right panel shows the average percentage of copartisans in discussion networks for each ethnoracial group. Vertical lines represent 95% confidence intervals.

As we discuss in Chapter 2, the way in which we operationalize copartisanship is flexible and might underestimate the degree of partisan homogeneity. Black respondents had the most homogeneous discussion networks, followed by Latinos, Asian Americans, and Whites. Whites had the most diversity in their discussion networks. Because African Americans affiliate so strongly with the Democratic Party (Frymer 2010) and their networks tend to be ethnoracially homophilous (Leighley and Matsubayashi 2009), it is not surprising that African Americans have the most homogeneous discussion networks in terms of partisanship. This is also consistent with Eveland and Appiah's (2019) comparison of White and Black discussion networks.

Partisan Composition by Nativity. In Figure 3.9, we examine the perceived partisan composition of political discussion networks by nativity, breaking out Asian- and Latin American–origin respondents. Again, our sample is not intended to be nationally representative of these groups, so Democratic party identification is likely to be overrepresented based on the characteristics of

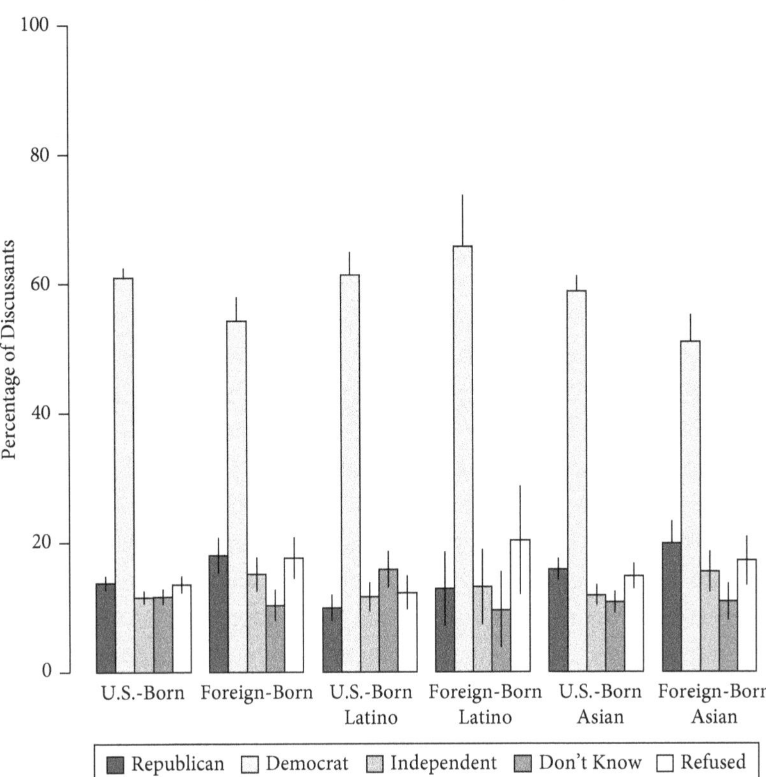

Figure 3.9. Partisanship by nativity. This figure shows the average percentage of each network's discussants that was perceived to identify with each political party. Vertical lines represent 95% confidence intervals.

our sample. However, we still observe some interesting patterns. Overall, our foreign-born respondents had significantly fewer Democrats in their networks than U.S.-born respondents ($p < .001$). Foreign-born respondents had significantly more Republicans ($p < .01$) and Independents ($p < .001$) in their networks than U.S.-born respondents. There was no statistically significant difference in the percentage of discussants for whom the respondent reported that he or she did not know the partisanship between U.S.- and foreign-born respondents.

These results are likely driven by Asian-origin respondents, given they outnumber those of other origins in our sample. Looking within Asian respondents, we can see that foreign-born Asian respondents had a significantly higher percentage of Republicans and Independents in their networks than U.S.-born Asian Americans respondents ($p < .05$). In contrast, U.S.-born Asian Americans respondents had significantly more Democrats in their networks than foreign-born Asian Americans respondents ($p < .01$). However, foreign-born and U.S.-born Asian Americans appear to be equally likely to report that they do not know the party identification of their discussants, as well as being equally likely to refuse to report the party identification of their discussants. While our Latino sample is substantially smaller than our Asian Americans sample, we see the opposite pattern. Specifically, we observe *suggestive* evidence that foreign-born Latino respondents were more likely to refuse to report the party identification of their discussants or report that they do not know the partisanship of their discussants than U.S.-born Latino respondents ($p < .10$). There are no statistically significant differences in the percentage of Democrat, Republican, or Independent network members between U.S.- and foreign-born Latino respondents.

Thinking about nativity by generation, we find that first-generation respondents had significantly fewer Democratic partisans in their discussion networks than second-generation respondents ($p < .05$). Foreign-born respondents had significantly more Republican partisans ($p < .05$) and Independents ($p < .05$) than U.S-born respondents. Importantly, first-generation respondents were also significantly more likely to refuse to report the partisanship of their discussants than respondents from other generations ($p < .05$), while second-generation respondents were significantly more likely to report that they did not know the partisanship of their discussants ($p < .05$).

Figure 3.10 presents the distribution of the percentage of copartisans in a respondent's discussion network by nativity. The right-hand panel shows the average percentage of copartisans in a discussion network by nativity.[11] Overall, the patterns of copartisanship are similar regardless of birthplace or the how we measured partisanship; most individuals find themselves in political discussion networks with copartisans. Even though both groups are in somewhat homogeneous networks in terms of partisanship, U.S.-born respondents were in significantly more homogeneous networks than foreign-born respondents ($p < .05$). The difference in copartisanship between foreign-born Latino and U.S.-born Latino respondents is statistically indistinguishable, while there is suggestive evidence that U.S.-born Asian Americans respondents have significantly more copartisans in their networks than foreign-born Asian-origin respondents ($p < .10$).

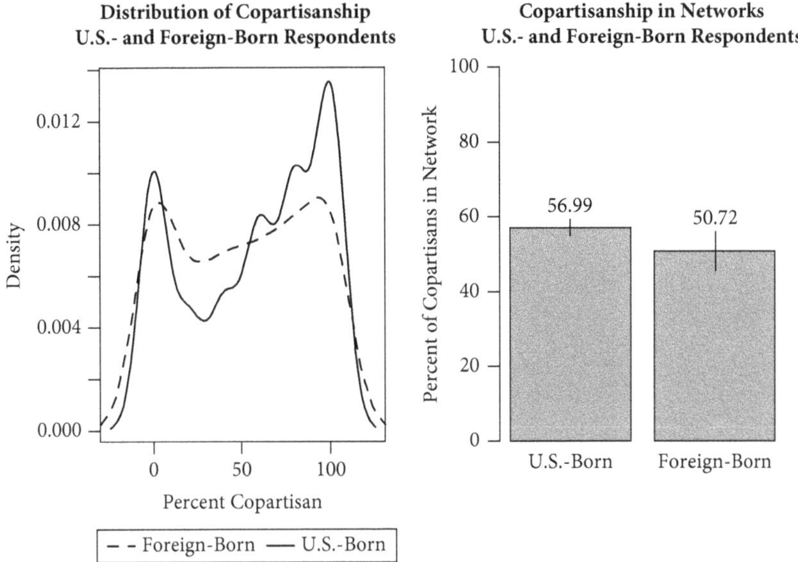

Figure 3.10. Copartisanship in discussion networks. The left panel shows the distribution of the percentage of copartisans in one's discussion network by nativity. The dashed line represents foreign-born respondents while the solid line represents U.S.-born respondents. The right panel shows the average percentage of copartisans in U.S.-born and foreign-born discussion networks. Vertical lines represent 95% confidence intervals.

Partisan Composition by Gender. Figure 3.11 shows the partisan composition of discussion networks for our male- and female-identified respondents. Much like what we observed for our analyses by ethnorace and nativity, both men and women in our sample had networks dominated by Democrats. Men had networks with a significantly greater percentage of Republicans ($p < .001$) and Independents ($p < .01$) than did women, while women had a significantly greater percentage of Democrats ($p < .001$) in their networks than did men. Men and women were equally likely to refuse to report the partisanship of their discussants, but there is suggestive evidence of an important difference in not knowing the partisanship of their discussants. Women reported being unaware of a greater percentage of their political discussants than men ($p < .10$).

Next, we analyzed the copartisanship by gender. Figure 3.12 shows the distribution of the percentage of copartisans in one's discussion network by gender (left) and the average percentage of copartisans in one's

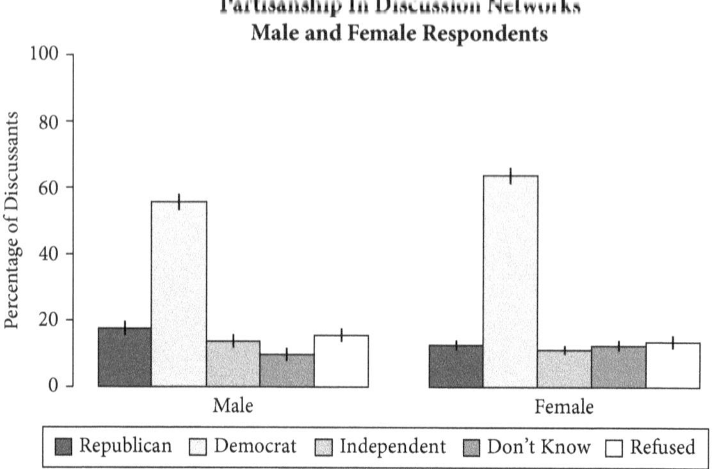

Figure 3.11. Percentage of discussants perceived to identify as Republicans, Democrats, or Independents, or for whom respondents refused to report or did not know the discussant's partisanship, by gender. Vertical lines represent 95% confidence intervals.

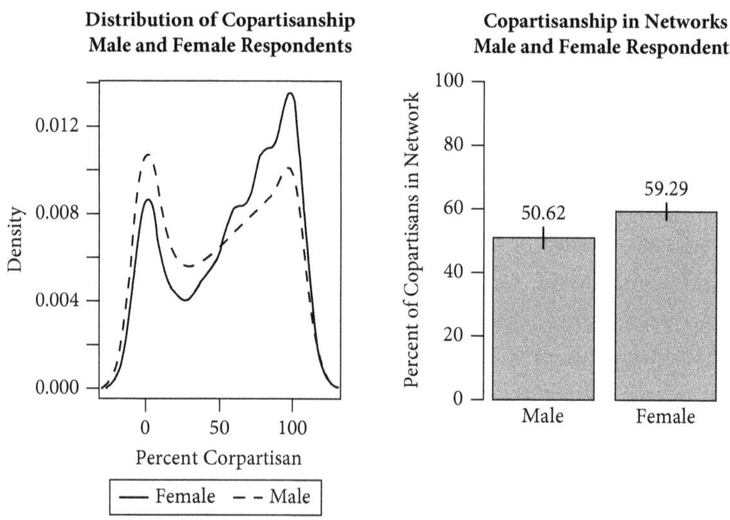

Figure 3.12. The left panel shows the distribution of the percentage of copartisans in male and female discussion networks. The right panel shows the average percentage of copartisans in male and female discussion networks. Vertical lines represent 95% confidence intervals.

network by gender (right). The results indicate that overall the distribution of copartisanship is similar for men and women, but women have a significantly greater percentage of copartisans in their networks than men. Male networks are composed of only about 50 percent copartisans, making their networks more diverse compared with female networks, which are composed of nearly 60 percent copartisans. Given that women across all ethnoracial groups except Asian Americans are more Democratic than their coethnic men, this may be the result, as we saw with Blacks, of women having fewer non-Democratic women available with whom to discuss politics. Or, as previous research has shown, because women tend to be more agreeable than men in studies that compare personality traits across gender, that could lead them to prefer to discuss politics with copartisans (Weisberg et al. 2011).

Discussion Frequency

The final network characteristic that we examine is the rate at which individuals discuss important matters with those in their networks. That is, individuals who engage in regular and daily conversations about current events and other important matters should be more positively inclined to participate in politics and be more politically efficacious (Huckfeldt and Sprague 1998). Additionally, having these everyday discussions should also be correlated with higher levels of political knowledge (Eveland 2004).

Given the importance of this network characteristic on a whole host of political outcomes and behaviors, we asked all respondents to report the degree to which they discuss politics, candidates, or elections with each of their named discussion partners. The response options ranged from 0 (never) to 4 (a great deal). Because of the documented disparities in the rates of political interest reported by non-whites versus Whites (Verba et al.), we expect similar differences in network discussion frequency across the ethnoracial groups. We might also expect less discussion about politics to occur in the networks of foreign-born individuals, relative to their U.S.-born counterparts, particularly if they understood the question to mean conversations about U.S. politics.

Figure 3.13 presents a bivariate distribution of discussion frequency rates by ethnoracial group, gender, and nativity. As we can see, our respondents certainly do not discuss politics with their networks on an everyday or constant basis. But consistent with our expectations, there are some ethnoracial

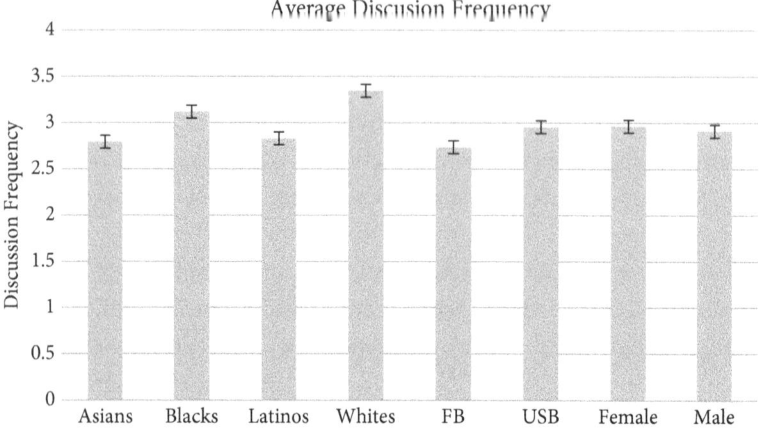

Figure 3.13. Average discussion frequency by ethnorace, nativity, and gender. FB denotes foreign born, and USB denotes U.S. born. Vertical lines represent 95% confidence intervals.

differences that emerge in the frequency of political discussion. In particular, we see that Whites discuss politics more often than do Latinos, Blacks, and Asians, and these differences are all statistically significant at $p < .05$. We observe that U.S.-born respondents discussed politics more frequently than foreign-born respondents ($p < .05$). Finally, as expected, we observe no significant differences in rates of discussion frequency by gender. Given this variation, the predictive power of this particular network attribute on political engagement and attitudes may vary as well, an idea we return to in Chapter 6 and in related work (Carlson, Abrajano, and García Bedolla 2019).

Political Engagement

We next analyze the level of political engagement in political discussion networks by ethnorace. Our measure of political engagement is based on our original survey in which participants self-reported the types of political activities in which they engaged. We measure classic political engagement using the standard scale used by the American National Election Studies. Specifically, respondents were asked to indicate whether they have done any of ten different political activities over the past 12 months: (1) signed a paper or online petition, (2) shared, reblogged, or retweeted news articles or petitions on social media, (3) attended a political speech, march, rally, or demonstration, (4) talked about politics on social media, (5) given money to a political candidate, (6) given money to an organization or cause, (7) volunteered for a political campaign or political cause, (8) contacted a government official either in person, by phone, email, social media, or with a letter, (9) talked to anyone and tried to show them why they would vote for or against one of the ballot initiatives or candidates, or (10) joined a local community organization. We examine the correlation between ego and alter self-reported political engagement.

Political Engagement by Ethnorace. We begin by analyzing the correlation between ego and alter political engagement by ethnorace. Because we have such small numbers of dyads with each ethnoracial combination (see Table 3.2), we broadly analyze differences between coethnoracial and non-coethnoracial dyads. We find that there is a statistically significant, positive correlation between ego and alter self-reported political engagement among coethnoracial dyads ($r = .36, p < .001$). In contrast, there is no statistically significant correlation between ego and alter political engagement among non-coethnoracial dyads ($r = -.07, p = .65$). Once again, these analyses could be underpowered to detect meaningful correlations, especially among our 47 non-coethnoracial dyads. Among coethnoracial social ties, at least, we can see that individuals tend to discuss politics with co-ethnics who have similar levels of political engagement.

In an effort to explore some of the nuances among ethnoracial groups, we analyze the correlation between ego and alter political engagement based only on the ego's ethnorace. There is a moderate, statistically significant, positive correlation between ego and alter political engagement among Asian American egos ($r = .26, p < .01$). However, there is not a statistically significant association between ego and alter political engagement among any other ethnoracial group explored (Black, Latino, or White). This is likely due to a statistical power issue. Because analyses of Black, Latino, and White egos are likely to be underpowered in this sample, we are hesitant to draw conclusions about there being a relationship between ego and alter engagement for Asians, but not for the other groups.

Political Engagement by Nativity. In our reduced sample, we can analyze nativity for only 202 dyads, but our analysis yields interesting results nonetheless. Overall, there appears to be a positive correlation between ego and alter political engagement, suggesting that individuals are more likely to discuss politics with people who are similarly engaged with politics. The correlation, however, is not particularly strong, with a Pearson's correlation coefficient of 0.23 ($p < .01$). Looking into nativity, there are a number of ways in which we can analyze the data, as shown in Table 3.3. One way is to focus on the correlation coefficients between ego and alter political engagement by nativity combination. For instance, the top left cell shows that the correlation between U.S.-born ego political engagement and a U.S.-born alter political engagement is 0.23 ($p < .01$). The results suggest that there is a positive correlation between ego and alter political engagement among both U.S.- and foreign-born egos (original respondents) when the discussant is U.S. born or either U.S. or foreign born, but not when the alter is foreign born. This could in part be due to the smaller number of foreign-born respondents in this sample.

Political Engagement by Gender. Table 3.4 shows the correlation coefficients between ego and alter political engagement by the respondent's gender. The results suggest that among both male and female egos, there was a statistically significant, positive correlation between ego and alter political

Table 3.3. Correlation Coefficients between Ego and Alter Political Engagement by Nativity

		Alter nativity		
		U.S.-born	**Foreign-born**	**Either**
Ego nativity	U.S.-born	0.23**	–.01	0.20*
	Foreign-born	0.49*	0.31	0.45*
	Either	0.25**	0.02	0.23**

Note: $^{**}p < .01$, $^{*}p < .05$.

Table 3.4. Correlation Coefficients between Ego and Alter Political Engagement by Gender

		Alter gender		
		Male	**Female**	**Either**
Ego gender	Male	0.23	0.47**	0.24*
	Female	0.32	0.22	0.21*
	Either	0.24*	0.30**	–.29***

Note: $^{**}p < .01$, $^{*}p < .05$.

engagement, regardless of the alter's gender. The same pattern occurred for alters. While this null result could be due to a lack of statistical power instead of signaling the lack of a relationship, it is interesting to note that there is not a statistically significant association between ego and alter political engagement when they are of the same gender. However, there is a strong correlation in political engagement between male egos and female discussants, suggesting that more mixed-gender networks may have a stronger impact on political engagement.

The correlations that we observe between ego and alter political engagement are largely echoed by what we found in our interviews. Many of the canvassers we interviewed, regardless of ethnorace or gender, indicated that many of their friends were already politically engaged. Many of interviewees also shared with us that they met many of their friends through canvassing or nonprofit civic engagement work. Yet, many canvassers shared that they still felt that their conversations had an impact in mobilizing people outside their immediate discussion or friend networks, suggesting that there is room for social influence in engagement beyond just homophilous selection. For example, one Asian American canvasser shared the following:

> But, then there are certain people in my social circles that, like say, right now I'm taking a health care interpreting certificate course and there are people who've been in . . . either been in health care or they've been a linguist, but that's like one of the few places where it's not politically charged I guess. But I've been able to talk to folks about the work I'm doing in just really cultivating that interest about what's going on and hey, like by being involved you can actually make a difference in, you know, I have in my little way and so I don't know. Yeah, my friends are either already canvassers or highly involved in the work or they're non-citizens.

We will return to these ideas in Chapter 6 as we delve more deeply into the relationship between discussion networks and political engagement.

The Determinants of Political Discussion Networks

Thus far, we have painted a comprehensive descriptive picture of what political discussion networks look like across ethnorace, nativity, and gender. The next logical step is to explore what factors best predict the three network characteristics of size, discussion frequency, and partisan homogeneity. To what extent do individual-level attributes such as education or age best predict the size of individuals' networks? Or perhaps it depends on where they live and with whom they interact? It could also be the case that it is a combination of both of these things.

The existing research related to this topic has demonstrated that both characteristics are critical in determining who participates in politics (and who does not).[12] Studies have repeatedly shown that socioeconomic status (SES), which includes individual-level factors such as age, occupation, and income, influences individuals' civic and political engagement, although we know that the impact of SES varies across ethnoracial groups, with White engagement most likely to be explained by these factors (Gurin 1984; Tate 1993; Fraga et al. 2006; Wong et al. 2011). These resources may also help to facilitate the development of one's political discussion networks.

Contextual factors also matter in helping us unpack the determinants of one's social networks. Since we know that individual-level socioeconomic characteristics strongly correlate with political participation, we would also expect individuals residing in high-socioeconomic status neighborhoods to be more politically engaged. In addition, involvement in civic, religious, or political organizations comprise a contextual resource that can have an important effect on political opportunity structures and engagement. As Wong (2006) and Verba et al. (1995) find, organizations help to develop individuals' civic skills; this, in turn, gives them the necessary skills to become more politically involved and engaged individuals. Wong's (2006) research, in particular, documents the critical role that these civic organizations play in immigrants' political integration and socialization processes (see also Ramakrishnan and Bloemraad 2011).

In Chapter 1, we discussed why political discussion networks are most likely to foster political engagement when they are larger, include more regular political discussion, and are homophilous in terms of partisanship. Connecting those research findings with what we know about the role that socioeconomic status and neighborhood context play in civic engagement, we would expect that homeowners, the more educated, and older individuals would have networks with these participation-enhancing characteristics. Similarly, we would expect those residing in areas with a high degree of contextual resources (e.g., high-status neighborhoods, access to membership in civic and religious organizations, etc.) to have political discussion networks that have these characteristics. Since we know that both the individual and contextual-level factors described above are strongly correlated with ethnoracial group membership, gender, and nativity, we hypothesize that non-whites, women, and the foreign born will be less likely to be situated in political discussion networks that have these characteristics.

To understand which factors help to explain our key network characteristics of interest—network size, frequency of political discussion in one's network, and network homogeneity, measured by the percentage of copartisans in one's network—we employ ordinary least squares (OLS) regression. Doing so allows us to control for a variety of factors to determine which of them are associated with the specific network characteristic of interest. Our explanatory variables account for resources at both the individual and contextual levels. The individual-level resources are: whether an individual is a renter (versus a homeowner), marital status, gender, age, and level of education. In the models, our renter variable takes the value of 1 if the respondent was a renter and 0 otherwise. For marital status, the variable takes the value of 1 if the respondent was married and 0 otherwise. Gender is coded such that a 1 indicates that the respondent is female-identified and a 0 indicates that the respondent is male-identified. Age is a continuous variable indicating how many years old each respondent was at the time of the survey. Finally, education is coded as a dichotomous variable whereby 1 indicates that the respondent has at least a college degree and 0 otherwise.

As for our contextual-level measures, we account for group membership in either a religious or secular organization; here secular organizations are defined as the respondent's self-reported membership in any of the following organizations: professional, neighborhood, community, labor union, ethnic and/or cultural, issue-oriented political (e.g., immigration, environment), political, civic and/or rotary.[13] We also consider the median income and percentage of high school graduates in the respondent's census tract.[14] Additionally, we control for the percentage of Blacks, Whites, Latinos, and Asian Americans in the respondent's census tract. All of these results may be found in the Appendix (Tables A3.1–A3.9).

Determinants of Network Size. For Blacks, Latinos, and Asian Americans, membership in a secular group is positively associated with the size of their political discussion networks (see Table A3.4). Religious group membership is also associated with larger political discussion networks for Latinos and Whites. The only other contextual factor that is associated with network size is the percentage of high school graduates in a neighborhood, although this is only for Asian Americans. The relationship is negative, such that a greater percentage of high school graduates is associated with fewer discussion partners among Asian Americans.

Only the contextual factors seem to influence network size for foreign-born and U.S.-born respondents (see Table A3.1). For both foreign-born and U.S.-born respondents, secular group membership positively predicts the size of their networks. Those who reported belonging to any secular group were likely to have more discussion partners in their networks. The coefficient size of secular group membership is larger in magnitude for the foreign-born than it is for U.S.-born respondents. A high percentage of high school graduates in one's neighborhood is negatively correlated with network size for both U.S.-born and foreign-born respondents. In this case, high-status neighborhoods are not correlated with our respondents having a political discussion network with more discussion partners.

Looking at gender (see Table A3.7), we find that, even though there are not statistically significant differences between men and women in terms of their network size, the factors associated with network size are also similar. For both men and women, living in a less educated neighborhood is associated with smaller political discussion networks. Similarly, belonging to a secular community organization is associated with larger discussion networks among men and women. At the individual level, however, we observe some differences between men and women. Having a college education was positively associated with network size for men, but not women. Age was also a statistically significant factor for men, but not women. The older men become, the smaller their discussion networks are likely to be. This could be due to the fact that men's friend networks are known to become smaller as they age, which can lead to social isolation (Neville et al. 2018).

Determinants of Discussion Frequency. Considering the determinants of discussion frequency by ethnorace (see Table A3.6), among Asian Americans, Blacks, and Latinos, we find that secular group membership is positively associated with frequent political discussion within one's networks. We detect no such relationship among Whites. Religious group membership was positively associated with discussion frequency among Asian and Latino respondents, but not among White or Black respondents. The other contextual-level factors were not associated with discussion frequency at the 5 percent level for any of the groups. At the individual level, age was positively associated with discussion frequency for Black and Latino respondents, but not for Asian or White respondents. Having a college education was positively associated with discussion frequency among Asians and Latinos, but not among Blacks or Whites.

In terms of nativity (see Table A3.3), being college educated, being older, being a renter, and membership in a secular or religious group are positively correlated with frequent political discussions among U.S.-born respondents. For foreign-born respondents, membership in a secular group is the only factor that is associated with discussion frequency, with the relationship being positive in nature. That is, foreign-born respondents in a secular group are more likely to engage in regular political conversations with their discussion partners, relative to foreign-born respondents who are not in a secular group.

Turning to gender (see Table A3.9), we find important contextual- and individual-level differences between men and women. Looking at the contextual factors, secular group membership is positively associated with discussion frequency for both men and women, but religious group membership is only positively associated with discussion frequency for women. At the individual level, we find that age is positively associated with discussion frequency for women, but not men. In contrast, having a college education and being a renter are positively associated with discussion frequency for men, but not women.

Determinants of Partisan Homogeneity. In terms of ethnorace (see Table A3.5), secular group membership is positively associated with the percentage of copartisans in Asian Americans' and Blacks' networks. Religious group membership for Asian Americans is also an important factor, but it is negatively correlated with partisan homogeneity. Age has different relationships with the partisan composition of Blacks' and Asian Americans' political discussion networks. Whereas age is negatively correlated with network homogeneity among Asian Americans, we see the opposite pattern among Blacks. As Asian Americans get older, they are less likely to have more homogeneous discussion networks, whereas Blacks are more likely to have less diverse (more homogeneous) discussion networks. Finally, for Blacks, the percentage of Whites in the neighborhood is positively associated with network partisan homogeneity, but this is only significant at the 10 percent level. We do not observe any statistically significant associations among our contextual- or individual-level factors and partisan homogeneity among Latino or White respondents.

When we compare the determinants of network partisan homogeneity for our foreign-born and U.S.-born respondents (see Table A3.2), we find that the factors associated with partisan composition among the U.S.-born respondents fail to be statistically significant in our foreign-born sample. For example, among our U.S.-born respondents, contextual-level resources exert much more power than do the individual-level resources in explaining the level of partisan homogeneity within one's political discussion network. Membership in secular groups is positively associated with having discussion partners with similar partisan preferences. On the other hand, we find a negative relationship between those who are members of religious groups and partisan homogeneity within one's political discussion network among the U.S.-born. Gender is the only individual-level factor that helps explain U.S.-born network homogeneity; as we have seen, being a woman is positively correlated with a larger share of copartisans in her network.

Interestingly, gender differences do not seem influential in this regard (see Table A3.8). Here, again, we see the importance of membership in a secular organization, which is positively associated with network copartisanship for men and women. And we again see age playing an important role only for men, with older men having fewer copartisans in their network. Neighborhood composition also seems to matter for men, with men being significantly less likely to have copartisans in their networks if they live in more diverse census blocks. Interestingly, that local context does not seem to have as much of a relationship with women's networks. One possible explanation is that, since women are much more likely than men to have family members as discussion partners, the composition of their networks is less influenced by their immediate neighborhood contexts.

What Can We Make of These Results?

In general, these results are consistent with those documented in earlier work by Leighley and Matsuyabashi (2009), but they also offer some new insights that help us to understand the partisan network homogeneity and the frequency of discussion for a given network. One of the main takeaways from our analysis is that the individual and contextual-level factors fail to consistently explain one's networks across all ethnoracial groups, nativity, and gender. In some instances, group membership is much more strongly associated with network size for Latinos than it is for Blacks, and in some cases, being a member of a secular or religious group has no bearing on the size of one's discussion network. All of this goes to show that understanding the factors that are associated with the various facets of political discussion networks are not the same across the board, which therefore implies that network effects on political behavior and attitudes may vary as well. At a minimum, our results underscore the fact that ethnoracial group members hold different social positions within U.S. society, have therefore had varied political experiences, and are subject to differential political opportunity structures. Not surprisingly, that could influence the structure and function of their political discussion networks.

Overall, our findings suggest that individual-level factors appear to have the strongest associations with network characteristics among Asian Americans, relative to the other ethnoracial groups. Asian Americans who are college educated are likely to have larger discussion networks, whereas being older is negatively correlated with the size of one's network. Being married results in a mixed effect for Blacks and Latinos; while it is positively associated with network size for Blacks, it has the opposite relationship for Latinos. We find that naturalized voters are embedded in smaller networks that are more politically diverse in terms of partisanship than those of the U.S. born. In terms of gender, we find that for men and women, being involved in a secular organization has an important effect on their network composition. For men, their networks seem to shrink with age, and they seem to be affected by their neighborhood contexts in ways that women are not. We note, however, that these tests are not causal in any way and can only identify correlational patterns.

Conclusion

This chapter provides an important foundation for understanding what political discussion networks look like for the major ethnoracial groups in the United States, and how they vary by nativity and gender. Our results make clear that the makeup and character of these political discussion networks vary in important ways across different groupings of our respondents. We also find that that the effects that individual-level and contextual-level factors have on network makeup vary across these groups. Previous research suggests that these three factors—network size, discussion frequency, and partisan composition—all affect how political discussion networks relate to political knowledge, attitude formation, and engagement. Our findings suggest that the opportunity structures available to individuals that influence the formation and character of their discussion networks are quite different across ethnorace, nativity, and gender. We will see in subsequent chapters that these differences are consequential in terms of our respondents' opinions about public policy and their civic engagement patterns.

4

Precursors to Political Engagement

Political Efficacy and Trust

Things are happening. Change is happening. We are overcoming the stigma of politics.

Male Latino canvasser, Community Coalition

The "stigma of politics," as our canvasser calls it, has long played a central role in the political experiences of communities of color in the United States. Laws and policies such as Jim Crow, The Chinese Exclusion Act, and countless others have prevented non-whites from becoming full-fledged participants in the U.S. political process (Smith 1997; King 2000). As a result of our long and sordid history of racially exclusionary political practices, many Black, Latino, and Asian voters can feel that their role in politics is minimal at best, and at worst, inconsequential or even inappropriate (Dawson 2000; García Bedolla 2009; Wong et al. 2011). Stigma, which is experienced by individuals who possess or are believed to possess some attribute, or characteristic, that conveys a social identity that is devalued in a particular social context (Garcia Bedolla 2005), is therefore a serious psychological factor that can affect voters' political engagement.

Feeling stigmatized from politics directly affects individuals' attitudes toward government and feelings of political efficacy and trust. Generally speaking, these attributes are typically what scholars refer to as the psychological resources that positively predict political participation and civic engagement (Garcia Bedolla 2005). Individuals who feel that they have a say in government believe that their vote matters and individuals who think that politicians care about them are the ones most likely to become involved in politics. Yet, those who are politically stigmatized are likely to feel that they can have little impact in the political process or that their participation is of little significance. As a result, they may be unlikely to become involved in

Talking Politics. Taylor N. Carlson, Marisa Abrajano, and Lisa García Bedolla, Oxford University Press (2020). © Oxford University Press.
DOI: 10.1093/oso/9780190082116.001.0001

politics. Such an explanation has helped us to understand the "racial gap" that exists in the political participation rates of non-whites and Whites (Tate 1993; García Bedolla 2005; Wong et al. 2011, García Bedolla and Michelson 2012).

What determines whether individuals feel politically empowered and trusting in government? Generally speaking, the existing research has found that the same factors that explain who participates in politics, such as one's level of education and income, can also help us to predict which individuals are politically trusting and efficacious (Verba et al. 1995; Delli Carpini and Keeter 1996). In this chapter, we contribute to these studies by examining whether political discussion networks also help to explain levels of political efficacy and trust, particularly among voters who have experienced stigma in their lives. While very little research on this subject matter exists, we have reason to believe that discussion networks could be important to explaining one's trust in government as well as one's feelings of political efficacy and perhaps as a countervailing force that help engage voters of color in politics. Given the positive relationship that has been found between political conversations and political engagement, we expect these discussions to exert a similarly positive effect on participants' likelihood of feeling politically efficacious and trusting of government, particularly among marginalized voters.

We therefore contend that these everyday political conversations may be crucial to engaging voters of color. Reflecting on the many conversations they had with potential voters, one of our male Asian American APEN canvassers said:

> I think it [canvassing] was really my motivation to get involved politically. I think when I think about my own personal theory of social change, electoral politics are certainly one important part of that. And so, just through my experience with canvassing and also as an activist on my college campus, I really saw the power of what kind of one-on-one conversations can achieve, although I have been interested in also different canvassing models. I just think it's an interesting way of trying to achieve social change, and there's parts of it that I'm not sure are so successful and there's other parts of it that I do think are. But really, first and foremost, canvassing has been a way for me to be involved within electoral politics.

Canvassing is relevant to our discussions because it entails having purposeful political conversations designed to try to shift individuals' behaviors. If individuals do not have these types of one-on-one conversations and only talk about politics infrequently and with a small number of individuals who, in turn, reside in communities that are not highly politicized, this could also influence their attitudes toward government and politics. While canvassing may capture a different type of social influence given that the conversations often occur between strangers instead of carefully chosen discussants, our qualitative interviews tell us that even conversations with strangers through canvassing can have an important impact on people's political efficacy and trust. Thus, it is crucial to understand the role that political discussion networks play in the development of the two key psychological factors that have been found to influence political behavior in the United States: trust and efficacy.

Why Political Trust in Government Matters

Levi and Stoker broadly define trust as a relationship that "involves an individual making herself vulnerable to another individual, group or institution that has the capacity to do her harm or betray her" (2000: 476). Political trust or trust in government, however, does not equate to the same type of trust that one might bestow on a friend. Instead, one's trust in government may suggest a belief that the government or elected official possesses the ability to perform a good job (Hardin, 2002). It can also be conceived of as a one-way form of trust, because it is the individual who trusts the political institution, with no expectations that the institution will reciprocate (Hardin, 2002). Looking at time series data on political trust, we see that political trust hit its peak in 1964, followed by an overall decline. Scholars attribute this downward trend to events such as Vietnam, Watergate, and the civil rights movement (Abramson, 1983; Markus, 1979). But even when the elected officials responsible for these events left office, this decline still continued. Scholars have pointed to the growing cynicism of television news reporting as the reason for these decreasing levels of trust (Chan, 1997; Patterson, 1994). The electorate's negative evaluations of Congress, and by extension the federal government, further contributed to this downward trend in political trust in the United States (Feldman 1983; Williams 1985).

Concern about the decline in political trust stems from the belief that trust is linked to political behavior. Those who feel that they have little impact on the political process or that their participation is of little significance may be expected to have little interest in politics. Similarly, the conventional wisdom is that individuals who are less trusting of government should also be less likely to participate and be involved in politics (Almond and Verba 1963; Stokes 1962). According to Putnam (2000), individuals who trust their fellow citizens should be more willing to meet and interact with others than those with less trust. The politically trusting should also be the ones that volunteer in their communities, participate in political events, and in general are the most engaged in political and civic affairs.

Despite the intuitive appeal of this argument, it has mixed empirical support. For instance, Rosenstone and Hanson (1993) find no difference in the likelihood of voting and levels of political interest among the most and the least trusting individuals. Miller (1974) reaches a similar conclusion, failing to observe a relationship between the decreasing turnout rates and low levels of government trust. In contrast, Shingles (1981) finds that politically distrustful individuals participate in more policy-related politics than more politically trusting individuals.

Several studies have found differences in the levels of political trust by ethnorace, particularly between Blacks and Whites. For instance, Blacks have been found to be less trusting of the government than Whites, specifically pertaining to government's efforts at racial equality (Abramson, 1983). Moreover, Shingles (1981) finds that political trust and efficacy play an important role in the participation rates of Blacks, though it depends on the particular policy issue. However, exploring why Blacks are less politically trusting than Latinos, as the trends from the ANES data suggest, has not received much attention in the research literature. One reason may be that Blacks hold a more pessimistic outlook on the future of race relations than Latinos, Whites, and Asians (Hajnal and Baldassare 2001). One of our Black interviewees from SCOPE offers another possible reason:

> Well, I think that a lot of them don't trust the government. Not being involved in how important voting is. I know at one time, our race [Blacks] wasn't allowed to vote, and now we're working at the voter registration, so I bring that up as an example sometimes, for the people who don't wanna actually get involved. Well, we couldn't even vote, but now you can go work there. I think it's mainly because of trust, because of some of the things that they've been promising and didn't do, or the money didn't come and it didn't show up. They see how we get the less of the stick. So how it's hard to believe in somebody that's holding the stick, the less end of it.

Some of these same mechanisms may also be observed in the Latino community. Michelson (2001) found that Puerto Ricans in the Chicago area who were born on the island were more trusting of the government than were long-time Puerto Rican residents. Her research on Mexican Americans yields similar results, where the greater one's level of acculturation into American society, the lower his or her level of government trust (Michelson 2003). Using a nationally representative sample of Latinos, Abrajano and Alvarez (2010) find that first-generation Latinos are much more trusting of the federal government than are later generation Latinos. They offer a fairly straightforward reason for this pattern—one that aligns with our theory as well: first-generation immigrants are generally more optimistic and enthusiastic about the economic opportunities that await them in their host country. As such, their views and attitudes toward government tend to be more positive than those of later generations. Although their study focused exclusively on Latinos, we would expect the same patterns among Asian Americans for similar reasons. Therefore, across ethnoracial groups, we expect levels of political trust to be highest among Whites, with Blacks being the least trustful. Asian Americans and Latinos should fall somewhere in between.

In light of the distinct political socialization processes experienced by many Asian Americans and Latinos, we would also expect intragroup variation in levels of political efficacy and trust toward government by nativity. Namely, we expect first-generation immigrants to be more trusting of the federal government than later generation community members. Immigrants who are new to the American political system may not only perceive it as being better than their homeland government but also give credence to the American dream and everything associated with this idea—freedom, democracy, and transparency. In time, and perhaps after a generation or so, non-whites may become more disenchanted and skeptical of the government as a result of negative experiences or interactions, but that is a question beyond the scope of our study. To the extent that we can explore differences in political trust within these communities, we expect immigrants' views and attitudes toward government to be more positive than those from later generations.

In terms of gender, studies have found mixed results, with women sometimes being less trustful than men, and other times with men more trusting (Catterburg and Moreno 2006). Given that, we expect it to be unlikely that we will find any significant gender differences in trust. If we do, it would likely be due to the intersection of gender and race, given that many of the women in our sample are women of color and we know Blacks, Latinos, and Asians have lower levels of government trust than Whites.

How Are Networks Related to Trust in Government?

The size of political discussion networks and frequency of political discussion, we hypothesize, should be positively associated with one's level of trust in government. That is, those who talk about politics on a regular basis and have a large number of political discussants within their networks should exhibit higher levels of government trust than those who do not. As one of our male Asian American APEN canvassers expressed, "I've been able to talk to folks about the work I'm doing in just really cultivating that interest about what's going on and hey, like by being involved you can actually make a difference in, you know?". We know that engaging in routine conversations with a large network of individuals is associated with greater levels of political interest (Huckfeldt and Sprague 1998); likewise, it should also be the case that these individuals view the government positively and have faith in it to do what is right. However, the fact that political trust varies considerably by ethnorace suggests that these network effects may not be enough to mitigate experiences with racial discrimination, particularly in dealings with government entities or officials.

Why Political Efficacy Matters

The concept of political efficacy is particularly salient for naturalized voters and voters of color in the United States, who oftentimes feel as if they lack a voice in politics, or that it would not be appropriate for them to get involved in the political process (García Bedolla 2015; Abrajano and Alvarez 2012; García Bedolla 2005). These sentiments are particularly pronounced in immigrant communities, with many naturalized, first-time voters feeling overwhelmed and intimidated by the myriad of laws and regulations surrounding the act of voting, as well as the countless candidate races and initiatives that can appear on the ballot. Take for example, a male Latino CoCo canvasser, who prior to his canvassing experience, "had this jaded belief that no matter what [he does], whatever they [elected officials] want to do is going to happen."

Additionally, the proliferation of voter identification laws in the last two decades and their deleterious effects on minority turnout (Hajnal et al. 2017; Atkeson et al. 2010; Barreto et al. 2009) may also depress feelings of political efficacy among voters of color. It therefore stands to reason that feelings of political efficacy will vary not only by nativity but also by ethnorace. Such variation can be attributed to the U.S. racial hierarchy as well as to the spate of recent laws that are explicitly designed to intimidate and dissuade voters of color from voting.

Considering the relationship between efficacy and gender, studies have generally found that women have lower levels of efficacy than men (Coffé and Bolzendahl 2010). These differences are seen as partially explaining differences in political engagement between men and women.

Political efficacy can be defined in two ways—internal and external. Traditionally, scholars have defined internal efficacy as the belief that one can understand and therefore participate in politics (García Bedolla and Michelson 2012: 17). The other type of efficacy, which is described as external, stems from the belief that an individual's action can exert an impact on government actions. Both of these feelings tap into a voter's self-esteem. As García Bedolla and Michelson convincingly argue, fostering these feelings of self-worth, or efficacy, is particularly critical for low-propensity voters of color; by doing so, it makes them feel that "they can and should act politically" (García Bedolla and Michelson: 17).

In light of this existing research, we expect variation to exist in feelings of political efficacy across ethnorace, nativity, and gender. Namely, we offer the following hypotheses: (1) Feelings of political efficacy should be greatest among Whites and men relative to non-whites and women; (2) because they have been in the United States longer, U.S.-born individuals should be more politically efficacious than the foreign born.

How Are Networks Related to Political Efficacy?

As we hypothesized about the role of discussion networks on political trust, we expect networks' relationship to political efficacy to be positive. That is, belonging in a network with a large number of discussion partners engaged in frequent conversations should be positively correlated with strong feelings of political efficacy. Yet it is possible that the effects of ethnoracial discrimination and intimidation may so pronounced as to dilute the impact of discussion networks on political efficacy. It is also possible that, if those stories are shared within political discussion networks, networks could deepen feelings of distrust rather than ameliorate them. This reality may therefore result in more muted, or possibly negative, network effects for Blacks, Latinos, and Asians, relative to Whites. In the section that follows, we outline the survey items and methodology that we use to test these hypotheses.

Data and Methods

Our main dependent variables of interest are political trust and political efficacy. We measure political trust with the following survey item: "How often can you trust the federal government in Washington to do what is right?" The response options ranged from 1 (never) to 5 (always), and thus higher scores are associated with more trust in government. Although some research has used a few different questions to measure trust in government, we were limited in the number of questions we could include on our survey, so we chose to focus on a comprehensive question.

We measure political efficacy using the question wording used by the American National Elections Study (ANES). Participants were asked to indicate the extent to which they agreed or disagreed with the following six statements regarding their feelings toward government:

(1) Sometimes politics and government are so complicated that a person like me can't really understand what's going on.
(2) I feel that I have a pretty good understanding of the important political issues facing our country.
(3) Public officials don't care much what people like me think.
(4) People like me don't have any say about what the government does.
(5) Voting is very difficult to do.
(6) Voting can make a difference in my life.

Respondents were then asked to rate the extent to which they agree or disagree with each statement, ranging from strongly disagree (1) to strongly agree (5). Four of these statements, all except (2) and (6), are reverse coded so that higher values represent more politically efficacious attitudes for all statements. We then create an aggregate political efficacy score by summing the responses to each of the six questions. For ease of interpretation, we rescale this variable to range from 0 (least politically efficacious) to 1 (most politically efficacious).

The primary independent variables of interest are the respondents' political discussion network characteristics, including network size, the reported frequency of discussion within the network, and network partisan homogeneity.[1] In our multivariate models, we also control for variables known to be predictors of political trust and efficacy, such as age, education, and political knowledge levels.

Political Trust by Ethnorace, Nativity, and Gender

First we examine the impact of network characteristics on political trust. Figure 4.1 Figure 4.1 presents the average level of political trust, rescaled to range between 0 and 1, by ethnorace, nativity, and gender. Looking at the distributions of levels of political trust among our respondents by ethnorace, we see that they are somewhat consistent with previous research. Asian American respondents report the highest levels of trust, significantly more than Whites ($p < .01$), Blacks ($p < .001$), and Latinos ($p < .001$). Considering that our Asian American respondents are the most likely to be foreign born in our sample (25.1 percent vs. 16.6 percent of the sample overall), it is understandable that their levels of political trust would be higher overall than those of the other ethnoracial groups given naturalized voters often have greater levels of trust than the U.S. born. Among our respondents, Whites and Latinos had statistically indistinguishable levels of trust in government. Our Black respondents reported the least amount of political trust among all the groups included in our study.

These patterns are reflected in the experiences of one our female SCOPE interviewees who canvasses Black neighborhoods in South Los Angeles. She says that

> "[Blacks] ain't got no problem in telling you 'I don't believe none of that crap, ain't nothing gonna change, ain't nothing changed, it's all gonna be the same, blah blah.' I get that a lot too. Sometimes some people can be persuaded to be undecided, or some people stick to what they believe in."

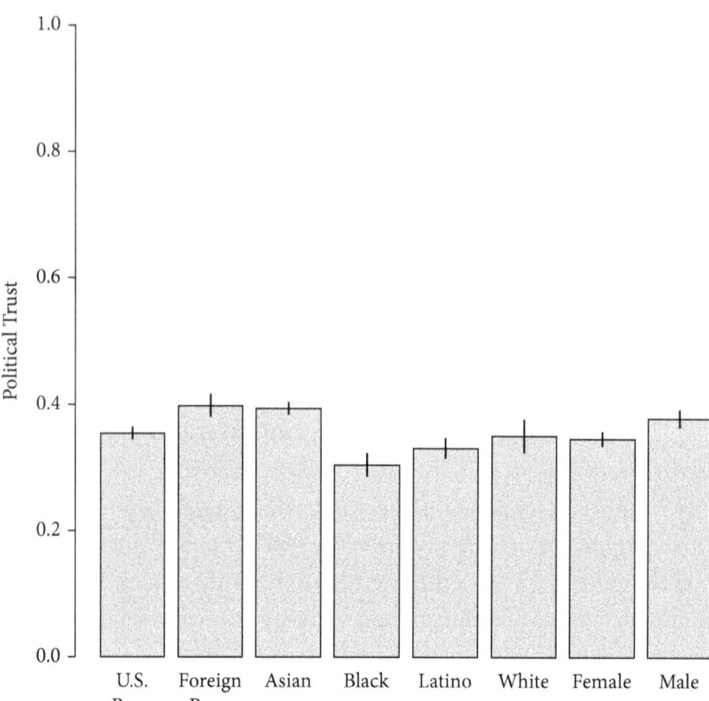

Figure 4.1. Average levels of political trust by ethnorace, nativity, and gender. Vertical lines represent 95% confidence intervals.

Similarly, a Black-idenfified SCOPE canvasser, said:

> Perhaps they [south Los Angeles residents] might be a little fearful, or they've had encounters in life with the government or something. Things such as, you know, okay. Take a person that may have gotten food stamps. Well they took my food stamps, I don't want to talk about that or whatever, you know. Or they reduced my check or whatever. Or they're giving me . . . things to that nature. They have some kind of, you don't want to say ill will, or distastefulness should one say . . . against the government of a small caliber. Maybe it's small to us, but maybe not them. [They'll say] I don't want to talk about that or whatever, they're [the government is] no good, they won't give me my raise, or whatever the case may be. So things to that nature which lets me know the persons who are doing this aren't

> the persons that are in authority to make these changes, these decisions for these persons are not all wrong. They're [elected officials] not just going to be sitting up there saying I'm not going to give you this, or whatever.

That question of trust—the belief that our democratic government is serving all people as it should and doing so fairly, is fundamental to a successful democratic political system. But we see in our survey results and in these quotes from canvassers that many Americans have experiences in their communities and work lives that lead them to question whether the "system" is to be trusted. That, in turn, logically can affect their willingness to participate in and trust that system.

Looking at nativity, consistent with our expectations, those born in the United States have significantly lower levels of political trust than the foreign born ($p < .001$). Our findings align with the existing research that finds differential levels of political trust among Latino immigrants, with second- and later generation Latinos possessing lower levels of trust than their foreign-born counterparts (Abrajano and Alvarez 2010; Michelson 2001). Again, the rationale for these varying levels of trust is rather straightforward; first-generation immigrants are generally more optimistic and enthusiastic about the economic and political opportunities that await them in their host country. Indeed, breaking these results down by generation, we find that first-generation Americans had the highest levels of trust. Specifically, first-generation respondents had significantly higher levels of trust than U.S.-born respondents ($p < .001$). Classic assimilation theory would also predict that as immigrants become more acculturated and integrated into the dominant society, their opinions will begin to mirror those of the majority, thereby gaining a more skeptical and cynical outlook of the federal government.

Looking at gender, males in our sample reported slightly higher levels of political trust than women ($p < .05$). Given the mixed results in previous research and the fact that these responses are from a very diverse group of men and women, it is difficult to ascertain whether this result is driven by gender or ethnoracial differences.

Network Characteristics and Political Trust by Ethnorace

Next, we analyze the relationship between political discussion network characteristics and political trust by ethnorace. In Table 4.1, we present the results

Table 4.1. Relationship between Network Characteristics and Political Trust, by Ethnorace

	Dependent variable: Political trust			
	Asian (1)	Black (2)	Latino (3)	White (4)
Percent copartisan	0.0003	0.001**	0.001**	0.0004
	(0.0002)	(0.0004)	(0.0004)	(0.001)
Network size	−0.019	0.055*	0.003	0.025
	(0.016)	(0.030)	(0.018)	(0.046)
Discussion frequency	−0.0002	−0.029	0.006	−0.005
	(0.011)	(0.019)	(0.016)	(0.028)
Political knowledge	0.015	−0.005	−0.025	0.032
	(0.015)	(0.024)	(0.022)	(0.034)
Female	−0.007	−0.057*	−0.049*	0.028
	(0.018)	(0.031)	(0.028)	(0.040)
Age	0.0004	0.002**	0.0001	−0.002
	(0.001)	(0.001)	(0.001)	(0.001)
College	0.015	0.018	0.002	0.022
	(0.022)	(0.031)	(0.029)	(0.046)
Constant	0.406***	0.034	0.314	0.196
	(0.088)	(0.147)	(0.111)	(0.264)
Observations	532	210	252	92
R^2	0.009	0.074	0.043	0.051
Adjusted R^2	−0.005	0.042	0.015	−0.028
Residual std. err.	0.201 (df=524)	0.209 (df=202)	0.216 (df=244)	0.174 (df=84)
F statistic	0.658 (df=7; 524)	2.313** (df=7; 202)	1.561 (df=7; 244)	0.649 (df=7; 84)

Note: *$p < 0.10$; **$p < 0.05$; ***$p < 0.01$.

from an OLS regression in which the dependent variable was political trust and the independent variables of interest were the network characteristics: network size, discussion frequency, and partisan homogeneity. Our results reveal that the predictive power of discussion networks on political trust is fairly limited. Partisan composition is the only network characteristic that is associated with political trust, and only among Black and Latino respondents. We find that a statistically significant, positive association between the percentage of copartisans in one's discussion network and the extent to which our Black and Latino respondents trust the government. However, the coefficients are small in magnitude. This means that when Blacks and Latinos are exposed to less disagreement in their discussion networks, they tend to have greater trust in government. There is suggestive evidence of a positive association between network size and political trust among Blacks as well ($p < .10$). Given that Blacks have notably low levels of political trust, it is important to note how political discussion networks might help to build trust. However, given that Blacks have good reason not to trust the government given their long history of discriminatory treatment at its hands, it may be difficult for political discussion networks to have a significant impact on their levels of trust.

We find few consistent patterns with regard to the individual-level characteristics. Black and Latino men seem to have slightly higher levels of trust in government than Black and Latina women, but gender is not associated with trust among White or Asian respondents. Age is positively associated with trust among Black respondents, such that older respondents had higher levels of trust than younger respondents. Otherwise, individual-level factors did not have a statistically significant effect on our respondents' reported political trust levels.

Network Characteristics and Political Trust by Nativity

Next, we explore the relationship between political discussion network characteristics and political trust by nativity. The results are presented in Table 4.2. Of our three different measures of discussion networks, only one is associated with political trust for U.S.-born respondents: the percentage of copartisans within their networks. Among the U.S. born, there is a significant and positive association between partisan homogeneity and political trust. Specifically, those who are in more homogeneous discussion networks—exposed to less partisan disagreement—have higher levels of trust in government, but the magnitude of this relationship is small. Such a relationship, however, is not evident among our foreign-born respondents. There is suggestive evidence of a statistically significant negative association between network size and political trust among the foreign-born respondents ($p < .10$), but we find no relationship between network size and trust among U.S.-born respondents. There is no statistically significant relationship between discussion frequency and political trust among our U.S.- or foreign-born respondents.

With regard to individual-level characteristics, only gender and education are significantly associated with trust in government, and only among the U.S. born. Specifically, among the U.S. born, men had higher levels of trust than women, and those with some college education had higher levels

Table 4.2. Relationship between Network Characteristics and Political Trust, by Nativity

	Dependent variable: Political trust	
	U.S. born (1)	Foreign born (2)
Percent copartisan	0.001***	−0.0002
	(0.0002)	(0.0005)
Network size	0.010	−0.048*
	(0.011)	(0.029)
Discussion frequency	−0.010	0.0003
	(0.008)	(0.022)
Political knowledge	0.004	0.032
	(0.011)	(0.030)
Female	−0.032**	−0.00002
	(0.013)	(0.035)
Age	−0.0002	0.0002
	(0.0005)	(0.001)
College graduate	0.028*	0.048
	(0.014)	(0.039)
Constant	0.292***	0.506***
	(0.061)	(0.172)
Observations	1,020	146
R^2	0.022	0.038
Adjusted R^2	0.015	−0.011
Residual std. err.	0.205 (df=1012)	0.207 (df=138)
F statistic	3.291*** (df=7; 1012	0.781 (df=7; 138)

Note: $^{*}p < 0.10$; $^{**}p < 0.05$; $^{***}p < 0.01$.

of trust than those without some college education, however this education result is only suggestive at the 10 percent level. Curiously, none of the individual-level variables in our model were significantly associated with political trust among our foreign-born respondents.

Network Characteristics and Political Trust by Gender

Even though we find, as expected from previous research, that women in our sample reported lower levels of political trust than men, the network factors

Table 4.3. Relationship between Network Characteristics and Political Trust, by Gender

	Dependent variable: Political trust	
	Female (1)	Male (2)
Percent copartisan	0.001***	0.0005*
	(0.0002)	(0.0003)
Network size	0.008	−0.003
	(0.014)	(0.015)
Discussion frequency	−0.013	−0.002
	(0.009)	(0.012)
Political knowledge	0.006	0.011
	(0.013)	(0.016)
Age	0.0001	−0.0005
	(0.001)	(0.001)
College	0.029*	0.026
	(0.017)	(0.022)
Constant	0.281***	0.336***
	(0.077)	(0.086)
Observations	703	464
R^2	0.016	0.012
Adjusted R^2	0.007	−0.001
Residual std. err.	0.202 (df = 696)	0.211 (df = 457)
F statistic	1.884* (df=6; 696)	0.959 (df=6; 457)

Note: *$p < 0.10$; **$p < 0.05$; ***$p < 0.01$.

that are most strongly associated with those levels of trust are the same for men and women. As Table 4.3 indicates, the percent of copartisans within the discussion network had a positive, statistically significant relationship with levels of political trust among men and women. While this relationship was substantively small for both genders, none of the individual-level characteristics were significantly associated with trust for men or women.

Political Efficacy, by Ethnorace, Nativity, and Gender

We now turn to our respondents' responses to the political efficacy scale, with survey responses disaggregated by ethnorace, nativity, and gender.

Table 4.4. Average Disagreement with Each Political Efficacy Statement

	U.S. born	Foreign born	Asian	Black	Latino	White	Female	Male
Sometimes politics and government are so complicated that a person like me can't really understand what's going on. (R)	3.18	2.98	2.96	3.54	3.11	3.55	3.09	3.28
I feel that I have a pretty good understanding of the important political issues facing our country.	3.87	3.80	3.72	4.09	3.89	4.03	3.77	4.01
Public officials don't care much what people like me think. (R)	2.55	2.54	2.60	2.52	2.38	2.70	2.55	2.53
People like me don't have any say about what the government does. (R)	3.11	3.02	3.04	3.20	3.09	3.19	3.15	3.04
Voting is very difficult to do. (R)	4.25	4.19	4.15	4.39	4.28	4.43	4.25	4.27
Voting can make a difference in my life.	3.85	3.71	3.77	3.98	3.82	3.86	3.91	3.74

Note: Each statement is measured on a scale that ranges from 1 (agree strongly) to 5 (disagree strongly). Items marked with (R) were reverse coded so that across all six items, higher values indicate a more efficacious attitude.

Table 4.4 presents the average responses to the political efficacy questions on the original 5-point agreement scales by nativity and ethnorace. The statements marked with "(R)" indicate that they were reverse coded so that higher values reflect more politically efficacious attitudes. For example, a 5 in response to "Voting can make a difference in my life" means that the respondent strongly agreed with that statement. The results in Table 4.4 suggest that substantial variation in feelings of political efficacy exists by ethnorace, nativity, and gender. For instance, U.S.-born respondents possessed higher levels of efficacy for all six statements than foreign-born respondents, though many of these differences were small, especially for "Public officials don't care much what people like me think."

Across ethnorace, Asians and Latinos tended to have less efficacious attitudes than Blacks and Whites on most statements. As expected, relative to Whites and Blacks, a larger number of Asians and Latinos, on average, agreed with the statement that politics was too complicated for them to understand. And although we hypothesized that Whites would report the highest levels of political efficacy out of all the groups, particularly when compared with Blacks, our results suggest otherwise. In fact, our Black respondents' feelings of political efficacy were generally on par with those of Whites.

Interestingly, we find no significant differences in feelings of political efficacy by gender when we look at overall levels of efficacy, but we do find some statistically significant differences across particular items. That being the case, the men and women in our sample view their role in government in quite a similar manner. However, when we look into each item of the scale, we uncover some important nuances that are masked by the null result in aggregate efficacy. Men were significantly more likely than women to disagree that politics and government are too complicated ($p < .001$), and more likely than women to agree that they have a pretty good understanding of the important political issues facing our country ($p < .001$). Women, in contrast, were more likely than men to disagree that people like them don't have any say about what the government does ($p < .05$). In other words, women were more likely than men to believe that public officials care what they think. Finally, women were more likely than men to agree that voting can make a difference in their lives ($p < .001$), even though there was no difference between men and women in how difficult they thought voting was.

In Figure 4.2, we provide the aggregate levels of political efficacy by ethnorace, nativity, and gender. Efficacy scores closer to 1 indicate higher levels of political efficacy, scores closer to 0 indicate lower levels of political efficacy. As one might surmise based on the results in Table 4.4, White and Black respondents possess the highest levels of political efficacy; these differences are significantly greater than those of Latinos and Asian Americans.[2] These results also suggest that Latinos felt slightly more politically efficacious than Asian Americans ($p < .05$). As such, our aggregate measure of political efficacy indicates that out of all the ethnoracial groups

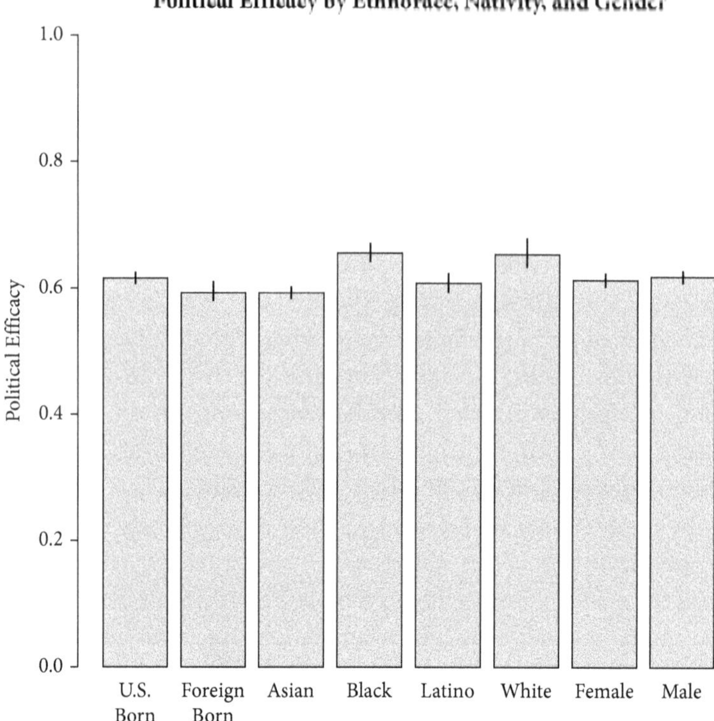

Figure 4.2. Average aggregate political efficacy. Vertical lines represent 95% confidence intervals.

that we examine, Asian Americans exhibit the lowest levels of political efficacy. This is consistent with other studies of Asian American political attitudes that have attempted to explain the "Asian paradox"—the fact that Asian Americans possess high socioeconomic status and relatively low levels of political engagement (Wong et al. 2011; Dobard et al. 2017).

Looking at how political efficacy intersects with nativity, we find that our U.S.-born respondents reported significantly higher levels of political efficacy than the foreign born ($p < .01$). Although, as expected, female-identified respondents expressed slightly lower levels of political efficacy, that difference was not statistically significant (Burns et al. 2001). Overall, these descriptive differences are consistent with what previous scholars have noted, particularly with respect to immigrant-origin groups (Bobo and Gilliam 1990; García Bedolla and Michelson 2012; Dobard et al. 2017).

Network Characteristics and Political Efficacy by Ethnorace

In this section, we turn to the relationship between network characteristics and political efficacy by ethnorace. Table 4.5 presents the results from an OLS regression in which the dependent variable was political efficacy, and our main independent variables of interest were network characteristics.[3] Recall that our multivariate model also controlled for other individual-level factors that could predict feelings of political efficacy. Given that we want to

Table 4.5. Relationship between Network Characteristics and Political Efficacy, by Ethnorace

	Dependent variable: Political efficacy			
	Asian (1)	Black (2)	Latino (3)	White (4)
Percent copartisan	0.0004**	0.001***	0.0003	0.001*
	(0.0002)	(0.0003)	(0.0003)	(0.0004)
Network size	0.011	−0.018	0.018	0.017
	(0.015)	(0.022)	(0.014)	(0.040)
Discussion frequency	0.051***	0.046***	0.030**	0.064**
	(0.009)	(0.014)	(0.013)	(0.025)
Political knowledge	0.048***	0.033*	0.036**	−0.039
	(0.012)	(0.017)	(0.017)	(0.029)
Female	−0.012	−0.016	−0.043*	−0.023
	(0.015)	(0.022)	(0.022)	(0.035)
Age	−0.0001	0.001	0.002*	−0.001
	(0.001)	(0.001)	(0.001)	(0.001)
College graduate	0.025	0.041*	0.032	0.020
	(0.018)	(0.023)	(0.023)	(0.040)
Constant	0.252***	0.398***	0.302***	0.460***
	(0.079)	(0.107)	(0.088)	(0.230)
Observations	523	207	247	92
R^2	0.132	0.183	0.127	0.134
Adjusted R^2	0.121	0.155	0.101	0.062
Residual std. err.	0.161 (df=515)	0.151 (df=199)	0.169 (df=239)	0.151 (df=84)
F statistic	11.222*** (df=7; 515)	6.381*** (df=7; 199)	4.958*** (df=7; 239)	1.855* (df=7; 84)

Note: $^{*}p < 0.10$; $^{**}p < 0.05$; $^{***}p < 0.01$.

understand within-group as well as across-group differences, we estimate the model separately for each ethnoracial group.

We find that some network characteristics are positively associated with political efficacy. Of our three different measures of network characteristics, it was the frequency of political discussion among one's discussion partners that was most consistently positively associated with higher levels of political efficacy across all ethnoracial groups. Regardless of ethnorace, we find that individuals who talk about politics regularly within their networks possess higher levels of political efficacy. As we hypothesized, engaging in everyday political discussions should be associated with a greater sense of political self-worth. Given that this relationship is robust across all ethnoracial groups, our results underscore discussion networks' potential to foster and develop feelings of political efficacy within the U.S. electorate even among marginalized group members.

The degree of partisan homogeneity in one's network was also a consistent predictor of political efficacy for all ethnoracial groups, with the exception of Latinos. The more copartisans in one's network, the greater the levels of political efficacy among Asian and Black respondents. Among Whites, this relationship is suggestive at the 10 percent level. Having like-minded individuals in one's network could possibly lead to a greater sense of political empowerment and agency and thereby lead one to see oneself as a meaningful and influential member of the polity. Why we fail to observe this relationship among Latinos could be that network copartisanship is unable to compensate for Latinos' comparatively smaller networks and other socialization mechanisms in the broader society that may negatively affect their feelings of personal efficacy. Our final network measure is network size. Across all groups, the size of one's network fails to predict their feelings of political efficacy.

Looking at the impact of individual-level characteristics indicates that among our non-white respondents, political knowledge is positively associated with political efficacy. However, the remaining individual-level characteristics are not associated with efficacy for any group except Latinos. Among Latinos, older respondents and men had higher levels of political efficacy than younger Latinos and women, but these patterns are only suggestive at the 10 percent level. We also observe suggestive evidence that Black respondents with a college education have higher levels of efficacy ($p < .10$). Overall, these findings offer some much-needed insight into the role that political discussion networks play in predicting feelings of political efficacy. Based on our analysis, we contend that these network effects, indeed, help to explain how politically efficacious one feels, but they do not operate uniformly across all ethnoracial groups. We also want to emphasize that the coefficients are generally small, indicating that the patterns may be statistically significant, but that the magnitude of the effects is small.

Network Characteristics and Political Efficacy by Nativity

Our next set of analyses employs the same models, but broken down by nativity instead of ethnorace. The results in Table 4.6 indicate that network characteristics are a stronger and more consistent predictor of political efficacy among the U.S.-born than among the foreign-born. We find that partisan homogeneity and discussion frequency are positively associated with increased levels of political efficacy among our U.S.-born respondents. Specifically, as political discussion networks become more homogeneous, with less exposure to disagreement, U.S.-born respondents have higher levels of political efficacy. However, there is no statistically significant relationship between partisan homogeneity and political efficacy among the foreign-born respondents. Network size does not appear to be associated with efficacy for either group. There is suggestive evidence at the 10 percent level that discussion frequency is positively associated with efficacy among foreign-born respondents. That is, regardless of nativity, those who discuss politics in their networks more often have higher feelings of political efficacy.

Beyond network characteristics, there are some important individual-level factors to note. First, political knowledge is significantly, positively associated with political efficacy among both the U.S.- and foreign-born respondents. Those who are more politically knowledgeable have higher levels of political efficacy. Beyond political knowledge, however, demographic factors only influenced political efficacy among the U.S.-born respondents. Specifically, among the U.S. born, men had higher levels of political efficacy than did women, and older respondents had higher levels of efficacy than younger respondents. In contrast, demographic factors are not significantly associated with political efficacy among foreign-born respondents.

Table 4.6 Relationship between Network Characteristics and Political Efficacy, by Nativity

	Dependent variable: Political efficacy	
	U.S. born (1)	Foreign-Born (2)
Percent copartisan	0.001***	0.001
	(0.0001)	(0.0004)
Network size	0.009	0.021
	(0.009)	(0.036)
Discussion frequency	0.048***	0.037*
	(0.006)	(0.020)
Political knowledge	0.026***	0.096***
	(0.008)	(0.026)
Female	−0.023**	0.048
	(0.010)	(0.030)
Age	0.001**	−0.0003
	(0.0004)	(0.001)
College	0.012	0.022
	(0.011)	(0.034)
Constant	0.312***	0.111
	(0.048)	(0.196)
Observations	1,005	143
R^2	0.135	0.190
Adjusted R^2	0.128	0.148
Residual std. err.	0.157 (df=997)	0.175 (df=135)
F statistic	22.144*** (df=7; 997)	4.515*** (df=7; 135)

Note: $^{*}p < 0.10$; $^{**}p < 0.05$; $^{***}p < 0.01$.

Network Characteristics and Political Efficacy by Gender

Burns et al. (2001) emphasize the importance of institutions—the family, workplace, churches, and community organizations—in explaining gender differences in political engagement. Our analysis of the degree to which the political discussion networks we are focusing on, which arguably are the product of the relationships and conversations that occur within those institutions, can help explain gender differences in feelings of political efficacy. As Table 4.7 demonstrates, we find that discussion frequency and partisan homogeneity are positively associated with efficacy for both men and

Table 4.7. Relationship between Network Characteristics and Political Efficacy, by Gender

	Dependent variable: Political efficacy	
	Female	Male
Percent copartisan	0.0003*	0.001***
	(0.0002)	(0.0002)
Network size	0.006	0.012
	(0.012)	(0.013)
Discussion frequency	0.044***	0.056***
	(0.007)	(0.010)
Political knowledge	0.034***	0.042***
	(0.010)	(0.013)
Age	0.002***	−0.001
	(0.004)	(0.001)
College	0.017	0.001
	(0.013)	(0.017)
Constant	0.290***	0.287***
	(0.063)	(0.071)
Observations	690	459
R^2	0.139	0.147
Adjusted R^2	0.132	0.135
Residual std. err.	0.155 (df = 683)	0.166 (df = 452)
F statistic	18.399*** (df=6; 683)	12.942*** (df=6; 452)

Note: *$p < 0.10$; **$p < 0.05$; ***$p < 0.01$.

women. However, the relationship between partisan homogeneity and political efficacy is only suggestive at the 10 percent level among women and the magnitudes are substantively small for both genders. We do not observe a statistically significant association between network size and efficacy for either gender. Political knowledge was significantly, positively associated with political efficacy for both men and women. For women, age is also statistically significant, with older women more likely to feel efficacious within politics.

Conclusion

We know from previous research that feelings of political efficacy and trust in government are important predictors of political engagement. The research on political discussion networks would lead us to assume that the structure and function of those networks influence both political efficacy and political trust. Yet, no study has systematically examined the relationship among political discussion networks, political efficacy, and trust. Nor have any of these analyses explored variation across the lines of ethnorace, nativity, and gender. Our goal in this chapter was to do just that.

As summarized in Table 4.8, we find that the impact of those political discussion network characteristics—size, discussion frequency, and partisan composition—varies in important ways by ethnorace, nativity, and gender. For each group, the network factors best able to predict levels of political trust and efficacy vary significantly.

Political discussion network characteristics appear to have little predictive power in explaining our respondents' levels of political trust. Greater partisan homogeneity is associated with higher levels of political trust for Latinos, Blacks, and U.S.-born individuals, as well as among men and women in our sample. Discussion frequency was not associated with political trust for any of the groups and network size was only associated with trust for Black and foreign-born respondents, but the results were suggestive and in opposite directions.

Table 4.8. Summary of Findings: Relationship between Network Characteristics and Political Trust and Efficacy

	Ethnoracial Group				*Nativity*		*Gender*	
	Asian	Black	Latino	White	Foreign-Born	U.S. born	Female	Male
Political efficacy								
Size								
Discussion frequency	+	+	+	+	+	+	+	+
Copartisanship	+	+		+		+	+	+
Political trust								
Size		+			–			
Discussion frequency								
Copartisanship		+	+			+	+	+

Note: Cell entries with a (+) denote that the discussion network characteristic coefficient was statistically and positively significant at at least the $p < .10$ level. Entries with (-) denote a negative coefficient at the $p < .10$ level.

Network effects on our respondents' feelings of political efficacy were more mixed. Looking at ethnorace, the frequency of political conversations was associated with greater feelings of political efficacy for all ethnoracial groups. Partisan homogeneity was associated with higher levels of political efficacy among all groups except Latinos. In terms of nativity, network effects exerted greater explanatory power in explaining the levels of political efficacy among U.S.-born individuals, compared with the foreign born. In fact, only discussion frequency helped to explain feelings of efficacy for our foreign-born respondents. Finally, network characteristics had a significant impact on political efficacy for men and women, and copartisanship within networks affected political trust among both male- and female-identified respondents.

These findings point to the need for future scholars to continue to investigate the role that discussion networks play in facilitating precursors to political engagement such as political trust and efficacy. We also encourage scholars to explore other important attitudinal predictors of political engagement and behavior (e.g., racial resentment, ethnocentricism, and discrimination) and how they might intersect with and/or mediate network effects.

Our findings underscore the need for scholars not to assume that political discussion networks operate in the same way for all members of the U.S. electorate. The variation we see in this chapter suggests that individual-level differences, social context, and other socializing factors such as a group's particular political history and relative social position in U.S. society play important roles in determining a person's network characteristics and also its impacts.

5

Political Discussion Networks and Information

> My friends schooled me on some of the propositions that were going through and what we needed and our community needed and I felt like I could reach out to more people as well.
>
> Female Latina canvasser, Community Coalition

As this quote from a Community Coalition canvasser highlights, talking about politics with friends and family can be an important source of information for individuals. Discussing politics generally improves citizens' knowledge of public affairs (Bennett et al. 2000), increases political sophistication among participants in face-to-face discussions (Gastil and Dillard 1999), and elevates opinion quality (Wyatt et al. 2000). Talking about politics on a regular basis also makes individuals more likely to know about the ins and out of politics, as well as general political facts (Eveland and Hively 2009).

In terms of the influence that discussion networks may play in explaining levels of political knowledge, the conventional wisdom is that frequency of political discussion with one's discussion partners will be positively associated with the amount of political information that one possesses. Individuals who discuss politics regularly with family and friends in their network are going to be more politically knowledgeable, especially if these discussions occur in heterogeneous networks, allowing individuals to be exposed to a wider variety of information (Eveland and Hively 2009). One of our male Asian American APEN canvassers pointed out how canvassing affected his levels of political knowledge:

> Well, I definitely know a lot more about these propositions [after canvassing], and especially with Prop 5, I just did not know the history that led up to that at all. And so, now I know that, and I would share that

Talking Politics. Taylor N. Carlson, Marisa Abrajano, and Lisa García Bedolla, Oxford University Press (2020). © Oxford University Press.
DOI: 10.1093/oso/9780190082116.001.0001

> history with everyone. So, definitely during that time, I was able to share that knowledge that was new. And then, I think when I talk with my friends about canvassing and what are the pros and cons of it, I feel like I have a much more tangible experience to draw upon.

However, as we demonstrated in Chapter 3, political discussion network characteristics vary along the lines of ethnorace, nativity, and gender, but the majority of scholarly findings on discussion networks and political knowledge come from mostly White samples. We also know that rates of political engagement and political knowledge, for historic and political reasons, vary in important ways across ethnoracial groups in the United States. Thus, it is reasonable to assume that the availability and quality of political information within individuals' political discussion networks will vary in important ways as well. In addition, the information to which individuals are exposed through political conversations could affect not only how much they know about politics, but also the attitudes they hold. In this chapter, we focus on the impact of political discussion network characteristics on: (1) political knowledge and (2) issue attitudes and policy preferences among Whites and non-whites.

Political Discussion Networks and Information Acquisition

The flow of information that passes through political discussion networks can be incredibly valuable for individuals, and we might imagine it to be of even greater import for naturalized votes who are not as frequently targeted and exposed to other types of political information, particularly those provided by political elites and campaigns (Abrajano 2010). Informal channels, such as political discussion networks, could help fill the informational void left by more formal political networks, such as campaigns, that often fail to target non-whites. These political discussions not only can foster greater issue awareness, but they can also lead to increased levels of political knowledge.

Political Discussion Networks and Political Knowledge

How exactly do these political conversations lead to a more aware and knowledgeable citizenry? There are three general explanations for the relationship between political discussion networks and political knowledge. The first explanation, which Eveland (2004) refers to as the exposure explanation, contends that individuals acquire information from their discussion partners in a way that is similar to getting information from the news media. Discussion is therefore just an additional way that individuals can acquire information. Political discussion can either supplement information acquired from other sources, such as the news media, or it can be a substitute for getting information from the news media. Political discussions could also provide individuals with an alternative perspective from what they get from the media. A Latino male Community Coalition canvasser shared how being exposed to political knowledge through canvassing gave him this type of alternative perspective on the importance of political engagement:

> So canvassing has been able to not only make me a more informed individual, I know the process of law now. I know why it's important to vote now. I know that it's not a privilege gesture. I know that it's not this one thing where people come together every 4 or 2 years. I know the importance of it now. And I'm able to deliver that with my loved ones, my friends, my community, and CoCo has helped me a lot in that. I didn't know those things before. I wasn't even really interested because I honestly had this jaded belief that no matter what I do, whatever they want to do is going to happen.

This type of exposure to political knowledge can be especially important for individuals who do not use the news media for political information, those who consume media from distinct sources, or those for whom information is not available in their preferred language.

Concerns over the exposure explanation have centered on the accuracy of the information being provided. Huckfeldt and Sprague (1995), for instance, find that more than half of those in their study reported having discussion partners with only an "average amount of political knowledge." Furthermore, individuals sometimes wrongly assume that those who are more engaged are more knowledgeable, leading them to rely on information from others whom they perceive to be more knowledgeable than they actually are (Ryan 2011). Beyond the possibility that individuals are discussing politics with those who only have an average amount of political knowledge (or less), individuals might strategically (or accidentally) misrepresent information as they communicate it to others. Ahn et al. (2014: 2) argue that "Political communication is not an antiseptic, politically neutral information transfer, and it is not necessarily an exercise in civic enlightenment. Rather, it is an extension of the political process in which some people are more influential than others." Even beyond deliberate, strategic efforts to mislead or persuade others, political information can become distorted through the telephone game (Carlson 2018; Aarøe and Petersen 2018), sometimes leading individuals to change their attitudes in response to biased, incomplete, or inaccurate information (Carlson 2019).[1] Thus, exposure alone is not sufficient to explain how political discussions can increase political knowledge and awareness.

The second explanation is what Eveland (2004) refers to as anticipatory elaboration. This perspective contends that the expectation of a forthcoming discussion leads to an internal motivation that then increases cognitive deliberation on new information. That is, in anticipation of the discussion, individuals will invest more heavily in processing the first piece of information to which they are exposed, as a form of preparation for later discussion of the subject matter. Proponents of this perspective argue that increased learning happens via information processing that occurs prior to future interpersonal communication (McLeod and Becker 1981). One of our Asian American APEN respondents described undergoing this type of anticipatory learning when preparing to canvass target voters: "you learn a lot [canvassing] . . . you also get to teach yourself about finance issues, not just what's going on in the world but like, how to actually make that phone call and make it worth[while] and bring results."

The third and final explanation is known as the discussion-generated elaboration. When individuals are required to provide a detailed explanation for their policy position, for example, it requires them to engage in meaningful information processing. As a result, it increases learning due to enhanced information processing *while* the discussion is taking place. Elaboration can occur in two ways—either self-generated or conversation partner–generated. Important for purposes of our discussion is the fact that different, dynamic processes are occurring within these political discussions, all of which affect how political information is relayed and understood within these conversations. A male Latino canvasser from Community Coalition described this exact phenomenon: "I've had actually a few instances like that where I've been able to explain something that somebody didn't quite understand before and the way I explained it to them gave them a different perspective." As such, the process of learning from others is, indeed, dynamic and is dependent on the personal interaction that one has with one's discussion partners.

All three of these explanations would lead us to hypothesize that political discussions with one's discussion partners will be positively correlated with higher levels of political knowledge. We therefore expect individuals who discuss politics a great deal with friends in their network to be more politically knowledgeable. This expectation draws on work by Eveland (2009), who posits a similar relationship. However, we expect variation to exist across our study population because of our respondents' relative social positions and the resulting levels of political knowledge and engagement available to them within their networks. Given the ethnoracial gap in political knowledge documented by early scholars such as Verba et al. (1995), one may expect to see the relationship between both the frequency and size of discussion networks to be less robust for non-whites than it is for Whites because non-whites have been found to be less politically knowledgeable than Whites.

Yet recent work by Abrajano (2015) and Pérez (2015) demonstrates that the specific types of political knowledge questions asked matter tremendously in assessing levels of political knowledge among ethnoracial groups. When ethnoracial group members are asked knowledge items that are specifically relevant to their group (e.g., "What political position does Sonia Sotomayor hold?"), they are more likely to answer the questions correctly. Thus, these recent studies suggest that the "racial gap" in political knowledge may largely be a result of the survey items being used. Thus, we specifically designed the political knowledge questions in our survey to be ones that are relevant and salient to non-whites in California (e.g., whether a photo ID is required to vote in CA).

Considering the relationship between network size and political knowledge, there is also the possibility that in addition to talking to others about politics on a regular basis, the size of one's network can contribute positively to the amount of political information available within it. Here, we would expect that as the size of one's network increases, so too would a person's political knowledge. Drawing largely on the exposure explanation, if individuals are exposed to information from a greater number of political discussants, they should be exposed to more information, thus making them more politically knowledgeable. Even drawing on more cognitive explanations, it is possible that with larger discussion networks there are more people with whom to anticipate discussions, leading individuals to more carefully process political information in preparation for future discussions. Given this, because the discussion networks for the foreign born in our sample are more heterogenous and smaller than those of the U.S. born, we hypothesize that they will not talk about politics in their networks as frequently as the U.S. born and that therefore their discussion networks will be less knowledgeable.

Our expectations in terms of gender are based on the finding that women's levels of political knowledge tend to be lower than men's and undervalued by their discussion partners, both male and female. We therefore expect our female respondents to have lower levels of political knowledge than men. In terms of network effects, the fact that women are assumed to be less knowledgeable regardless of their knowledge levels leads us to expect that we will not find that networks have a positive effect on political knowledge for women. In contrast, we assume they will have a positive effect for men.

Political Discussion Networks and Policy Attitudes

Regular and repeated discussions on political matters can lead individuals to hold views that reflect and are similar to those with whom they discuss politics. Studies have shown that most individuals interact with those who are like-minded in political affiliation and preferences (Huckfeldt and Sprague 1988). As the seminal work by Huckfeldt and Sprague (1988) demonstrates, individuals intentionally construct informational networks that correspond to their own political preferences, yet there is still more disagreement in political discussion networks than we might otherwise expect (Huckfeldt, Johnson, and Sprague 2004). Thus, if we think about this from a partisan lens, Democrats are likely going to engage in conversations with Democrats, and Republicans are likely going to engage in conversations with Republicans. The general consensus from the existing research is that those in homogeneous discussion networks (all the same political party) will hold attitudes consistent with those of their respective parties. In contrast, those in heterogeneous discussion networks, which include discussants from different political parties, might be less "polarized" in their attitudes (e.g., Huckfeldt and Sprague 1995; Huckfeldt et al. 2004; Levitan and Visser 2009).

As we have stressed repeatedly, these expectations are reasonable for Whites because these studies included largely White samples. However, we do not know whether these assumptions will hold for non-whites and naturalized voters, nor how they might differ across diverse men and women (see Leighley and Matsubayashi 2009). We saw in Chapter 2 that political discussion networks (both in terms of the composition and determinants) vary across ethnoracial groups, by nativity, and by gender. Given the strong relationship between ethnoracial group membership and party identification for Blacks and Whites, it will be difficult to disentangle whether a policy attitude is influenced by ethnorace or party. However, we do expect to find a strong relationship among group membership, party preferences, and policy attitudes. Among Latinos and Asians, we would expect this relationship to be less strong, given that their party identification levels are weaker than those of Whites or Blacks.

Among our foreign-born respondents, their partisan preferences and familiarity with U.S. politics likely are still being developed. Therefore, their policy attitudes may be less influenced by the partisan homogeneity of their networks, relative to the U.S. born. Given that foreign-born individuals are also less likely to think of themselves in the same partisan terms as U.S.-born Whites (Hajnal and Lee 2011), the role of partisan attachments may play out differently within their networks. Finally, we saw in Chapter 3 that our female respondents' networks included more copartisans than men's; it stands to reason that those differences will have an impact when considering the role that partisanship plays in attitude formation within networks.

Assessing the Relationship between Networks and Political Knowledge

To test our hypotheses, we focus on our two dependent variables of interest: political knowledge and policy opinions. With regard to the former, most existing studies rely on "textbook" political knowledge questions (e.g., "How many members of Congress are required to override a Presidential Veto?") or hard political facts (e.g., "Who is the Chief Justice of the U.S. Supreme Court?"). While such questions capture knowledge of "hard political facts," they fail to actually measure the amount of information an individual has that is relevant and important to their everyday political lives.[2] In light of this fact, as well as existing studies highlighting the importance of developing political knowledge questions that are relevant to the group being interviewed (Abrajano 2015; Pérez 2015), we developed a battery of novel political knowledge survey items. As we discussed in Chapter 2, our three knowledge questions asked participants to indicate whether the following statements were true or false: (1) you must present a valid form of identification every time you vote in California; (2) all registered voters can vote by mail in California; (3) naturalized U.S. citizens can register to vote. All three of these survey items, in our view, are highly salient to California voters, and having knowledge of these voting requirements and restrictions is important because it indicates that individuals know the steps necessary to become participants in the electoral process.

Policy Opinions. For measures of policy opinions, we examine two issues that are of high salience to our respondents: environmental issues and social and/or criminal justice reform issues. We focused on these issues because they are the ones around which our partner community organizations focused their outreach efforts during the 2016 election. Many studies have shown the disproportionate presence of particulate contamination and toxic waste in low-income areas (Bullard and Chavis, Jr., 1999). As a result, Blacks and Latinos have been found to have higher rates of exposure to pollutants compared with their White counterparts.[3] One simply needs to recall the recent events in Flint, Michigan, to understand how access to such basic items such as clean and safe drinking water disproportionately affects disadvantaged communities.

The survey items pertaining to the environment asked respondents the extent to which they agree or disagree with the following statements: (1) climate change is a threat to California's economy; (2) affordable and accessible solar energy programs should be made available to low-income residents and renters; (3) local projects and programs that address climate change and make our city greener should also produce good-paying local jobs with benefits.[4]

The other issue area we examine, criminal justice, is a pressing concern within many communities of color (Alexander 2010; Soss and Weaver 2017). The "tough on crime" policies that characterized much of the 1990s, particularly California's Three Strikes sentencing law enacted in 1994, have experienced some reversal in recent years. In 2014, California voters supported Proposition 47, which classified "nonserious and nonviolent crimes" as misdemeanors as opposed to felonies. Because of this, one of our organizations wanted to assess respondents' opinions on less punitive ways of addressing gang violence and a more rehabilitative approach to criminal justice. Respondents were asked the extent to which they agree or disagree with these three statements: (1) increased access to recreation activities would help reduce gang violence in your neighborhood; (2) creating more youth centers and recreation centers is a solution to gang activity; (3) California should eliminate bail fees for nonviolent offenses.

Measuring Discussion Networks. For our main independent variables of interest (measures of political discussion networks), we again consider three aspects of one's political discussion networks—the size of the discussion network, frequency of political discussion, and partisan homogeneity.[5] To determine which the policy opinions of political discussants are associated with an individual's policy opinions, we examine the percentage of Democrats in one's network. This conceptualization differs from our standard measure of partisan homogeneity, which examines the number of copartisans in one's network. We examine the percentage of Democrats in one's network to see whether the respondent adopts similar attitudes as his or her network. The idea is that for most of these policy issues, Democrats should be in favor, while Republicans should be against. Thus, if the percentage of Democrats in one's network is positively associated with agreement on the issues of criminal justice and climate change after also controlling for respondent partisanship, then we can infer that a respondent has similar attitudes as those in his or her network, and a network effect exists above and beyond the effect of partisanship. In the case of these two particular issue areas, we would expect Democratic Party identifiers to hold less restrictive views on climate change and criminal justice.

Of course, there are other possible factors that could explain issue attitudes and levels of political knowledge aside from one's discussion networks, in particular, those pertaining to socioeconomic or demographic characteristics. Thus, in our models that seek to explain issue attitudes, we control for factors that pertain to the respondent's demographic and political characteristics—education level, age, partisan affiliation, gender, and political knowledge levels.[6] The controls that we include in our models explaining political knowledge are the following: gender, education level, and age. We also want to be clear that we do not solve the endogeneity problem in our empirical analyses; we are unable to isolate a causal relationship among these factors. It is entirely possible—perhaps likely—that individuals who hold these policy attitudes or are more knowledgeable prefer to associate with others who share the same attitudes or are also knowledgeable. Given that both of the dependent variables in our models are ordinal in nature, we use ordinary least squares (OLS) analysis as our estimation technique. Similar to our earlier analyses, we estimate these models separately for each ethnoracial group, as well as by nativity (foreign born versus U.S. born), and gender.

Findings

Discussion Frequency and Political Knowledge

Before we discuss the results from our multivariate models, it is helpful to begin with some basic descriptive statistics. Table 5.1 compares the levels of political knowledge by ethnorace, nativity, and gender, including both the number and percentage of correct answers for the given group. Comparing the percentage of correct answers by ethnoracial group, we find that more than a majority of Asians and Latinos, and almost a majority of Blacks (48 percent), correctly answered 2 out of the 3 knowledge questions. In contrast, Whites were the most likely to correctly answer all three knowledge questions (49 percent). Thus, despite our attempt to design political knowledge survey items that would be relevant for non-white respondents, the political knowledge "racial gap" appears to persist. This gap is most acute

Table 5.1. Number and Percentage of Respondents with Each Number of Correct Political Knowledge Questions, by Ethnorace, Nativity, and Gender

	Number/percent of questions answered correctly				N
	0	1	2	3	
Ethnorace					
Asians	4 (0.2%)	125 (7%)	964 (56%)	618 (36%)	1711
Latinos	4 (0.5%)	72 (10%)	465 (62%)	205 (27%)	746
Blacks	4 (0.7%)	59 (10%)	291 (48%)	248 (41%)	602
Whites	3 (1.4%)	22 (10%)	83 (39%)	103 (49%)	211
Nativity					
Foreign born	1 (0.2%)	51 (9%)	330 (57%)	202 (35%)	584
U.S. born	14 (0.5%)	249 (9%)	1566 (54%)	1053 (37%)	2882
Gender					
Male	6 (0.4%)	94 (7%)	724 (53%)	540 (40%)	1364
Female	7 (0.3%)	188 (10%)	994 (55%)	621 (34%)	1810

between Whites and Latinos, with a 22 percentage-point difference in the proportion of who answered all three questions correctly, followed by Asians (13 percentage-point difference) and finally Blacks (8 percentage-point difference).

That these gaps are so sizable raises two potential implications regarding the influence of networks and political knowledge. On the one hand, if individuals are in heterogeneous networks in terms of political knowledge, networks could help alleviate political knowledge gaps by the most knowledgeable members of a network informing the least informed members. On the other hand, if individuals are in homogeneous networks in terms of political knowledge, the knowledge disparities might be amplified through political discussion, with the least knowledgeable discussing politics among themselves, isolated from their more knowledgeable counterparts. Either possibility makes the role of political discussion networks in expanding or limiting political knowledge even more vital to explore.

Breaking down political knowledge by nativity reveals little difference in the knowledge levels of U.S.-born and foreign-born respondents. Irrespective of nativity, the modal category was answering 2 out of 3 knowledge questions accurately. About a third of both foreign- and U.S.-born respondents answered all three questions correctly.

In terms of gender, the modal category for both men and women was correctly answering 2 out of the 3 questions. Among those who answered all of the questions correctly. However, a larger percentage of men versus women did so (38 percent versus 33 percent). These gender discrepancies support the existing research by Huckfeldt and Sprague (1995) and others (Ihme and Tausendpfund 2018). Overall, these comparisons of political knowledge by ethnorace, nativity, and gender show that ethnorace affects political knowledge levels more than nativity. And, as expected, women in our sample generally had lower levels of political knowledge than men.

Next, we present our multivariate analysis to determine whether political discussion network characteristics are associated with political knowledge levels. The results by ethnorace are presented in Table 5.2, Table 5.3 summarizes our results by nativity, and Table 5.4 reports our results by gender. The findings reveal important variation across the four ethnoracial groups in our sample. What is most striking is the differential effect of political discussion networks on knowledge. In the full model that includes all of our controls, we only find a positive association with frequency of political discussion and levels of political knowledge for Asian Americans. That

Table 5.2. Relationship between Discussion Frequency and Political Knowledge by Ethnorace

	Dependent variable: Number of political knowledge questions answered correctly			
	Asian (1)	Black (2)	Latino (3)	White (4)
Discussion frequency	0.043***	0.001	0.026	0.050
	(0.016)	(0.027)	(0.020)	(0.051)
Network size	0.032***	0.051***	0.006	0.094***
	(0.011)	(0.020)	(0.015)	(0.035)
Female	−0.090**	−0.024	−0.031	−0.257***
	(0.035)	(0.062)	(0.050)	(0.104)
College	0.037	0.211***	0.192***	0.204*
	(0.043)	(0.063)	(0.050)	(0.122)
Age	0.002	0.006***	0.005**	0.013***
	(0.001)	(0.002)	(0.002)	(0.004)
Constant	1.989***	1.767***	1.863***	1.312***
	(0.070)	(0.119)	(0.088)	(0.224)
Observations	1,170	445	595	160
R^2	0.037	0.080	0.053	0.191
Residual std. err.	0.591 (df=1164)	0.628 (df=439)	0.589 (df=589)	0.645 (df=154)
F statistic	9.016*** (df=5; 1164)	7.679*** (df=5; 439)	6.652*** (df=5; 589)	7.267*** (df=5; 154)

Note: *$p < 0.10$; **$p < 0.05$; ***$p < 0.01$.

is, talking about politics on a regular basis is associated with having more political knowledge only among Asian Americans. For Blacks, Latinos, and Whites, engaging in regular and frequent political conversations fails to have a statistically significant effect on levels of political knowledge. Instead, it is the *size* of one's discussion network that is positively associated with his or her knowledge level. We observe this positive association between network size and political knowledge among all groups except Latinos. The findings also suggest that demographic characteristics, such as education (for all except Asian Americans), gender (in the case of Whites and Asian Americans), and age (for all except Asian Americans) are also correlated with higher levels of political knowledge.

Table 5.3 Relationship between Discussion Frequency and Political Knowledge by Nativity

	Dependent variable: Number of political knowledge questions answered correctly	
	U.S. born (1)	Foreign born (2)
Discussion frequency	0.030**	0.051*
	(0.012)	(0.027)
Network size	0.036***	0.017
	(0.008)	(0.020)
Female	−0.061**	−0.152**
	(0.027)	(0.062)
Some college	0.130***	0.198***
	(0.028)	(0.071)
Age	0.006***	−0.002
	(0.001)	(0.002)
Constant	1.799***	2.074***
	(0.049)	(0.126)
Observations	2,132	391
R^2	0.067	0.056
Adjusted R^2	0.065	0.043
Residual std. err.	0.602 (df=2126)	0.609 (df=385)
F statistic	30.657*** (df=5; 2126)	4.546*** (df=5; 385)

Note: * $p < 0.10$; ** $p < 0.05$; *** $p < 0.01$.

These results offer some support for our contention regarding the importance of talking about politics frequently on levels of political knowledge. As scholars have noted, those situated in larger networks, with more political discussants, are expected to be exposed to more political information, especially when those networks include individuals who have greater political knowledge levels (Lake and Huckfeldt 1998). While we do not have measures of most their discussion partners' political knowledge levels, we do know that both Blacks and Whites have larger networks than Latinos and Asian Americans, and as a result, they may be getting more information from these discussion partners, even if they are not engaging with them on an everyday basis.

Table 5.4. Relationship between Discussion Frequency and Political Knowledge by Gender

	Dependent variable: Number of political knowledge questions answered correctly	
	Female	Male
Discussion frequency	0.052***	0.010
	(0.014)	(0.016)
Network size	0.031***	0.036***
	(0.010)	(0.012)
College	0.117***	0.167***
	(0.035)	(0.039)
Age	0.005***	0.005***
	(0.001)	(0.001)
Constant	0.031***	0.036***
	(0.010)	(0.012)
Observations	1,471	1,053
R^2	0.062	0.053
Adjusted R^2	0.059	0.049
Residual std. err.	0.614 (df=1466)	0.591 (df=1048)
F statistic	24.221*** (df=4; 1466)	14.672*** (df=4; 1048)

Note: *$p < 0.1$; **$p < 0.05$; ***$p < 0.01$.

For Asian Americans, however, frequent political conversations with their discussion networks seem to be beneficial to their political learning. It could be the case that, when these political conversations happened frequently within their networks, they helped to make up for their relatively smaller networks. Although Asian Americans' frequency of political discussion with their discussion partners was significantly lower than those of Blacks or Whites, our findings suggest that these conversations are still valuable to them in becoming more informed and aware of politics, and more specifically, on the rules of voting. On a broader level, our findings support one of the main tenets that we have put forth in the book—political discussion networks do not operate uniformly across the U.S. electorate, and that different aspects of one's networks (conceptualized here in terms of network size and frequency of political discussion), differentially influence individuals' political orientations and inclinations depending on their relative social position (in this case, their levels of political knowledge).

We now turn to our results that compare the effects of political discussion network characteristics on political knowledge based on nativity. These results are presented in Table 5.3. The results from our multivariate models indicate that discussion frequency is positively associated with higher levels of political knowledge for both foreign-born and U.S.-born respondents.[7] Although we had hypothesized that frequency of political discussion would be a stronger predictor of knowledge for U.S.-born respondents relative to the foreign born, we are encouraged to find that regular political conversations are also positively associated with knowledge levels for the foreign born. This positive relationship suggests that social networks can help naturalized voters integrate politically and learn about the U.S. political system, which contributes to our scholarly understanding of the way political discussion networks can help or hurt how the foreign born get socialized politically into the host country.

Our results also indicate that network size is positively associated with political knowledge for U.S.-born respondents; however, no such relationship exists for their foreign-born counterparts. Thus, both the size of the network and frequency of political discussion within a network exert a positive impact on political knowledge for U.S.-born respondents. Being college educated, older, and male is also positively associated with higher levels of political knowledge for U.S.-born respondents. Among the foreign born only educational level and gender are significantly associated with political knowledge levels.

Our next set of estimates, presented in Table 5.4, examine whether any gender differences exist in the relationship between discussion network characteristics and political knowledge. Here, we see that network size is positively and statistically significantly associated with political knowledge for both men and women. However, discussion frequency is only positively associated with political knowledge for women. Education and age were both positively associated with political knowledge among men and women.

Discussion Networks and Policy Preferences

Next, we analyze the relationship between discussion networks and the sorts of policy positions individuals hold. For the two issue areas on which we focus, climate change and criminal justice, there do not appear to be significantly divergent attitudes among our respondents across the ethnoracial groups.[8] The same can be said when we disaggregate policy opinions by nativity. In the case of gender, however, significant differences do arise when it comes to issue opinions on the environment.

When we examine the bivariate distributions of policy responses, by ethnorace, nativity, and gender, several interesting patterns emerge. First, Blacks and Latinos in our sample tended to be the most progressive on these issues, whereas Whites tended to adopt more restrictive positions. Asian Americans tended to fall somewhere in between. Again, it is important to keep in mind that many of these differences are not statistically significant and that the similarity in attitudes is likely due to our sample of primarily progressive and Democratic party-identified individuals. When we examine issue preferences by nativity, the general pattern that emerges is that U.S.-born respondents tended to have a more progressive position on climate change and criminal justice than their foreign-born counterparts. And while the differences are not statistically significant, they are consistent in terms of direction across all six issues that we examine.[9]

Gender distinctions on the issue of climate change do exist, such that women in our sample were significantly more likely than were men to strongly agree that climate change is a threat to California's economy, support affordable solar energy programs for low-income residents, and favor local projects that address climate change. These findings are consistent with the existing research by Pearson et al. (2017), who find a gender gap in climate change opinion, such that women express greater concern for the environment, relative to men. Also consistent with previous research, the women in our sample also expressed more progressive stances on the criminal justice issues than did the men, across all three of the issues that were included in the survey (Applegate et al. 2002; Carll 2017).

We now move on to our statistical models that examine the role of one's discussion networks in explaining policy opinions on the environment, while controlling for both contextual and individual-level attributes. The estimates, presented by ethnoracial group, may be found in the appendix. We also performed a similar analysis but disaggregated the sample by nativity and gender. While we expected the percentage of Democrats in one's discussion network to be most strongly associated with issue attitudes, for all three issues it was only consistently statistically significant for Asian American and White respondents. The percentage of Democrats in one's network was positively associated with having more liberal climate change policy opinions among Black respondents in two out of our three issues, though the results are only statistically significant at the 10 percent level for one of these. But among Latinos, the partisan composition of their network, as measured by the percentage of Democrats in the network, fails to explain any of their attitudes on climate change. Looking at network size, we observe inconsistent patterns across groups and specific issues.

At the individual level, the only factor that consistently is associated with climate change opinions is an individual's partisanship, with Republicans less supportive of policies that address climate change than Democrats. The fact that we find that the proportion of Democrats in Asian Americans' and Whites' networks is positively associated with agreement on the issues of climate change even after we control for their partisanship suggests that a network effect exists above and beyond individual-level partisan attachments for some, but not all, groups.

Our results by nativity suggest that percentage of Democrats in one's network and discussion frequency were consistently, positively associated with having more liberal climate change attitudes for both U.S.-born and foreign-born respondents. Network size was positively associated with having more liberal climate change policy attitudes among the U.S. born, but not among the foreign born. Party identification also had a statistically significant impact on these attitudes. Specifically, Democrats had more favorable attitudes toward the climate change policies than did Republicans, as we expected.

Looking at gender, for all three climate change questions, political discussion network characteristics—percentage of Democrats within their network, network size, and discussion frequency—had a positive and significant association with whether our female respondents held progressive views about climate change. We find no relationship among our male respondents for network size, but discussion frequency and the percentage of Democrats in their networks did affect men's climate change attitudes. This suggests that the role that political discussion networks play in the development of policy opinions is different for women than it is for men, a question worth exploration in future research (e.g., Karpowitz and Mendelberg 2014).

Criminal Justice Issues. We analyzed three different policy opinions pertaining to criminal justice and we present these results, by ethnoracial group, nativity, and gender, in the appendix. Consistent with our previously mentioned findings, our results suggest that the percentage of Democrats in the network exerts a powerful effect on criminal justice attitudes. For all groups studied except Blacks, and across almost all the criminal justice issues we asked about, there was a positive, statistically significant association between the percentage of Democrats in the network and having more progressive policy attitudes. This network characteristic's lack of explanatory power among Blacks could be due in part to the very small number of Black Republicans in our data set (27 out of 527). It could also be that these issues, given the prevalence of discussions about policing within Black communities over the past few years and the advent of the Movement for Black Lives, are thought of more in ethnoracial than partisan terms among Blacks. Looking at gender, discussion frequency is positively associated with progressive policy attitudes among both women and men, for all three issues studied.

Table 5.5 summarizes the policy attitude results. We would be remiss not to discuss one important concern that is particularly acute in this chapter's analyses—the issue of endogeneity plaguing studies of homophily. It is unclear whether we observe opinion similarity in our respondents' political

Table 5.5. Summary of Findings: Relationship between Network Attributes and Policy Attitudes

	Ethnoracial group				*Nativity*		*Gender*	
	Asian	Black	Latino	White	Foreign Born	US Born	Female	Male
Climate change issues								
Percentage of Democrats	+++	++		+++	++	+++	+++	+++
Network size	+	+	+	++		+++	+++	
Discussion frequency	+++		+++	+	++	+++	+++	+++
Social justice issues								
Percentage of Democrats	+++		++	++	++	+++	+++	++
Network size			+		+			
Discussion frequency	+++	++	+		++	+++	+++	+++

Note: (+) entry indicates that the network attribute coefficient was positive and statistically significant for one specific policy issue, (++) means the coefficient was positive and statistically significant for two specific policy issues, and (+++) means the coefficient was positive and statistically significant for all three specific policy issues. Cell entries with (–) mean that the coefficient was negative and statistically significant.

discussion networks because individuals have chosen to discuss politics with others who have the same opinions or whether individuals change their opinions over time to conform to the group. This distinction can be conceptualized as selection versus social influence (Bello and Rolfe 2014). Furthermore, Song and colleagues (2015) contend that a difference exists between political and accidental selection. That is, individuals could choose their political discussants based on their political views (political selection), or they could select their political discussants based on apolitical factors, such as age, ethnorace, family ties, or gender, that correlate with political views, thus creating a spurious correlation between an individual's political views and his or her discussants' views. Disentangling the influence of selection or social influence is a challenge, and our qualitative interviews help us to gain some insights into this process. In cases in which individuals are canvassed, they can gain information through accidental selection. As one Latino male Community Coalition interviewee observes:

> [J]ust like with any conversation where there's politics or not, there's agreements and disagreements and it just gives us both different perspectives but I know for a fact that I definitely changed people's opinions, perspectives and not because I want them to think like me or anything, just because they didn't quite know the full facts or something or had wrong information, maybe some outdated information, who knows?

Resolving this endogeneity question lies beyond the scope of our analysis. However, since, as we saw in Chapter 3, a significant proportion of these network members are family members rather than close friends, it stands to reason that some of these discussants are not politically chosen. That suggests that policy attitude homophily within their networks is likely a result of a combination of selection and influence. Teasing out those threads more precisely should be the focus of future research.

Conclusion

The goal of this chapter was to determine the role that one's discussion network plays in facilitating information flows that influence an individual's level of political knowledge as well as his or her policy opinions and preferences. As Table 5.6 highlights, we considered two key ways that networks can foster

Table 5.6. Summary of Findings: Relationships between Network Attributes and Political Knowledge

	Ethnoracial group				*Nativity*		*Gender*	
	Asian	Black	Latino	White	Foreign Born	U.S. Born	Female	Male
Network attribute								
Size	+	+		+		+	+	+
Discussion Frequency	+				+	+	+	

Note: (+) entry indicates that the network attribute coefficient was positive and statistically significant.

information flows: frequency of political discussion within the network and the size of the network. The findings suggest that network size explains increased levels of political knowledge for 3 out of the 4 ethnoracial groups in our study, whereas discussion frequency only helps to explain levels of political knowledge for Asian Americans. Larger networks are correlated with gains in political knowledge for Asian Americans, Blacks, and Whites.

By carefully testing each of these hypotheses by ethnoracial group, nativity, and gender, we found that our empirical evidence supports the conventional wisdom regarding the importance of political discussion networks in enabling individuals to become more politically knowledgeable and in the formation of issue preferences. However, our results indicate that network effects are not uniform across these social positions. When we compared network effects between U.S.-born and foreign-born respondents, we generally find them to have more predictive power for U.S.-born respondents. Our gender analysis revealed that although networks were found to affect the issue attitudes of both men and women, the magnitude of the effects was much greater for women.

Why are network effects not as important for Blacks in explaining their issue attitudes and knowledge levels, even though they have had a longer presence in the United States and are probably more politically socialized into U.S. politics than members of the two immigrant-origin groups in our sample (Latinos and Asian Americans)? This likely has to do with their socialization patterns overall, particularly through institutions that exist outside Blacks' political discussion networks. Studies have shown the important impact the Black church and other institutions have had on Black political integration patterns and policy preferences (Dawson 2001). This also helps to explain high levels of African American voter turnout, relative to their socioeconomic status. At a minimum, our analysis suggests that the impact of political discussion networks on political knowledge and policy preferences varies in important ways across groups. In addition, these differences must be understood within the context of each group's historical and current political experiences and their relative social position within U.S. politics.

6
The Impact of Political Discussion Networks on Civic and Political Engagement

> I'm part of the community, and I believe that by me knowing [people], I could tell five other people and those same people could tell . . . make our community aware what's going on. Because here, I'm from South Central and we don't really . . . we don't . . . most of us don't vote. We say we're gonna vote but we don't. But we expect change and we never commit to it, and that's where canvassing comes in 'cause we go door to door explaining to people things that they didn't . . . they weren't aware about.
>
> Male Latino canavasser, Community Coalition

As the quote from this canvasser aptly highlights, discussion networks, indeed, have the potential to exert an influence on political engagement and participation. This is especially true if we consider that the content of these conversations includes direct appeals to mobilize individuals to vote and participate in politics. Moreover, the canvasser acknowledges the importance of being a part of his community as key to his ability to disseminate information about the importance of voting not only to his networks but also potentially to others' networks. Both the political discussion network and political participation literatures emphasize the importance of political discussion networks for political engagement, yet we know very little about how network characteristics impact engagement across different types of community members. In this chapter we explore how network size, the frequency of political discussion, and partisan homogeneity impact our respondents' civic and political engagement. As we have demonstrated throughout this book, ignoring the nuances in how discussion networks affect political outcomes

Talking Politics. Taylor N. Carlson, Marisa Abrajano, and Lisa García Bedolla, Oxford University Press (2020). © Oxford University Press.
DOI: 10.1093/oso/9780190082116.001.0001

across diverse groups is a problem—one that we seek to address further in this chapter.

How Do Political Discussion Networks Impact Political Engagement?

The same three network-level factors that we have been discussing thus far—network size, discussion frequency, and partisan homophily—have been found to affect political engagement. There is a general consensus among scholars that individuals in larger political discussion networks can be expected to be more politically engaged (Knoke 1990; Lake and Huckfeldt 1998). To the extent that we view discussing politics as an important form of political engagement (e.g., Huckfeldt and Sprague 1995; Mutz 2006), the more an individual discusses politics, the more likely he or she is to engage in other forms of political behavior.

There is considerable debate about the impact of the partisan composition of political discussion networks—or political disagreement—on political engagement. Mutz (2002, 2006) argues that exposure to alternative political views can make people more tolerant of those on the other side of the aisle at the cost of making individuals politically apathetic. She argues that individuals who are exposed to multiple, disagreeable points of view are more likely to feel cross-pressured, second-guess their initial views, and ultimately opt out of political participation. On the other hand, Scheufele and colleagues (2004) argue that individuals in heterogeneous political discussion networks are *more* likely to participate. The authors suggest that exposure to different views increases knowledge and political interest and inspires information-seeking behavior that can be politically mobilizing. Some more recent work suggests that individuals might react differently to disagreement, which could explain how they respond with either more or less political engagement (Lyons et al. 2016).

In Chapter 3 we demonstrated important variation in the partisan composition of our respondents' political discussion networks—that is, the amount of disagreement to which individuals were exposed—based on ethnorace, nativity, and gender. We found that Black respondents were in the most homogeneous networks, followed by Latinos, and that Asian Americans and Whites had relatively lower levels of partisan homogeneity in their networks.

It was also the case that individuals who were born outside the United States were exposed to more partisan disagreement in their political discussion networks than the U.S. born. We also found that women were more likely than men to have copartisans in their networks.

Thus, there is an ongoing debate about how disagreement within political discussion networks affects political behavior, and we found important differences in the partisan makeup of political discussion networks along ethnorace, nativity, and gender. Based on past work that found important differences among voters of color in terms of their responsiveness to mobilization contact (García Bedolla and Michelson 2012), we hypothesize that the impact of political discussion network characteristics on political engagement will vary by ethnorace, nativity, and gender.

Closing the Theoretical and Empirical Gap

In light of the social positioning of non-white groups in the United States (see Chapter 1), we hypothesize that ethnoracial group membership, nativity, and gender could influence an individual's political discussion network and the impact of that network on his or her political engagement. First, we consider network size. In Chapter 3, we saw that non-whites and those born outside the United States are in smaller discussion networks than Whites and those born in the United States, which is consistent with previous research (Leighley and Matsubayashi 2009). As one of our Japanese-origin APEN canvassers stressed, for the foreign born, being within networks that include political engagement can advance political knowledge, as we discussed in Chapter 5, and have a mobilizing effect:

> Actually, my partner was involved in the first federal court case on the whole like Monsanto Roundup case, which was amazing. I'm glad he got to be a part of it and I was thinking how much that affects Japan too and like they're very few regulations as far as, yeah, like pesticides and chems we use on like in agriculture and it was really, unfortunately, Japanese people don't get to vote directly on legislation, which is sad, but it . . . but for the longest I thought like activism and organizing was like, unique to . . . I kind of like associate it with being American in some way, the more I get involved and especially after like working with APEN I really think that it's changed. It

> might look differently in like different cultures and countries but it does need to happen and you can't do it without the participation of the public en masse, so definitely in the future, I have been thinking about ways to how to like bring this like my learning and experience back home and have like mobilized people.

Thus, networks can expose the foreign born to opportunities for political engagement.

We expect network size to be positively associated with political engagement. This is the relationship predicted by previous research, but this has not been substantially tested across different ethnoracial groups. Klofstad and Bishin (2014) examine the impact of political discussion networks on campaign participation among immigrants. They find a positive, bivariate relationship between network size and campaign participation, but this effect does not hold once alternative explanations, such as personal resources and assimilation, are considered. Following Klofstad and Bishin (2014), we should expect differential effects of network size on political engagement based on nativity. However, we examine far more forms of political engagement than campaign participation, which could yield different relationships with network size as well.

On the one hand, we might expect the relationship between network size and political engagement, broadly construed, to operate in the same way regardless of ethnorace and nativity, especially if those who are most engaged are more likely to find themselves in larger networks. However, it is possible that ethnoracial and nativity differences could lead individuals in larger discussion networks to be less engaged. For instance, if individuals view political discussion as a sufficient level of engagement, they might not see the utility in engaging any further. Alternatively, larger political discussion networks could increase the likelihood of exposure to disagreement, which could have a demobilizing effect.

In terms of gender, there has been little research exploring the relationship among gender, network size, and political engagement. We do know that women in our sample had the same size networks as men and reported discussing politics equally frequently, leading us to assume that the impact of network size and discussion frequency should not vary significantly by gender. However, we also know women tend to have more copartisans in their networks, suggesting that discussion frequency could have a unique impact on their engagement patterns because they have less disagreement within their networks than men. In general, there is little research that would lead us to a clear set of expectations about how political discussion networks affect men and women's political engagement.

Thinking about the effects of partisan composition, we expect the variation in partisan composition of political discussion networks to produce distinct effects on political engagement across ethnoracial groups. If, as the existing research has shown, partisan identification is less meaningful to Latinos and Asian Americans than it is for Whites and Blacks, we might expect (de) mobilizing effects of partisan homogeneity. Moreover, partisan disagreement might not be as relevant to engagement if our respondents' partisan attachments are not salient or meaningful to them, as we know is true for the foreign born, Latinos, and Asian Americans (Hajnal and Lee 2011). This could mean that the disagreement avoidance mechanism may not operate in the same way for these respondents as it does for Whites. In short, there is still much to be learned regarding the effect of political discussion networks for non-whites, the foreign-born, and women.

Empirical Tests

In this chapter we examine the relationship among our three main network characteristics and three forms of engagement. The full details on how we measure each of our network characteristics (network size, partisan homogeneity, and discussion frequency) were discussed in Chapter 2. These network characteristics serve as the independent variables used in this chapter. The dependent variables include self-reported civic engagement, self-reported political engagement, and validated voter turnout, which we define in detail below.

Measuring Engagement

Our dependent variables of interest involve engagement—civic and political. We measure civic and political engagement using self-reported data from our original survey in which respondents reported the civic and political activities in which they had engaged over the past 12 months. Because self-reported data can be susceptible to social desirability bias that could systematically distort our results, we also measure political participation using validated voter turnout data from the California voter file.

Self-Reported Civic Engagement. We measured civic engagement by asking respondents to indicate whether they are involved in any community organizations, such as religious groups, labor unions, or cultural organizations.[1] We then construct a civic engagement variable by totaling the number of groups with which the respondent reported being involved.

Self-Reported Political Engagement. Our measure of political engagement draws on the survey items used in the 2016 American National Election Studies (ANES). Specifically, respondents were asked to indicate whether they had done any of ten different political activities over the past 12 months.[2]

Validated Turnout. Since we can match our survey respondents with the California voter file, we are able to objectively measure each respondent's vote history. Our measure calculates the total number times in last five statewide elections in which the respondent turned out to vote.[3] This captures the November 2012 presidential election, June 2014 primary, November 2014 general election, June 2016 primary, and November 2016 presidential election. Our measure of vote history thus, ranges from 0 (the respondent did not vote in any of the last five elections) to 5 (the respondent voted in all five elections).

Findings

Below, we analyze the effect of network characteristics on civic engagement, political engagement, and validated voter turnout. We present both descriptive results and results from ordinary least squares regressions that control for other variables that could affect the relationship among network characteristics, ethnorace, nativity, gender, and engagement.

Civic Engagement

We first present descriptive statistics to provide a sense for the types of community activities in which respondents in our sample engaged. Table 6.1 shows the percentage of respondents in each group who reported engaging in each activity in our civic engagement index, by ethnorace, nativity, and

Table 6.1. Self-Reported Participation in Civic Engagement Activities, by Nativity, Ethnorace, and Gender

	U.S. born	Foreign born	Asian	Black	Latino	White	Female	Male
Religious group	24.17	23.80	21.74	37.32	18.84	25.86	24.5	24.4
Neighborhood or community Organization	20.25	15.24	15.65	30.89	15.35	25.86	20.72	18.7
Labor union	11.82	6.89	7.03	19.29	12.01	13.22	10.9	11.58
Professional organization	25.11	26.72	28.41	26.25	17.63	29.31	25.27	26.09
Ethnic/cultural organization	13.95	13.57	15.07	16.96	11.40	6.32	13.79	13.8
Issue-oriented political organization (e.g., environmental, immigration, etc.)	9.94	7.52	8.48	12.86	5.47	13.79	9.81	9.17
Political party	17.55	9.81	13.70	23.04	12.46	21.84	15.07	19.15
Civic association (e.g., Rotary Club, Lions Club)	4.25	2.51	4.20	5.71	1.67	4.60	3.14	4.72
Other	8.43	8.77	7.17	9.46	9.88	12.07	8.72	8.55

gender. Across all groups, involvement in professional organizations and religious groups was most common. Black respondents, who were the most engaged overall, were more likely to engage in a neighborhood or community organization than a professional organization. Whites were more likely than members of other ethnoracial groups to be involved in a professional organization. Consistent with Lee and Hajnal's (2011) findings, we find partisan attachments are stronger among our U.S. born respondents; those born in the United States (17.6 percent) were nearly twice as likely to report being involved in a political party than the foreign born (9.8 percent). Similarly, Whites (21.8 percent) and Blacks (23 percent) were substantially more likely to report involvement with a political party than were the Asian Americans (13.7 percent) and Latinos (12.5 percent) in our sample. This pattern is consistent for other political activities, such as involvement in issue-oriented political organizations. While not particularly common for any group, our non-white respondents were more likely to report being involved in ethnic or cultural organizations than were White respondents (6.3 percent).

By gender, the types of activities our respondents reported engaging in varied in important ways. Women were more likely than men to report being a member of a neighborhood or community organization (20.7 percent vs. 18.7 percent) and an issue-oriented political organization (9.8 percent vs. 9.2 percent). Men were more likely than women to report being part of a political party (19.2 percent vs. 15 percent) and a labor union (11.6 percent vs. 10.9 percent). Table 6.1 shows important variation in the types of community involvement in which our respondents engaged, depending on their social position.

In Figure 6.1, we present the average number of civic engagement activities in which individuals reported engaging. Overall, participants in our sample were not involved in a large number of community activities, with the overall average being only 1.3 out of 9 possible activities. Although individuals in our sample were not extremely engaged in their communities based on their responses, there is considerable variation when we disaggregate the results by ethnorace, nativity, and gender. U.S.-born respondents engaged in significantly more activities than foreign-born respondents. Looking at ethnorace, Black respondents reported the greatest levels of engagement in their communities, followed by Whites. Asian Americans engaged in fewer activities than Blacks or Whites. One of our female Asian American canvassers suggests that the reason for this low level of nonelectoral participation

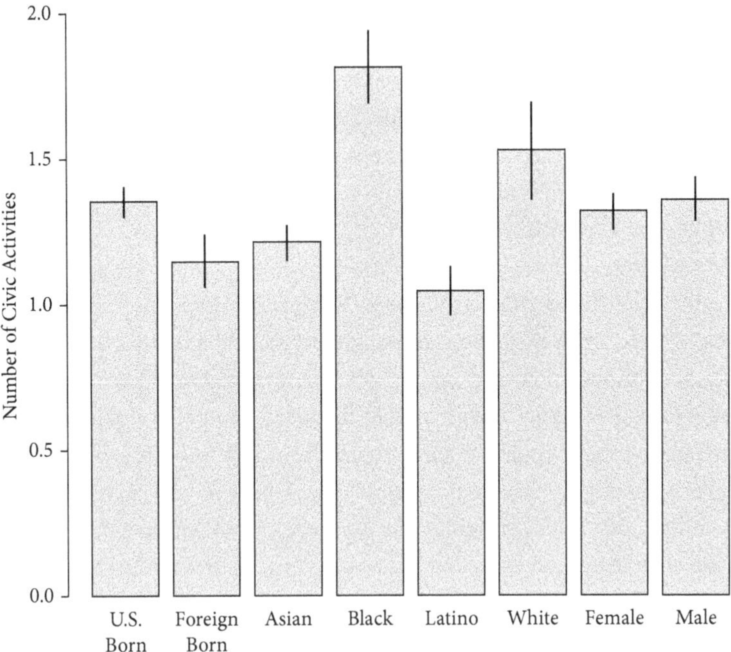

Figure 6.1. "Civic Engagement by Ethnorace, Nativity, and Gender". The description of the figure needs to be corrected to reflect this order as well: ethnorace, nativity, and gender.

among Asian Americans may be due to preconceptions about what political engagement entails:

> I think the first thing that I do [as a canvasser] is kind of like demystify, kind of like changing the preconceptions about like activism, like it's not [just] rallies and marches and protests [that] are like really, really important but especially with my Japanese friends, they have a lot of . . . that's just like very foreign to them. So it's kind suggesting that they could sign petitions and put in your signature for certain things even if you are not a constituent. There are letter drives and things like that.

While this canvasser acknowledges that it is a slow process, she recognizes the importance of her organizing efforts, and their potential to produce long-term change in people's engagement patterns.

Latinos in our sample reported the lowest levels of civic engagement across our four ethnoracial groups. Such patterns are consistent with the existing research that finds differential rates of political participation along the lines of ethnorace (Leighley 2001; Verba et al. 1995; Dobard et al. 2017; Abrajano and Alvarez 2012). One of our male Latino CoCo canvassers spoke to the difficulties he has faced trying to mobilize Latino voters and that changing attitudes toward political participation requires changing people's sense of their own social position and power:

> [I canvassed] 18 individuals that were, Mexicanos, Hispanos, even an Asian couple, they all opened their doors and actually heard what I had to say. But more importantly, were enjoying it to where they were like, "okay, we're going to vote for that." It wasn't off of the jaded perspective that no matter what we say, they're going to still do what they want. It was more "I feel what you're saying and I feel your passion. And I believe you right now." And I was like, "Yes!" It's important that we believe that we have the power to make change instead of feeling like we're going to continuously be inferior to everyone else.

Civic engagement activities tend to foster a sense of collective empowerment and reflect the political opportunity structures available to particular ethnoracial groups. Latinos' low levels of engagement are influenced by important ethnoracial differences in those opportunity structures. With regard to gender differences, although men reported participating in more civic activates than did women, this difference fails to reach statistical significance at conventional levels.

Civic Engagement by Ethnorace. Table 6.2 presents the results from OLS regressions in which we separately analyze the relationship between network characteristics and civic engagement by ethnorace. While these results could be underpowered to detect statistically significant differences, they suggest that across ethnorace is not associated with civic engagement. These results suggest that civic engagement levels are not determined by partisan composition within a network.

Next, we can see that network size is positively associated with civic engagement only among Latinos, the U.S. born, and men. We see here that the influence of network size on civic engagement varies across ethnoracial groups. Among our respondents, discussion frequency had a significant, positive association with civic engagement among all ethnoracial group

Table 6.2. Relationship between Network Characteristics and Civic Engagement, by Ethnorace

	Dependent variable: Number of civic engagement activities selected			
	Asian (1)	Black (2)	Latino (3)	White (4)
Percent copartisan	0.004	0.001	0.001	−0.001
	(0.002)	(0.003)	(0.002)	(0.003)
Network size	0.017	0.194	0.186**	0.295
	(0.100)	(0.209)	(0.081)	(0.289)
Discussion frequency	0.418***	0.251*	0.313***	0.127
	(0.069)	(0.128)	(0.078)	(0.193)
Political knowledge	0.248***	−0.185	−0.177	0.673***
	(0.095)	(0.168)	(0.113)	(0.220)
Female	−0.050	−0.290	−0.064	0.128
	(0.116)	(0.223)	(0.143)	(0.277)
Age	0.002	0.035***	0.002	0.006
	(0.005)	(0.007)	(0.005)	(0.009)
College	0.318**	0.203	0.450***	0.016
	(0.140)	(0.221)	(0.150)	(0.306)
Constant	−0.881	−0.985	−0.612	−2.164
	(0.565)	(1.010)	(0.537)	(1.710)
Observations	438	187	223	76
R^2	0.134	0.179	0.187	0.194
Adjusted R^2	0.119	0.147	0.160	0.111
Residual std. err.	1.178 (df=430)	1.383 (df=179)	1.022 (df=215)	1.089 (df=68)
F statistic	9.469*** (df=7; 430)	5.591*** (df=7; 179)	7.061*** (df=7; 215)	2.341** (df=7; 68)

Note: $^{*}p < 0.01$; $^{**}p < 0.05$; $^{***}p < 0.01$.

members except Whites, though this is only suggestive at the 10 percent level among Blacks.

Network characteristics do not appear to explain levels of civic engagement among our White respondents. This is likely driven by the notion that Whites are socialized into civic engagement differently than other ethnoracial group members, leaving networks to have a smaller impact on their civic engagement than individual-level characteristics.

Turning to the individual-level characteristics, we see that political knowledge exerts a mixed effect on civic engagement. Among Asian American and Whites, there is a positive association between political knowledge and civic engagement, such that those who are more knowledgeable are also more civically engaged. However, there is no statistically identifiable association between political knowledge and civic engagement among Black respondents.

Demographic characteristics such as gender, age, and education also present mixed results. Gender is not associated with civic engagement among any of the ethnoracial groups. Age is only positively associated with civic engagement among Black respondents. Looking across ethnoracial groups, education only positively explained Latino and Asian Americans civic engagement patterns.

Ultimately, political discussion network characteristics appear to be important factors in explaining civic engagement among non-whites. For White respondents, only political knowledge explained their levels of civic engagement, yet several network and individual-level characteristics offered explanatory value for non-whites. This again underscores the point that previous research relying on predominantly White samples may be glossing over important nuances in our understanding of the relationship between political discussion networks and civic engagement.

Civic Engagement by Nativity. We now turn to the impact of network characteristics on civic engagement by nativity. Table 6.3 presents the results from an OLS regression in which the dependent variable is the number of civic engagement activities selected and the independent variables are the percentage of copartisans in one's political discussion network, network size, and discussion frequency, controlling for several covariates. Overall, these findings indicate that network characteristics impact civic engagement differently by nativity. Although our limited sample sizes make it difficult to interpret null results as true nulls, the estimates still offer some suggestive patterns. First, partisan homogeneity—the percentage of copartisans in one's network—does not appear to be associated with civic engagement among those born in the United States or those born outside the United States. Although those born outside the United States in our sample were in less homogeneous networks overall, we find

Table 6.3. Relationship between Network Characteristics and Civic Engagement, by Nativity

	Dependent variable: Number of civic engagement activities selected	
	U.S. born (1)	Foreign born (2)
Percent copartisan	0.0004	0.004
	(0.001)	(0.003)
Network size	0.143**	0.243
	(0.066)	(0.163)
Discussion frequency	0.377***	0.187
	(0.049)	(0.116)
Political knowledge	0.097	0.023
	(0.068)	(0.165)
Female	-0.097	-0.025
	(0.086)	(0.196)
Age	0.015***	-0.004
	(0.003)	(0.007)
College	0.253***	0.169
	(0.090)	(0.213)
Constant	-1.312***	-0.733
	(0.371)	(0.948)
Observations	864	127
R^2	0.160	0.093
Adjusted R^2	0.153	0.039
Residual std. err.	1.206 (df=856)	1.069 (df=119)
F statistic	23.341*** (df=7; 856)	1.733 (df=7; 119)

Note: *$p < 0.10$; **$p < 0.05$; ***$p < 0.01$.

no evidence that partisan homogeneity is associated with civic engagement among either group.

In contrast to partisan homogeneity, network size is positively associated with civic engagement among the U.S. born, but not the foreign born. Individuals born in the United States in larger political discussion networks report being engaged in more community activities. Given previous work on the importance of social capital and social networks for civic engagement (e.g., Putnam 2000), it should not be surprising that the size of one's network is positively associated with civic engagement. It was unclear from previous research, however, in what ways we should expect this to differ by nativity. Yet, we find evidence that network size is not associated with civic engagement among foreign-born respondents.

The results in Table 6.3 also demonstrate that a positive association exists between the frequency of political discussion and civic engagement; however, this is only true for those born in the United States. Among the U.S. born, those who discuss politics more frequently are engaged in more community activities than those who discuss politics less frequently. This difference could be driven by the types of community activities in which the U.S. born and foreign born are more likely to be engaged. For instance, those born in the United States are far more likely to report being involved in a political party than those born in another country. Another possibility is that the content of political discussions among the U.S. born and the foreign born might be substantively different in a way that is positively associated with civic engagement.

Even beyond the network characteristics, the individual-level factors and control variables have different relationships with civic engagement based on nativity. We do not find evidence that political knowledge is associated with civic engagement for either group. Recalling the descriptive findings presented in Table 6.1, our foreign-born respondents were most likely to report involvement in the least political of the community activities we asked about: religious and professional organizations. It is possible that these activities are not related to political knowledge because they are not politically oriented.

Considering other demographic variables, we can see that age and education are positively associated with civic engagement among those born in the United States, but not those born in another country. Specifically, older and college-educated U.S.-born respondents are more civically engaged. Both age and education are strong predictors of civic engagement overall in the American politics literature, but these factors do not seem to predict civic engagement among the foreign born in our sample.

Civic Engagement by Gender. In terms of gender differences, our findings related to civic engagement are similar to what we found in terms of political efficacy, as shown in Table 6.4. Discussion frequency was significantly, positively associated with civic engagement for both men and women in our sample. Network size, however, was only a significant predictor of civic engagement among the men in our sample. Partisan homogeneity was not significantly associated with civic engagement for

Table 6.4. Relationship between Network Characteristics and Civic Engagement, by Gender

	Female (1)	Male (2)
Percent copartisan	–0.0003	0.003
	(0.001)	(0.002)
Network size	0.114	0.187**
	(0.087)	(0.089)
Discussion frequency	0.362***	0.363***
	(0.057)	(0.075)
Political knowledge	0.063	0.188*
	(0.078)	(0.104)
Age	0.015***	0.009*
	(0.003)	(0.004)
College	0.240**	0.234*
	(0.104)	(0.139)
Constant	–1.123**	–1.610***
	(0.468)	(0.526)
Observations	612	380
R^2	0.147	0.149
Adjusted R^2	0.139	0.136
Residual std. err.	1.174 (df=605)	1.232 (df=373)
F statistic	17.399*** (df=6; 605)	10.902*** (df=6; 373)

men or women. We find suggestive evidence at the 10 percent level that political knowledge is significant for men, but not for women. Having a college education and being older were both positively and significantly associated with civic engagement for both men and women in our sample; however, these relationships were only significant at the 10 percent level among men.

Self-Reported Political Engagement

Turning from civic engagement to political engagement, we next examine how network characteristics are associated with self-reported engagement in a variety of political activities. We begin by showing how political

Table 6.5. Percentage of Respondents in Each Group Who Reported Engaging in Each Political Activity

	U.S. born	Foreign born	Asian	Black	Latino	White	Female	Male
Signed a paper or online petition	61.5	54.1	55.5	69.4	58.6	67.6	64.5	55.9
Shared, reblogged, or retweeted news articles on social media	50.4	42.6	44.4	53.0	48.3	60.1	52.1	45.9
Attended a speech, march, rally, or demonstration	23.5	13.6	15.2	31.2	27.7	23.0	23.6	20.2
Talked about politics on social media	47.5	41.5	42.1	54.9	44.7	53.5	47.7	46.1
Given money to a political candidate	19.2	18.2	17.7	25.9	13.3	22.5	19.2	20.6
Given money to an organization or cause	27.5	21.6	24.7	33.7	17.5	39.4	28.2	25.7
Volunteered for a campaign or cause	9.5	7.8	6.9	15.1	8.8	8.9	9.7	9.1
Contacted a government official	22.8	16.1	17.0	34.8	16.8	31.0	23.5	20.9
Talked to anyone to try to show them why they would vote for or against a ballot initiative or candidate	50.4	49.5	48.6	51.9	45.5	63.4	50.9	48.9
Joined a local community organization	9.0	6.7	6.5	15.3	7.7	8.0	10.2	7.4

engagement varies by ethnorace, nativity, and gender. Table 6.5 presents the percentage of respondents in each group who reported engaging in each political activity. When it comes to ethnorace, there is not one group that is uniformly more engaged across all these activities. Black respondents, for instance, were the most likely to sign a petition; attend a speech, march, or rally; talk about politics on social media; donate money to a political candidate; volunteer for a campaign or cause; contact a government official; and join a local community organization. On the other hand, White respondents were the most likely to share news articles on social media, donate money to a political organization or cause, and talk to others to explain why they should vote for or against a ballot initiative or candidate. There was no political activity, however, in which Asian Americans or Latinos were most likely to engage. Looking at nativity, we find that a greater portion of those born in the United States reported engaging in all activities than the foreign born. In terms of gender, the women in our sample reported being more engaged than men in every activity other than donating money to a political candidate.

Across all the ethnoracial groups, signing petitions was the most common form of political engagement respondents reported. Although the most common form of engagement, the percentage of respondents who reported signing a petition varied dramatically by ethnorace, nativity, and gender. Black respondents were the most likely to sign a petition (69.4 percent), followed closely by White respondents (67.6 percent); Latino (58.6 percent) and Asian American (55.5 percent) respondents were far less likely to report signing a petition. About 7 percentage points more U.S.-born respondents reported signing a petition than did foreign-born respondents. Women were 9 percentage points more likely than men to report signing a petition.

Looking at the number of activities in which individuals reported engaging, our respondents were not very politically engaged, but they reported engaging in more political activities than civic activities on average. As shown in Figure 6.2, the average respondent engaged in 3.1 political activities, which is greater than the average number of community activities in which respondents reported engaging.

The pattern for political engagement looks remarkably similar to the pattern for civic engagement shown in Figure 6.1. Looking at ethnorace, Blacks and Whites reported the highest levels of political engagement, with Asian Americans and Latinos being the least politically engaged. These patterns are consistent with recent studies looking at political engagement by ethnorace in California, which

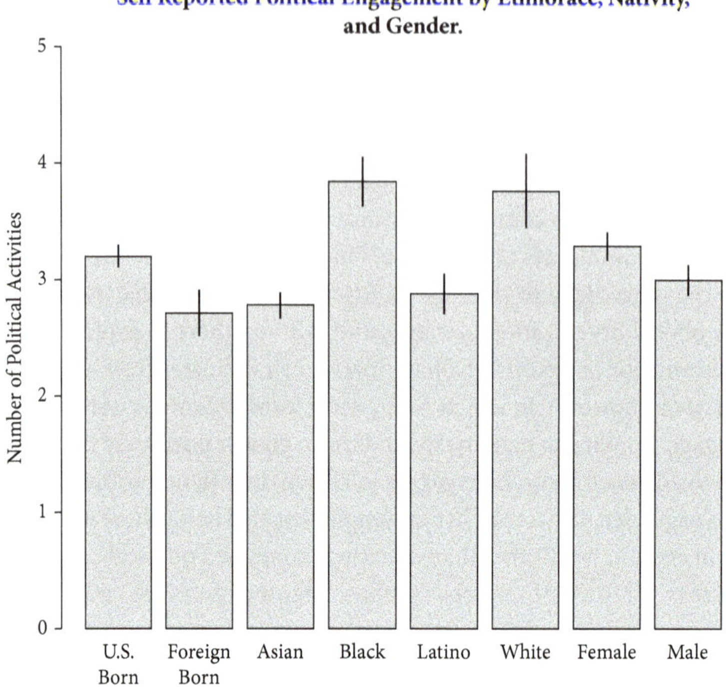

Figure 6.2. Average number of political engagement activities selected by ethnorace, nativity, and gender. Vertical lines represent 95% confidence intervals.

found very similar patterns of engagement across groups (Dobard et al. 2017). Those born in the United States were engaged in significantly more political activities than those born in another country. Finally, women were significantly more likely to report engaging in political activities than men.

Self-Reported Political Engagement by Ethnorace. First, we explore variation in the relationship between network characteristics and political engagement by ethnorace. Table 6.6 presents the results from an OLS regression in which the dependent variable is self-reported political engagement and the independent variables of interest are the political discussion network characteristics: network size, discussion frequency, and partisan homogeneity. Each column of Table 6.6 includes the results for a different ethnoracial group. Overall, the results suggest that discussion frequency is positively associated with self-reported political engagement for all ethnoracial groups, but partisan homogeneity and network size are not.

Table 6.6. Relationship between Network Characteristics and Political Engagement, by Ethnorace

	Dependent variable: Number of political engagement activities selected			
	Asian (1)	Black (2)	Latino (3)	White (4)
Percent copartisan	0.007***	0.004	0.001	0.012*
	(0.003)	(0.004)	(0.004)	(0.006)
Network size	0.426**	−0.159	0.343**	0.132
	(0.165)	(0.332)	(0.170)	(0.539)
Discussion frequency	1.065***	1.310***	1.301***	1.157***
	(0.111)	(0.203)	(0.163)	(0.332)
Political knowledge	0.834***	0.567***	0.060	0.726*
	(0.147)	(0.261)	(0.229)	(0.398)
Female	0.224	0.152	−0.179	0.255
	(0.183)	(0.337)	(0.288)	(0.475)
Age	−0.019**	0.001	−0.010	−0.012
	(0.007)	(0.011)	(0.011)	(0.017)
College	−0.194	0.587*	0.563*	−0.353
	(0.223)	(0.346)	(0.302)	(0.538)
Constant	−3.907***	−1.494	−2.329**	−2.346
	(0.921)	(1.615)	(1.116)	(3.119)
Observations	512	212	254	92
R^2	0.284	0.257	0.283	0.246
Adjusted R^2	0.274	0.231	0.262	0.183
Residual std. err.	2.005 (df=504)	2.298 (df=204)	2.221 (df=246)	2.047 (df=84)
F statistic	28.543*** (df=7; 504)	10.064*** (df=7; 204)	13.862*** (df=7; 246)	3.908*** (df=7; 84)

Note: *$p < 0.10$; **$p < 0.05$; ***$p < 0.01$.

Looking first at partisan homogeneity, the results indicate that the percentage of copartisans in one's network is positively associated with political engagement only among Asian Americans. There is suggestive evidence at the 10 percent level that partisan homogeneity is positively associated with political engagement among Whites. As discussed in Chapter 3, Asian Americans had some of the most diverse political discussion networks, with only just over half of their discussants being copartisans. In contrast, Black respondents are in very homogeneous networks, with about

62 percent of their discussants being copartisans. Floor or ceiling effects stemming from the underlying levels of partisan homogeneity could drive some of what we are finding here.

Next, network size is positively associated with political engagement for Asian Americans and Latinos. Talking about politics on a regular basis with one's discussion partners was the variable that was most positively correlated with political engagement across all ethnoracial groups, with the magnitude of those effects varying in important ways.

Finally, we turn from network characteristics to individual-level characteristics. Political knowledge is positively associated with political engagement among Asian American and Black respondents, with suggestive evidence at the 10 percent level among White respondents, but no evidence of a statistically significant relationship among Latino respondents.

The demographic characteristics present no consistent pattern with respect to their relationship with political engagement by ethnorace. Gender fails to predict political engagement for any group, and age only predicts engagement among Asian Americans, but the direction of the relationship is counterintuitive given what we have learned from studies on political engagement that focused on White Americans (e.g., Wolfinger 1980; Rosenstone and Hanson 1993). For our Asian American respondents, we see a negative association between age and political engagement, such that younger Asians in our sample are more likely to report engaging politically than older Asians. This is consistent with findings from Dobard et al. (2017) whereby millennial Asian Americans were found to be more politically engaged across a variety of political activities than Asian American adults overall.

Finally, education is positively associated with political engagement among Blacks and Latinos, but these relationships are only significant at the 10 percent level. Of course, we would not claim that these findings suggest that education, gender, and age have no bearing on political engagement, but rather that after controlling for other characteristics, particularly political discussion network characteristics, we find that the relationships are less robust.

Ultimately, discussion frequency is strongly, positively associated with political engagement across all ethnoracial groups, above and beyond the impact of individual-level covariates traditionally used to explain political engagement. Partisan homogeneity is positively associated with political engagement only among Asian American respondents, and possibly White respondents. Network size was positively associated with political engagement only among Asian Americans and Latino respondents. Thus, we find general support for the notion that there are important nuances in the effects that political discussion network characteristics have on political engagement across ethnoracial groups.

Self-Reported Political Engagement by Nativity. In this next section, we examine the relationship between the various types of network characteristics on political engagement by nativity. Table 6.7 presents the OLS regression results for which the number of reported political engagement activities is the dependent variable; network size, discussion frequency, and partisan

Table 6.7. Relationship between Network Characteristics and Political Engagement, by Nativity

	Dependent variable: Number of political engagement activities selected	
	U.S. born (1)	Foreign born (2)
Percent copartisan	0.005**	0.010*
	(0.002)	(0.005)
Network size	0.346***	0.115
	(0.114)	(0.304)
Discussion frequency	1.298***	0.760***
	(0.083)	(0.233)
Political knowledge	0.522***	0.916***
	(0.111)	(0.314)
Female	0.016	0.843**
	(0.140)	(0.372)
Age	-0.001	-0.019
	(0.005)	(0.014)
College	0.071	-0.129
	(0.150)	(0.419)
Constant	-3.772***	-2.123
	(0.635)	(1.812)
Observations	1,008	142
R^2	0.282	0.242
Adjusted R^2	0.277	0.203
Residual std. err.	2.138 (df=1000)	2.176 (df=134)
F statistic	56.178*** (df=7; 1000)	6.126*** (df=7; 134)

Note: *$p < 0.1$; **$p < 0.05$; ***$p < 0.01$.

homogeneity are our independent variables. The estimates indicate that political discussion network characteristics are strongly associated with political engagement for both those born in the United States and the foreign born. Regardless of nativity, a positive association exists between the percentage of copartisans in one's network and one's self-reported level of political engagement, but this is only significant at the 10 percent level among foreign-born respondents. Those in more homogeneous discussion networks—exposed to less disagreement—report being more politically engaged. This supports Mutz's (2006) argument that disagreement, or exposure to heterogeneous discussion networks, can be associated with disengagement. While we cannot test her proposed mechanism, that individuals feel cross-pressured and ultimately become politically ambivalent, we find support for a positive relationship between partisan homogeneity and political engagement.

Our estimates also demonstrate a statistically significant and positive association between network size and self-reported political engagement, but only among U.S.-born respondents. Individuals born in the United States situated in larger and more politically homogenous political discussion networks are more politically engaged, relative to those in smaller and more heterogeneous networks. This finding is consistent with the results we presented earlier for some ethnoracial groups. Frequency of political discussion within one's network is also significantly associated with political engagement for both the U.S. and the foreign born. Given that several of the political activities in our political engagement index directly relate to political discussion (e.g., talking about politics on social media, talking to others about your opinions on the candidates or ballot initiatives), it is understandable why frequency of political discussion is strongly related to these political engagement measures.

Our model also accounts for individual-level characteristics that have traditionally explained political engagement. Political knowledge is positively associated with political engagement for both the U.S. and foreign born. Rather surprisingly, this finding stands in contrast to the relationship between political knowledge and *civic* engagement, in which the relationship was not significant for either group. Interestingly, age does not seem to explain political engagement levels for either the U.S.-born or foreign-born respondents. Among the foreign born, being female was positively associated with political engagement, suggesting that foreign-born women are more politically engaged than foreign-born men.

Overall, we find that network characteristics are strongly associated with political engagement, regardless of nativity. Some network characteristics, such as discussion frequency and partisan homogeneity, appeared to impact our

U.S.- and foreign-born respondents' reported political engagement in the same way and much more so than the individual-level characteristics. This could, in part, be due to the network characteristics being derived from explicitly *political discussion* networks, which should theoretically be more closely linked to political engagement than civic engagement. Possibly, a different name generator that derives a broader political discussion network might be more closely linked to civic engagement. Though in light of previous research showing little difference in networks based on the name generators used (Klofstad et al. 2009), this explanation does not seem to be particularly compelling.

Self-Reported Political Engagement by Gender. Women reported participating in more political activities than did men, and this difference is statistically significant at the $p < .05$ level. As the findings in Table 6.8 indicate, for the men and women in our sample, network size, discussion frequency, and

Table 6.8. Relationship between Network Characteristics and Political Engagement, by Gender

	Dependent variable: Number of political engagement activities selected	
	Female (1)	Male (2)
Percent copartisan	0.004*	0.006**
	(0.002)	(0.003)
Network size	0.287*	0.347**
	(0.162)	(0.141)
Discussion frequency	1.121***	1.454***
	(0.101)	(0.121)
Political knowledge	0.724***	0.393**
	(0.136)	(0.160)
Age	0.004	−0.015**
	(0.006)	(0.007)
College	0.062	−0.010
	(0.185)	(0.216)
Constant	−3.436***	−3.622***
	(0.869)	(0.829)
Observations	694	457
R^2	0.252	0.310
Adjusted R^2	0.245	0.301
Residual std. err.	2.187 (df=687)	2.082 (df=450)
F statistic	38.561*** (df=6; 687)	33.732*** (df=6; 450)

partisan homogeneity all have a positive and statistically significant impact on their reported levels of political engagement. The relationship between partisan homogeneity and political engagement, as well as between network size and political engagement, are significant at the 10 percent level among women. Political knowledge, we find, is significantly associated with political engagement for men and women.

Validated Turnout

Beyond self-reported political engagement, we also examine validated voter turnout. Since we rely on information from the California voter file, we overcome the measurement problems associated with self-reported voter behavior (Shaw et al. 2000). Most individuals have the tendency to say they voted when asked in a survey, even if they did not (Presser 1990; Silver et al. 1986). For instance, survey respondents from the 1992 ANES overreported their rates of turnout by 12 percentage points from the base rate of turnout.

Looking at our sample overall, the average respondent voted in 2.4 of the 5 most recent statewide elections.[4] Breaking this down by ethnorace, nativity, and gender, we see a similar pattern in voter turnout, as shown in Figure 6.3. Black respondents had the highest rates of vote propensity followed by Whites and Asians, who voted at statistically indistinguishable rates. Latinos voted in the fewest elections compared with all other ethnoracial groups. Those born in the United States voted in significantly more recent elections than the foreign born. Although turnout rates for men were slightly higher than for women, this difference is not statistically significant at conventional levels.

There are two notable differences in the type of political engagement captured in our self-reported measure and those presented here. First, the self-reported measures could overestimate the levels of engagement, given that social desirability bias might lead individuals to overreport the extent to which they engage in political activities. Moreover, the extent to which one feels pressured to overreport political engagement could vary systematically by ethnorace, nativity, or network characteristics. Those in larger political discussion networks and those who discuss politics more frequently could feel a stronger attachment to a social norm that one should be politically engaged, thus leading individuals to overreport their political engagement activities.

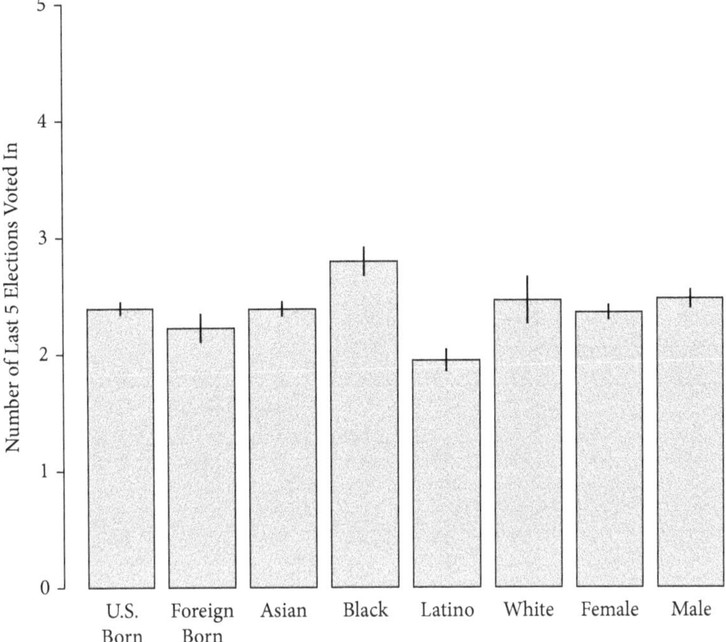

Figure 6.3. Average number of elections voted in, out of the five most recent statewide elections, by ethnorace, nativity, and gender. Vertical lines represent 95% confidence intervals.

Second, the types of political activities in our self-reported index are different from and do not include the act of voting. Many of the political activities we asked about are relatively "low-cost" forms of engagement in terms of time and resources. Talking about politics or sharing news articles on social media is relatively low-cost compared with turning out to vote. Turning out to vote has arguably more barriers to participation than most forms of engagement in our index, which could make it more difficult for networks to have a measurable impact over socioeconomic factors. Similarly, the types of activities in our engagement index are often quite social, such as talking about politics on social media, discussing politics with someone, or even attending a rally. Any of these activities might be more directly influenced by political discussion network characteristics than more individualistic activities such as voting.

Validated Turnout by Ethnorace. Table 6.9 shows the results from OLS regressions broken out by ethnoracial group in which the dependent variable is the number of the past five elections in which the respondent voted, and the independent variables of interest are discussion network characteristics. In contrast to the results for civic and self-reported political engagement, we find that only discussion frequency exerted statistically identifiable effects on validated voter turnout. We detect a statistically significant, positive association between discussion

Table 6.9. Relationship between Network Characteristics and Validated Turnout, by Ethnorace

	Dependent variable: Number of last five elections voted in			
	Asian (1)	Black (2)	Latino (3)	White (4)
Percent copartisan	0.002	0.0004	0.001	0.005
	(0.001)	(0.002)	(0.002)	(0.004)
Network size	0.047	0.148	0.035	-0.503
	(0.090)	(0.183)	(0.088)	(0.370)
Discussion frequency	0.193***	0.163	0.224***	0.513**
	(0.063)	(0.112)	(0.084)	(0.228)
Political knowledge	0.331***	0.342**	0.318***	-0.145
	(0.084)	(0.144)	(0.117)	(0.273)
Female	-0.023	0.240	0.012	-0.301
	(0.103)	(0.185)	(0.148)	(0.324)
Age	0.023***	0.049***	0.024***	0.027**
	(0.004)	(0.006)	(0.006)	(0.011)
College	0.435***	0.293	0.518***	0.372
	(0.127)	(0.190)	(0.154)	(0.369)
Constant	-0.279	-1.542*	-0.534	2.085
	(0.506)	(0.892)	(0.575)	(2.135)
Observations	536	213	258	93
R^2	0.154	0.347	0.220	0.182
Adjusted R^2	0.143	0.325	0.198	0.115
Residual std. err.	1.159 (df=528)	1.269 (df=205)	1.146 (df=250)	1.405 (df=85)
F statistic	13.728*** (df=7; 528)	15.577*** (df=7; 205)	10.072*** (df=7; 250)	2.703** (df=7; 85)

Note: $^*p < 0.10$; $^{**}p < 0.05$; $^{***}p < 0.01$.

frequency and validated turnout among all ethnoracial groups except Blacks.

In contrast to the relationship between network characteristics and validated turnout, individual-level factors were more influential in explaining turnout patterns across all groups in our sample. Political knowledge was positively associated with turnout among all ethnoracial groups except for Whites. We find that age is positively associated with turnout among all ethnoracial groups. This result stands in contrast to the finding that age was negatively associated with self-reported political engagement among Asian American respondents. However, this difference could be driven by variation in the types of political activities examined in the self-reported political engagement index, compared with turning out to vote. Education was positively associated with turnout only among Asian American and Latino respondents. That is, Asian American and Latino respondents with a college education voted in significantly more elections than Asian American and Latino respondents without a college education.

Overall, we find that network characteristics are less robust indicators of validated turnout across our respondents. Individual-level characteristics, such as political knowledge and demographics, have a much larger impact on validated turnout across all ethnoracial groups than the network factors studied here. This differs from civic and self-reported political engagement in which we showed that network characteristics had a greater impact on our respondents' engagement.

Validated Turnout by Nativity. Building on the self-reported political engagement, Table 6.10 shows the results from an ordinary least squares regression in which the dependent variable is the number of elections in which the respondent voted between November 2012 and November 2016. The independent variables of interest are the political discussion network characteristics examined throughout this book: network size, discussion frequency, and partisan homogeneity.

The results indicate that discussion frequency is positively associated with voter turnout among our U.S.-born and foreign-born respondents; however, this pattern is only significant at the 10 percent level among foreign-born respondents. Individuals who discuss politics more often (discussion frequency) turned out to vote in more elections, regardless of nativity.

For both U.S.- and foreign-born respondents, political knowledge was positively associated with validated voter turnout; those who were more

Table 6.10. Relationship between Network Characteristics and Validated Voter Turnout, by Nativity

	Dependent variable: Number of the last five elections voted in	
	U.S. born (1)	Foreign born (2)
Percent copartisan	0.002	0.001
	(0.001)	(0.003)
Network size	0.038	0.175
	(0.063)	(0.178)
Discussion frequency	0.214***	0.235*
	(0.046)	(0.133)
Political knowledge	0.280***	0.591***
	(0.061)	(0.181)
Female	−0.019	0.087
	(0.077)	(0.213)
Age	0.032***	0.047***
	(0.003)	(0.008)
College	0.485***	−0.065
	(0.083)	(0.238)
Constant	−0.488	−2.696**
	(0.347)	(1.058)
Observations	1,031	149
R^2	0.243	0.277
Adjusted R^2	0.238	0.241
Residual std. err.	1.195 (df=1023)	1.277 (df=141)
F statistic	46.900*** (df=7; 1023)	7.708*** (df=7; 141)

Note: *$p < 0.1$; **$p < 0.05$; ***$p < 0.01$.

politically knowledgeable turned out to vote in more elections. Similarly, among both U.S.- and foreign-born respondents, age was significantly and positively associated with validated turnout. Similar to what we found with political engagement more broadly, education is only significantly associated with turnout among the U.S.-born respondents. Those born in the United States who have a college education turned out to vote in significantly more recent elections than those who do not have a college education. In contrast, there is no significant association between college education and turnout among those born outside of the United States.

Validated Turnout by Gender. Table 6.11 shows the relationship between network characteristics and validated turnout by gender. For women, discussion frequency and the percentage of copartisans in their networks positively predict their voter turnout. However, the relationship between partisan homogeneity and turnout is only significant at the 10 percent level. For men in our sample, only discussion frequency is positively associated with turnout. Network size was not significantly associated with

Table 6.11. Relationship between Network Characteristics and Validated Voter Turnout, by Gender

	Dependent variable: Number of the last five elections voted in	
	Female (1)	Male (2)
Percent copartisan	0.002*	0.001
	(0.001)	(0.002)
Network size	-0.022	0.112
	(0.084)	(0.086)
Discussion frequency	0.187***	0.304***
	(0.055)	(0.072)
Political knowledge	0.295***	0.349***
	(0.073)	(0.096)
Age	0.032***	0.032***
	(0.003)	(0.004)
College	0.430***	0.379***
	(0.100)	(0.129)
Constant	-0.240	-1.277**
	(0.453)	(0.501)
Observations	710	471
R^2	0.237	0.240
Adjusted R^2	0.230	0.231
Residual std. err.	1.189 (df=703)	1.263 (df=464)
F statistic	36.345*** (df=6; 703)	24.483*** (df=6; 464)

Note: *$p < 0.1$; **$p < 0.05$; ***$p < 0.01$.

turnout among men or women. As we saw with self-reported political engagement, having higher levels of political knowledge, being older, and having a college degree positively impact voter turnout among women and men.

Conclusion

Political discussion networks play an important role in getting us to be civically and politically engaged citizens. From volunteering on campaigns to reblogging or sharing a tweet about politics, we tend to act politically when we are engaged and interact with others. In this chapter, we analyzed the various ways in which political discussion network characteristics impact three forms of engagement: civic, political, and validated voting behavior. Our analysis made clear that the relationship between political discussion network characteristics and engagement is more nuanced than previous research has suggested.

Existing research on partisan homogeneity argues that it can either encourage or discourage political engagement. On the one hand, exposure to political disagreement (heterogeneity) could inspire individuals to seek more information and subsequently engage more in politics (Scheufele et al. 2004). On the other hand, exposure to disagreement might lead individuals to feel cross-pressured, which can create feelings of ambivalence, leading individuals to opt out of political engagement (Mutz 2002, 2006).

Our results, which are summarized in Table 6.12, align more strongly with Mutz's argument, as we find that individuals who are in more homogeneous discussion networks, and therefore may be exposed to less disagreement, are more likely to engage in some types of political activity. But it is important to note that the effect of partisan homogeneity is not consistent across civic and political activity, nor across ethnorace, nativity, or gender. Moreover, we find virtually no evidence that partisan homogeneity is associated with validated turnout in any of our comparison groups, with the exception of some suggestive evidence that women in more homogeneous networks voted in more elections than did men. While we do not claim to settle the debate about whether partisan homogeneity causes individuals to engage or disengage in politics, we provide some evidence that it has a mobilizing effect, at least for political activities other than voting and among some groups of participants. More importantly, our analysis makes clear that the effects of partisan homogeneity on political engagement are not always uniform across all subsets of the U.S. electorate.

As Table 6.12 highlights, for self-reported forms of civic and political engagement, network size is positively associated with engagement among Asian Americans and Latinos. However, looking at validated turnout, network size fails to explain voting for any of the ethnoracial groups studied. Thus, network size appears to be influential for everyday forms of engagement, many of which have fewer barriers to participation.

Discussion frequency, in contrast, was a more consistent predictor of political and civic participation across ethnorace, nativity, and gender. Talking about politics on a regular basis with one's discussion networks is correlated with greater levels of turnout and participation in nonelectoral political

Table 6.12. Summary of Findings: Predictive Power of Network Attributes on Political and Civic Engagement

	Ethnoracial group				*Nativity*		*Gender*	
	Asian American	Black	Latino	White	Foreign born	U.S. born	Female	Male
Political Engagement								
Size	+		+			+	+	+
Discussion frequency	+	+	+	+	+	+	+	+
Copartisanship	+			+	+	+	+	+
Validated Turnout								
Size								
Discussion frequency	+		+	+	+	+	+	+
Copartisanship							+	
Civic Engagement								
Size			+			+		+
Discussion frequency	+	+	+			+	+	+
Copartisanship								

Note: Cell entries with a (+) indicate that the network characteristic coefficient was positive and statistically significant at $p < .05$ level.

activities for all ethnoracial groups. It was also the most consistent predictor of becoming civically involved across all groups. We also find that all three network characteristics helped to explain the levels of political engagement for U.S.-born respondents, men, and women.

Ultimately, our results demonstrate that the relationship between network characteristics and engagement is nuanced. It varies by ethnorace, nativity, and gender. In addition, the predictive power of political discussion networks also differs depending on the type of civic or political activity in question. Among our respondents, turning out to vote seems less affected by political discussion networks than other types of civic and political engagement. Some of our findings are directionally consistent with previous research, but we find that the magnitude of these effects varies substantially, relative to an individual's social position in the United States. We hope our findings make a strong case for the importance of accounting for political discussion networks in any studies that seek to understand the political behavior of individuals along the lines of ethnorace, nativity, and/or gender.

7
Conclusion
Political Discussion Networks and the New American Electorate

Because we experience politics in community, decades of social science research has investigated the role that our peers, by way of our family, friends, acquaintances and coworkers, influence our political actions and behaviors. The conclusions drawn from these research endeavors all support the notion that whom we talk to about politics matters a great deal in the way we formulate our political thoughts, and whether or not we decide to become engaged and active participants in the polity. At the same time that many of these landmark studies were being conducted, the United States has experienced rapid demographic and ethnoracial change. What was once a country predominantly comprised of White Americans is now much more ethnoracially diverse, with a large share of this diversity stemming from the considerable waves of immigration commencing in the mid- to late-1960s. By 2050, the U.S. Census estimates that Latinos will be 30.2 percent of the population, Asian Americans 7.8 percent, and Blacks 13 percent. Whites, who were estimated to be 62.4 percent of the U.S. population in 2015 will drop down to 46.3 percent of the population by 2050.[1]

What this means, then, is that virtually all of what we know about the importance of political discussion networks in explaining political attitudes and behaviors pertains to *White* Americans. This critical gap in the existing literature is where our research efforts come into play. In this book, our goals were threefold. First, we conducted a detailed comparative analysis of differences in political discussion network characteristics across and within ethnoracial groups. Second, we argued that the makeup of those discussion networks is affected by their ethnoracial group membership, nativity, and gender. Finally, in light of the important relationship that exists between partisan attachments and ethnoracial group membership, we suggested that political discussion network analysis needs to consider the ethnoracial composition

Talking Politics. Taylor N. Carlson, Marisa Abrajano, and Lisa García Bedolla, Oxford University Press (2020). © Oxford University Press.
DOI: 10.1093/oso/9780190082116.001.0001

of political discussion networks in order to understand how these networks serve to socialize network members into politics.

The empirical analysis that we provide is novel, given that virtually *no* existing studies have examined whether political discussion networks are positive predictors of political engagement, turnout, efficacy, and level of political knowledge for ethnoracial groups, the foreign born, or women from diverse backgrounds, to the extent that we do here.[2] Given the importance that political discussion networks have been found to play in explaining nearly all aspects of political behavior in the United States, it is long overdue to determine whether the same can be said for groups of individuals whose social position and, thus, political experiences and opportunity structures in the United States, differ markedly from those of the White majority.

With our analysis, we build on the political discussion network literature by providing a detailed comparative analysis of differences in political discussion network characteristics across ethnorace, nativity, and gender. We contribute to the existing research in American politics by demonstrating how social positions and the types of political opportunity structures that accompany them become reflected in each group's social networks. Finally, we reveal the impact that networks can exert on a whole host of behavioral and attitudinal outcomes that are the mainstays in studies of political behavior—civic and political engagement, turnout, political trust and efficacy, as well as political knowledge and policy opinions. Without a doubt, our analyses reveal the wide-ranging explanatory power of political discussion networks for U.S. political behavior. At a minimum, our results show how focusing solely at the individual level as the main driver of political actions misses the important ways in which individuals interact with their social context. Such interactions have the potential to explain their political behavior and how the experience of that intersection is mediated by their experiences of marginalization and privilege.

Chapter 2 began with a discussion of why there is such a dearth in research devoted to the political discussion networks of voters of color. As a way to rectify this shortcoming, we described the original survey that we designed and fielded on a diverse sample of California voters, both in terms of their ethnorace as well as their nativity. This survey data serves as the basis for most of our analyses. To supplement the survey data, we also conducted a series of in-depth interviews with canvassers from three California grassroots-based organizations, all of whom are charged with talking to voters about current political issues and events.

In Chapter 3, we provided a detailed descriptive picture of discussion networks, comparing them across ethnorace, nativity, and gender. We unpacked the types of social connections that comprise political discussion networks across groups who hold different social positions in the United States. We also examined the extent to which discussion networks are homogenous along political dimensions such as partisanship, political engagement, and political knowledge.

Chapter 3 continues on to assess how key political discussion network characteristics (size, partisan homogeneity, and frequency of political discussion) vary by ethnorace, nativity, and gender. As expected, we find important differences in political discussion networks between each of these groups that suggest that there are systematic differences in the composition of political discussion networks due to variation in our respondents' relative social position and the impact that has on individuals' political opportunity structures. For instance, Whites have the largest average discussion networks, with about 4 discussants on average, whereas Latinos' and Asian Americans' networks only have about 3 discussants, out of 5 total. These patterns are consistent across other nationally representative surveys, even if they lack large samples of non-whites. Additionally, we find that naturalized voters are embedded in smaller networks that are more politically diverse in terms of partisanship than those of the U.S. born.

One of the main takeaways from Chapter 3 is that the individual and contextual-level factors fail to consistently explain one's network across the four ethnoracial groups that we examine. In some instances, religious or secular group membership is much more strongly associated with network size, and in other cases, being a member of a secular or religious group has no bearing on the size of one's discussion network. However, in terms of organizational membership, belonging to a secular organization is more consistently associated with discussion network characteristics than is membership in a religious organization across our sample.

Chapter 4 turned its focus to the impact of discussion network characteristics on two important precursors to political engagement—political trust and political efficacy. These attitudinal measures are important because individuals who feel that they have say in government, believe that their vote matters, and think that politicians care about them are the ones most likely to become involved in politics (García Bedolla 2005). Yet those who feel they have little impact in the political process or that their participation is of little significance may be unlikely to become involved in politics. Citizens who exhibit high levels of trust in their government are also the ones who are habitual voters and are politically active between elections, attending political meetings and volunteering on campaigns.

In this chapter, we tested the contention that political discussion networks have the potential to foster greater trust in government and feelings of political efficacy. Overall, our analyses lend support for this contention, with important variations along the lines of ethnorace, nativity, and gender. For instance, consistent with previous research, Asian Americans and Latinos in our sample tended to have less efficacious attitudes than Blacks and Whites, suggesting that feelings of political agency among these groups are not as great as for others. And while we hypothesized that Whites would report the highest levels of political efficacy out of all the ethnoracial groups, particularly when compared with Blacks, our results suggest otherwise. In fact, Blacks' feelings of political efficacy in our sample are generally on par with those of Whites. The same can be said for women versus men.

Finally, in our multivariate models that examine the predictive power of network characteristics vis á vis other individual-level factors, we find that network effects are positively associated with political efficacy to a larger degree than with political trust. Notably, how often one engages in political discussion with his or her network predicts higher levels of political efficacy for all ethnoracial groups. In line with our expectations, we find that network characteristics are a stronger and more reliable predictor of political efficacy among the U.S. born than for the foreign-born.

With regards to political trust, we also find important variation across ethnorace and nativity; gender differences on the issue of political trust, however, were more muted. Consistent with the existing research, those born in the United States had significantly lower levels of political trust than those born in another country. Asians exhibited the highest levels of trust in government, followed by Whites, Latinos, and Blacks at the bottom. Rather interestingly, the predictive power of discussion networks to explain levels of political trust was not as robust as the other precursor to engagement we explored: political efficacy. Overall, our analysis indicated that network characteristics unevenly predicted feelings of political trust across our ethnoracial groups as well as by nativity and gender. The point here again is that network properties are not associated with political outcomes in the same way across all the ethnoracial groups in our sample.

In Chapter 5, we examined the relationship among discussion network characteristics, political knowledge, and policy attitudes. Most striking, we found that differential effects exist with regard to the relationship between political discussion networks and levels of political knowledge. In the full model that includes all of our controls, we only find a positive association with frequency of political discussion and levels of political knowledge for Asian Americans. Among Asian Americans, Blacks, and Whites, the size of their political discussion networks was positively associated with levels of political knowledge. That is, those who are situated in larger networks, which presumably means that they have access to more information, are associated with higher levels of political knowledge. In fact, our findings also reveal that discussion frequency is positively associated with higher levels of political knowledge for both foreign-born and U.S.-born respondents. Network effects also operated differently for men and women in our sample.

Concerning policy positions, our analysis reveals that regular and repeated discussions on political matters can lead individuals to hold views that align with those with whom they discuss politics. This finding is consistent with much of the political discussion network literature—both observational and experimental—but we note that in our case we cannot be sure that it is these frequent discussions that are causing individuals to adopt similar views, or whether individuals are choosing to have frequent discussions because they know that they already agree on these policy issues.

Here, we focus on two specific policy issues that are of great relevance to non-white voters—climate change and criminal justice. While we expected that the percentage of Democrats in one's discussion network to be most strongly associated with respondents' policy attitudes, it was not associated with policy climate change policy opinions among Latinos, nor criminal justice issues among Blacks. This means that Latinos and Blacks might be more resistant to social influence from their networks when it comes to climate change and criminal justice attitudes, respectively, than are Whites and Asian Americans.

Beyond the directional, partisan impact of discussion networks on climate change attitudes, we considered the impact of frequency of discussions. Among both U.S.-born and foreign-born respondents, how often they discuss politics within their networks is also positively associated with recognizing the negative economic impact of climate change. Those who talk about politics on a frequent basis are more likely to adopt this position, relative to respondents who report more infrequent political conversations.

We found similar results when looking at our respondents' attitudes toward criminal justice policy. When we examine this relationship across ethnoracial groups, the percentage of Democrats in one's discussion network is not positively associated with issue agreement on criminal justice for Black respondents. These findings suggest that political discussion networks, as measured by the percentage of Democrats in the network, exert the strongest impact on the criminal justice attitudes of Asian Americans, Latinos, and Whites. We recognize that some concerns over endogeneity may arise with this analysis. However, it is important to keep in mind that our efforts are aimed at understanding whether there is opinion homophily, the extent to which it varies among ethnoracial and nativity groups, and its relative impact on other political behaviors. Thus, our analysis prevents us from determining whether individuals from some ethnoracial groups are more or less likely to be *persuaded* by their networks' opinions. However, it seems that there is at least some variation in sensitivity to the partisan preferences of one's discussion networks across the ethnoracial groups in our study.

Our final set of empirical analyses, presented in Chapter 6, focused on the relationship between discussion networks and the behaviors that have most preoccupied political scientists: political and civic engagement. Namely, we look at participation in civic activities, self-reported measures of political participation, as well as validated voter turnout. Our results, generally speaking, align with the existing research documenting the positive relationship between discussion network activity and political participation. However, we find important differences depending on the type of behavior in question. While discussion frequency is positively associated with political participation regardless of ethnorace or nativity, turnout is less strongly associated with political discussion network characteristics.

When we examine differential effects by gender, we find that all three network characteristics are positively associated with self-reported political engagement among both men and women, yet the magnitude of the effect varies in important ways across the different types of activities we explore. Discussion frequency was positively associated with validated turnout for both men and women. These findings help us better understand what particular aspects of discussion networks help to foster civic and political engagement among Whites and non-whites, naturalized voters, and women, and which ones do not.

Research Implications

After reading this book, we hope to have provided ample evidence to convince readers about the importance of informal, political conversation in explaining and understanding the political behavior of individuals along the lines of ethnorace, nativity, and gender. As we have articulated throughout this book, it is imperative to recognize that political discussion networks fail to operate uniformly across different social positions. We are cautiously optimistic that the scope of the empirical analyses has made this point quite compelling. In light of this reality, we encourage political discussion and network scholars more broadly to use a diverse sample of individuals whenever possible. As we discussed earlier, the reality is that the demographics of the U.S. electorate are changing rapidly, and researchers must be acutely cognizant of these changes in order to generate research that accurately reflects the study population. We believe that one of our responsibilities as social science scholars is to be fully aware of the fact that the populace is rapidly changing both in terms of where they come from and what their political opportunity structures are, and how that translates into their political orientations, experiences, and sense of political agency. We will now highlight some of the major themes that emerge from our study.

The Importance of Community. One of the main takeaways from our qualitative data is the importance of community for understanding political behavior. As we asserted at the onset of this chapter, people's experiences with politics do not occur in an isolated vacuum. Instead, they occur in conversation with others, and those others could be our friends, family members, coworkers, or acquaintances. Consider the quote from this male Latino Community Coalition canvasser:

> I think it's important for my community to talk about what the issues are. I think politics brings the division of Republican and Democrat and then the belief of, I'm on this side and you're on that side. I think in order for community to be able to remain a community instead of [turning] into Democrat, Republican and Libertarian, it's one of the issues that is affecting us and how these issues can be remedied. Then we walk into the realm of politics without being contaminated with a view of politics but actually coming in there with a real perspective of what the solutions are to the problems that are there.

Our call to account for the salience of one's community is also a call to move beyond an individualistic explanation of political behavior and political attitudes in the United States. By doing so, scholars have the opportunity to more accurately and fully explain why individuals choose to vote for one candidate or another, and what factors best predict attitudes on policy issues or trust in government. Given the technological advancements of today, whereby collecting data and information is easier than it ever has been, the types of research questions political scientists attempt to answer can also be significantly broadened and expanded.

Accounting for Intersections. Ideally, our analysis would account for the intersectional nature of ethnorace, nativity, and gender. However, due to the limited sample sizes of each of these categories, conducting such an analysis was simply unfeasible. But our findings are suggestive that the intersection of experiences of marginalization and privilege affect the network and community contexts within which individuals are embedded and their resulting impact on political behavior. Individuals may choose some proportion of their network discussants, but their agency in making their choices is not absolute; they will be limited by the types of individuals with whom they come into contact on a regular basis. Those connections, in turn, are reflections of their neighborhoods, workplaces, church membership, and other institutional factors. We know from previous research that the composition of these spaces varies by ethnorace, nativity, gender, and class.[3] Understanding the determinants and effects of political discussion networks, then, needs to take into consideration how these intersections interact with a person's social context and subsequently affect how they move through and engage with the political and civic world.

Talking Politics Matters. We hope that our findings have made it abundantly clear and convincing that informal conversations about politics have an important impact on how individuals think about politics and whether or not they choose to become politically and civically engaged. Our qualitative interviews also suggest that these informal conversations may be even more impactful for voters of color given that their political opportunity structures, as a function of their social positions, are often more limited than those of White Americans. Having these types of discussions and conversations may be one way to ameliorate existing differences in political participation levels. Again, we recognize that measuring exactly how individuals interact with one another can be difficult and is something that has plagued researchers, yet one can imagine that the advance of sophisticated and innovative data collection processes could help to alleviate this problem.

Future Research Efforts

Our research only begins to scratch the surface on the role that discussion networks play in the political behavior and attitudes across diverse groups of voters. Despite its limitations, we believe our study provides important insights and lays the foundation for future research. We urge scholars to conduct network studies in other areas of the country where a sizable ethnoracial population exists, and/or with a large number of naturalized voters. As Hero (2000) has documented, state context and culture vary significantly and those differences have policy consequences. It is likely that network effects will differ based on contextual factors as well. It also goes without saying that the national origins of both the Latino and Asian American population vary substantially across the United States (García Bedolla 2014; Wong et al. 2011), which we know can impact their political orientations and viewpoints. Additionally, the context of reception for immigrants also varies by state and region and would therefore be another factor to consider.

While there is a wealth of research on gender and democratic deliberation, as well as gender and political attitudes and engagement, we believe that the research presented here opens up possibilities for additional inquiries at the intersection between gender and political discussion networks. In particular, we think that scholars could focus on further unpacking how discussion varies between women of different ethnoracial groups, especially since previous research has shown that non-white women are influential in grassroots mobilization efforts (García Bedolla 2005).

Given the results presented in this book, it is important to at least discuss the generalizability of political discussion network findings that cannot explicitly be compared across groups. Beyond improving our understanding and the generalizability of political discussion network research, we believe that this research provides ample opportunities to better understand political engagement among non-white voters. It is important to note that the research presented in this book, like much political discussion network research, analyzes networks as they existed at the time of data collection. However, considering how and when individuals develop their networks could be important for explaining why some of the patterns observed in our analysis exist. It will be especially worthwhile to consider when and how immigrants form their political discussion networks relative to those born in the United States. As immigrants aim to learn about and become engaged in the American political system, it is possible that informal political discussion networks might have a powerful influence on shaping both their political knowledge and their political engagement. Understanding when and how political discussion networks form and change over time during the political socialization process could inform our understanding of political engagement in important ways.

We also encourage scholars to consider possible interventions to increase the frequency of political discussion among ethnoracial group members and naturalized voters. The frequency of political discussion within one's network was one of the most consistent predictors of political engagement in our sample, as well as the precursors to engagement. Yet, we found that non-whites discuss politics less frequently than their White counterparts. As such, considering ways to increase political discussion among non-whites could lead to more engagement. Researchers could also consider strategies to increase discussion network size, which we also found to be important for engagement.

Another research path worth exploring is a network-based approach to mobilizing non-white voters. Extant research on mobilization indicates that social pressure and network effects can powerfully increase turnout (e.g., Bond et al. 2012; Gerber, Green, and Larimer 2008), but this research does not explore the extent to which the results are the same across ethnoracial groups. As García Bedolla and Michelson (2012) demonstrate, not all mobilization strategies operate in the same manner across all groups. Together with the results presented in our book, it stands to reason that mobilization efforts could take on a network-based approach with lower propensity voters of color, potentially increasing their engagement across numerous types of civic and political activities.

Since the behavioral revolution, political science has studied political behavior almost exclusively at the individual level. Similarly, the vast majority of the research in the field has failed to fully consider how marginal social positions—being non-white, an immigrant, or a woman—are associated with individuals' relationships to the political system. But to understand U.S. politics today we need to better understand how community-level relationships, narratives of inclusion or exclusion, and information sharing shape our politics. Without such a nuanced and multifaceted approach we will continue to tell only part of the story.

Appendix

Chapter 2 Appendix

A2.1 Invitation Emails

Original Survey and Black Oversample

You are being invited to participate in a research study titled Collaborative Study of Integrated Voter Engagement. This study is being conducted by Professor Marisa Abrajano from the University of California, San Diego and Professor Lisa García Bedolla from the University of California, Berkeley. You were selected to participate in this study because you have been previously contacted by one of the following organizations: APEN, CoCo, SCOPE, or Working Partnerships USA.

The purpose of this research study is to understand civic engagement and participation in your community, as well as your social and political networks. If you agree to take part in this study, you will be asked to complete an online survey. This survey will ask about your political opinions on several policies, past political engagement activities, the people you talk with about important matters and politics, and basic demographic and political information. It will take you approximately 10–12 minutes to complete. After you complete the survey, you will be eligible to receive a $5 Amazon gift card.

Your participation in this study is completely voluntary and you can withdraw at any time by simply exiting the survey. You are free to skip any question that you choose.

If you have questions about this project, you may contact the researcher(s), [REDACTED]. If you have any questions concerning your rights as a research subject, you may contact the [REDACTED].

Latino Oversample

(En Español abajo)

You are being invited to participate in a research study titled Collaborative Study of Integrated Voter Engagement. This study is being conducted by [REDACTED]. You were selected to participate in this study because you have been previously contacted by one of the following organizations: [REDACTED].

The purpose of this research study is to understand civic engagement and participation in your community, as well as your social and political networks. If you agree to take part in this study, you will be asked to complete an online survey. This survey will ask about your political opinions on several policies, past political engagement activities, the people you talk with about important matters and politics, and basic demographic and political information. It will take you approximately 10–12 minutes to complete. After you complete the survey, you will be eligible to receive a $5 Amazon gift card.

Your participation in this study is completely voluntary, and you can withdraw at any time by simply exiting the survey. You are free to skip any question that you choose.

If you have questions about this project, you may contact the researcher(s), [REDACTED]. If you have any questions concerning your rights as a research subject, you may contact the [REDACTED].

Lo/a invitamos a participar en un estudio de investigación titulado "Estudio colaborativo de la participación integral de los votantes." Este es un estudio realizado por la [REDACTED]. Usted fue seleccionado/a para participar en este estudio porque ha sido contactado/a antes por una de las siguientes organizaciones: [REDACTED].

El propósito de este estudio es entender su compromiso cívico y su participación en asuntos de su comunitarios. Asimismo queremos conocer sus redes sociales y políticas. Esta encuesta le preguntará acerca de sus opiniones políticas, sobre varias políticas públicas, sobre su participación en actividades políticas en el pasado, sobre las personas con las cuales usted discute sobre la política y otros asuntos importantes. También le pediremos información básica sobre sus características demográficas y sus opiniones políticas. Le tomará aproximadamente 10–12 minutos para completar la encuesta. Al concluir, usted será elegible para recibir una tarjeta de regalo de Amazon de $5.

Su participación en este estudio es completamente voluntaria, y usted puede dejar de participar en cualquier momento simplemente abandonando la encuesta. Usted puede omitir una respuesta a cualquiera de las preguntas de la encuesta.

Si tiene preguntas sobre este proyecto, puede comunicarse con la(s) investigadora(s), [REDACTED]. Si tiene alguna pregunta sobre sus derechos como sujeto de esta investigación, puede comunicarse con la Oficina del Programa de Protecciones de Investigación Humana de [REDACTED].

Snowball Sample

You are being invited to participate in a research study titled Collaborative Study of Integrated Voter Engagement. This study is being conducted by [REDACTED]. You were selected to participate in this study because you were identified by a friend/family member has identified you as someone they discuss politics with. The purpose of this research study is to understand civic engagement and participation in your community, as well as your social and political networks. If you agree to take part in this study, you will be asked to complete an online survey. This survey will ask about your political opinions on several policies, past political engagement activities, the people you talk with about important matters and politics, and basic demographic and political information. It will take you approximately 10–12 minutes to complete. After you complete the survey, you will be eligible to receive a $5 Amazon gift card.

Your participation in this study is completely voluntary and you can withdraw at any time by simply exiting the survey. You are free to skip any question that you choose. If you have questions about this project, you may contact the researcher(s), [REDACTED]. If you have any questions concerning your rights as a research subject, you may contact the [REDACTED]. Clicking on the link below will take you to the survey.

****

Lo/a invitamos a participar en un estudio de investigación titulado "Estudio colaborativo de la participación integral de los votantes." Este estudio está siendo realizado por [REDACTED]. Usted fue seleccionado para participar en este studio porque usted fue identificado por un amigo o miembro de la familia que lo identificó como alguien con quien discute la política. El propósito de este estudio es entender su compromiso cívico y su participación en asuntos de su comunidad. Asimismo queremos conocer sus redes sociales y políticas. Esta encuesta le preguntará acerca de sus opiniones políticas, sobre varias políticas públicas, sobre su participación en actividades políticas en el pasado, sobre las personas con quien usted discute sobre la política y otros asuntos importantes. También le pediremos información básica sobre sus características demográficas y sus opiniones políticas. Le tomará aproximadamente 10–12 minutos para completar la encuesta. Al concluir, usted será elegible para recibir una tarjeta de regalo de Amazon de $5. Su participación en este estudio es completamente voluntaria, y usted puede dejar de participar en cualquier momento simplemente abandonando la encuesta. Usted puede omitir una respuesta a cualquiera de las preguntas de la encuesta.

Si tiene preguntas sobre este proyecto, puede comunicarse con la(s) investigadora(s), [REDACTED]. Si tiene alguna pregunta sobre sus derechos como sujeto de esta investigación, puede comunicarse con la Oficina del Programa de Protecciones de Investigación Humana de [REDACTED].

A2.2 Survey Instrument

Original Survey–English

Below is the survey instrument used in the original survey wave, fielded in the weeks following the November 2016 election. Questions in italics were *not* included in the Latino-Black oversample fielded in April 2017, or the Latino-Black snowball sample.

1. During the last six months, did you talk with anyone face-to-face, on the phone, by email, or in any other way about government or elections, or did you not do this with anyone during the last six months?
   a. Yes, in the last six months I talked with someone about government or elections
   b. No, in the last six months I did not talk with someone about government or elections
   c. Refused
2. What are the first and last names of the people who you talked with about important matters? Please be sure not to type the same name for two different people. If two

people have the same name, please be sure to type two different names below, like "John" and "John Junior" or "older John" and "younger John." To "Refuse" this question, simply type "Refused" into each box.

a. First and Last Name of Person #1
b. First and Last Name of Person #2
c. First and Last Name of Person #3
d. First and Last Name of Person #4
e. First and Last Name of Person #5

3. How would you describe your relationship with each person below? [names from Q2 piped in]
   a. This person is my spouse/partner
   b. This person is my parent
   c. This person is my child
   d. This person is a close friend
   e. This person is my coworker
   f. This person is an acquaintance to me
4. How often do you discuss politics, candidates, or elections with each person? [names from Q2 piped in]
   a. Never
   b. Rarely
   c. Occasionally
   d. A moderate amount
   e. A great deal
5. How would you describe each person's political party identification? [names from Q2 piped in]
   a. Strong Republican
   b. Republican
   c. Weak Republican
   d. Independent
   e. Weak Democrat
   f. Democrat
   g. Strong Democrat
   h. Don't know
6. For each of the following, please indicate how strongly you agree or disagree with the statement. [Agree strongly, agree somewhat, neither agree nor disagree, disagree somewhat, disagree strongly, refused]
   a. Sometimes politics and government seem so complicated that a person like me can't really understand what's going on
   b. I feel that I have a pretty good understanding of the important political issues facing our country
   c. Public officials don't care much what people like me think
   d. People like me don't have any say about what the government does
   e. Voting is very difficult to do
   f. Voting can make a difference in my life
7. How often can you trust the federal government in Washington to do what is right?
   a. Always
   b. Most of the time
   c. About half the time

   d. Some of the time
   e. Never
   f. Refused
8. Please indicate whether you think the following statements are True or False: [True, False, Refused]
   a. You must present a valid form of ID every time you vote in California
   b. All registered voters can vote by mail in California
   c. Naturalized U.S. citizens can register to vote
9. Some people don't pay much attention to political campaigns. How interested would you say you have been in the political campaigns so far this year?
   a. Very much interested
   b. Somewhat interested
   c. Not much interested
   d. Refused
10. *In 2016, Hillary Clinton ran on the Democratic ticket against Donald Trump for the Republicans. Do you remember who you voted for?*
    a. *Hillary Clinton*
    b. *Donald Trump*
    c. *I don't remember*
    d. *Refused*
    e. *Other*
11. In talking to people about elections, we often find that a lot of people are not able to vote because they aren't registered, they get sick, or they just don't have time. Why do you think that people in your community do not vote? Please check all that apply
    a. They forget
    b. They aren't eligible or don't think they're eligible
    c. They are not registered
    d. They do not want to vote
    e. They don't have time
    f. They could not get time off of work
    g. They are sick
    h. The polls are not open at convenient times
    i. They had trouble getting to the polling station
    j. The candidates do not appeal to them
    k. Refused
12. As you may know, political parties or community organizations try to talk to as many people as they can about the election. Did anyone contact you this year?
    a. *Yes*
    b. *No*
    c. *Refused*
13. Now we'd like to ask you about activities that some people do related to politics at the local, state, or national level. Have you done any of these things in the past 12 months? Please check all that apply.
    a. Attended a political speech, march, rally, or demonstration
    b. Signed a paper or online petition
    c. Shared, reblogged, or retweeted news articles or petitions on social media
    d. Talked about politics on social media

  e. Contacted a government official either in person, by phone, email, social media, or with a letter
  f. Given money to a political candidate
  g. Given money to an organization or cause
  h. Volunteered for a political campaign or political cause
  i. Talked to anyone and try to show them why they should vote for or against one of the ballot initiatives or candidates
  j. Joined a local community organization
  k. Refused

14. Some people participate in groups and organizations while others do not. Do you currently belong to, volunteer with, attend meetings of, or pay dues for any of the following types of groups? Please check all that apply.
  a. Religious group
  b. Neighborhood or community organization
  c. Labor union
  d. Professional organization
  e. Ethnic/Cultural organization
  f. Issue-oriented political organization (e.g. environment, immigration, etc.)
  g. Political party
  h. Civic association (e.g. Rotary Club, Lyons Club)
  i. Other (please explain):
  j. Refused

15. Please indicate the extent to which you agree with each of the following statements [strongly agree, agree, neither agree nor disagree, disagree, strongly disagree, refused]
  a. Climate change is a threat to California's economy
  b. Affordable and accessible solar energy programs should be made available to low-income residents and renters
  c. Local projects and programs that address climate change and make our city greener should also produce good-paying local jobs with benefits

16. Please indicate the extent to which you agree with each of the following statements. [strongly agree, agree, neither agree nor disagree, disagree, strongly disagree, refused]
  a. Increased access to recreation activities would help reduce gang violence in your neighborhood
  b. Creating more youth centers and recreation centers is a solution to gang activity
  c. California should eliminate bail fees for non-violent offenses

17. Have you heard of Proposition 55?
  a. *Definitely yes*
  b. *Probably yes*
  c. *Might or might not*
  d. *Probably not*
  e. *Definitely not*
  f. *Refused*

18. *IF DEFINITELY YES, PROBABLY YES, or MIGHT OR MIGHT NOT for Q17: Which of the following best describes what Proposition 55 is about?*
  a. *Extending the personal income tax increases on incomes over $250,000 approved in 2012 for 12 years in order to fund education and health care.*

b. *Prohibiting the legislature from passing any bill until it has been in print and published on the Internet for 72 hours prior to the vote.*
c. *Increasing the cigarette tax to $2.00 per pack, with equivalent increase on other tobacco products and electronic cigarettes.*
d. *Increasing parole and good behavior opportunities for felons convicted of nonviolent crimes and allowing judges, not prosecutors, to decide whether to try certain juveniles as adults in court.*
e. *Repealing the 1998 Proposition 227 the "English in Public Schools" initiative, thus allowing for non-English languages to be used in public educational instruction.*
f. *Refused*

19. *IF "EXTENDING THE PERSONAL INCOME TAX INCREASES . . . " for Q18: That's. right. Proposition 55 is about extending the personal income tax increases on incomes over $250,000 approved in 2012 for 12 years in order to fund education and health care. What is your position on Proposition 55?*
    a. *I voted yes (in favor of extending the income tax to fund education and health care)*
    b. *I voted no (against extending the income tax to fund education and health care)*
    c. *I did not vote on this proposition*
    d. *I don't remember*
    e. *Refused*
20. *IF "EXTENDING THE PERSONAL INCOME TAX INCREASES . . . " was NOT selected for Q18: Actually, Proposition 55 is about extending the personal income tax increases on incomes over $250,000 approved in 2012 for 12 years in order to fund education and health care. What is your position on Proposition 55?*
    a. *I voted yes (in favor of extending the income tax to fund education and health care)*
    b. *I voted no (against extending the income tax to fund education and health care)*
    c. *I did not vote on this proposition*
    d. *I don't remember*
    e. *Refused*
21. *Did anyone contact you about Proposition 55?*
    a. *Yes*
    b. *No*
    c. *Refused*
22. *IF YES TO Q21: Who contacted you about Proposition 55?*
    a. *Prop 55 campaign*
    b. *Local community organization*
    c. *Friend or Family*
    d. *Other (please explain):*
    e. *Don't remember/don't know*
    f. *Refused*
23. *IF YES TO Q21: How were you contacted about Proposition 55? Please check all that apply.*
    a. *By phone*
    b. *In person at my home*
    c. *In person at a public place, such as a grocery story*
    d. *By email*
    e. *On social media*
    f. *By mail*
    g. *Refused*

24. With which racial group do you most strongly identify?
    a. White
    b. Black or African American
    c. American Indian or Alaska Native
    d. Asian
    e. Native Hawaiian or other Pacific Islander
    f. Latino or Hispanic
    g. Other
    h. Refused
25. What is the highest level of school you have completed or the highest degree you have received?
    a. No high school
    b. Some high school
    c. High school graduate – high school diploma or equivalent (for example, GED)
    d. Some college but no degree
    e. Bachelor's Degree
    f. Graduate or Professional Degree
    g. Did not go to school in the United States
    h. Refused
26. What language do you primarily speak at home with your family?
    a. Only English
    b. Mostly English
    c. Only Spanish
    d. Mostly Spanish
    e. Spanish and English equally
    f. Only Chinese
    g. Mostly Chinese
    h. Chinese and English equally
    i. Other
    j. Refused
27. In what state, country, or territory were you born?
    a. A U.S. state or D.C.
    b. Puerto Rico
    c. Another U.S. Territory (Guam, American Samoa, U.S. Virgin Islands)
    d. Another country (please specify):
    e. Refused
28. Where were your parents born?
    a. Both parents born in the U.S.
    b. One parent born in the U.S.
    c. Neither parent born in the U.S.
    d. Refused
29. IF A "A US STATE OR DC" IS NOT SELECTED FOR Q27: In what year did you arrive in the U.S.? To refuse this question, type "Refuse"
30. Where would you place yourself on this scale, or haven't you thought much about this?
    a. Extremely liberal
    b. Liberal
    c. Slightly liberal

d. Moderate; middle of the road
e. Slightly conservative
f. Conservative
g. Extremely conservative
h. Haven't thought much about it
i. I don't think of myself in these terms
j. Refused

31. Thank you for your participation in this survey. We would also like to invite the five friends you mentioned that you talk to about politics to participate in the survey. Please provide the email addresses for the five friends you listed earlier. To Refuse this question, type "Refuse" in each box. [pipe in names from Q2]
32. Would you be willing to be contacted again? If so, please provide the name and address of a person who is likely to know where you can be reached in case your address changes in the near future. To Refuse this question, type "Refuse" in each box.
    a. Name of person who will know where you can be reached
    b. Street address
    c. City/state/country/zip or postal code
    d. Email address
    e. Telephone number (including area code)

Latino Oversample (Spanish Translation)

Redes Políticas

1. Durante los últimos seis meses, ¿ha hablado usted con alguien cara a cara, por teléfono, por correo electrónico o de cualquier otra forma sobre el gobierno o las elecciones?, o ¿no hablo con nadie sobre el gobierno o las elecciones en los últimos seis meses?
    a. Sí, en los últimos seis meses hablé con alguien sobre el gobierno o las elecciones
    b. No, en los últimos seis meses no hablé con nadie sobre el gobierno o las elecciones
2. Por favor, ¿Podría darnos el nombre y el apellido de las personas con quienes usted habló sobre el gobierno o las elecciones?

    Asegúrese de no escribir el mismo nombre para dos personas diferentes. Si dos personas tienen el mismo nombre, favor de escribir dos nombres diferentes a continuación, por ejemplo, 'Juan' y 'Juanito' o 'Juan el más viejo' y 'Juan el más joven'. Para 'no contestar' esta pregunta, simplemente escriba 'no contesta' en cada cuadro.
    a. El nombre y el apellido de persona #1
    b. El nombre y el apellido de persona #2
    c. El nombre y el apellido de persona #3
    d. El nombre y el apellido de persona #4
    e. El nombre y el apellido de persona #5
3. ¿Cómo describirá su relación con cada uno de ellos?
    a. Esta persona es mi esposo/a o pareja
    b. Esta persona es mi padre/madre
    c. Esta persona es mi hijo/a
    d. Esta persona es otro pariente
    e. Esta persona es un amigo/a cercano/a
    f. Esta persona es mi compañero/a de trabajo
    g. Esta persona es un/a conocido/a mia

4. ¿Con qué frecuencia discute de política, candidatos o elecciones con cada una de estas personas?
   a. Nunca
   b. Rara vez
   c. De vez en cuando
   d. Con frecuencia moderada
   e. Mucho
   f. No quiero responder
5. ¿Cómo describirá el partido político con el cual identifica cada persona?
   a. Sumamente Republicano/a
   b. Republicano/a
   c. Algo Republicano/a
   d. Independiente
   e. Algo Demócrata
   f. Demócrata
   g. Sumamente Demócrata
   h. No se
   i. No quiero responder

Eficacia Política

6. Para cada una de las siguientes preguntas, favor de indicar cuánto está de acuerdo con cada declaración. Las opciones de respuesta son:
   a. Totalmente en desacuerdo
   b. Algo en desacuerdo
   c. Ni de acuerdo ni en desacuerdo
   d. Algo de acuerdo
   e. Totalmente de acuerdo

   A veces, los asuntos políticos y del gobierno son tan complicados que una persona como yo no puede comprender lo que está realmente ocurriendo.

   Siento que tengo buena comprensión de los problemas políticos mas importantes que se enfrentan en nuestro país

   A los funcionarios públicos no les importa mucho lo que piensa la gente como yo

   La gente como yo no puede afectar lo que hace el gobierno

   Es muy difícil votar

   Votar puede hacer una diferencia en mi vida

7. ¿Con qué frecuencia cree que el gobierno federal (en Washington, D.C.) hace lo correcto?
   a. Siempre
   b. Casi siempre
   c. Más o menos la mitad de las veces
   d. A veces
   e. Nunca
   f. No quiero responder

Conocimientos sobre Política

8. Por favor, indique si considera que las siguientes afirmaciones son Verdaderas o Falsas:
   a. En California, usted tiene que presentar una forma válida de identificación cada vez que va a votar.

b. Todos los votantes registrados pueden votar por correo en California
c. Los ciudadanos estadounidenses naturalizados se pueden registrar para votar

Involucramiento Político

9. Algunas personas no prestan mucha atención a las campañas políticas. ¿Qué tan interesado estuvo usted en las campañas políticas del año pasado?
   a. No muy interesado
   b. Algo interesado
   c. Muy interesado
   d. No quiero responder
10. Al hablar con la gente sobre las elecciones, a menudo encontramos que muchas personas no pueden votar porque no están registradas, o no votan porque están enfermos o simplemente no lo hacen porque no tuvieron tiempo. ¿Por qué cree usted que las personas de su comunidad no van a votar? Favor de marcar todas las respuestas que corresponden.
    a. Se olvidan
    b. No están habilitadas o no piensan que están habilitadas
    c. No están registradas
    d. No quieren votar
    e. No tienen tiempo
    f. No obtienen permiso para salirse del trabajo
    g. Están enfermas
    h. Las urnas de votación no están abiertos en horas convenientes
    i. Es difícil llegar a las urnas de votación
    j. Los candidatos no les atraen
    k. No quiero responder
11. Como usted sabe, los partidos políticos o las organizaciones comunitarias suelen intentar de hablar sobre las elecciones con tantas personas como sean posible. ¿Alguien lo/a contactó el año pasado?
    a. Sí
    b. No
    c. No quiero responder

Actividades de Participación Política

12. Ahora nos gustaría preguntarle sobre las actividades políticas en que ha participado al nivel local, al nivel estadual, o al nivel nacional. ¿Ha hecho usted alguna de estas cosas en los últimos 12 meses?
    a. Firmar una petición impresa o en internet
    b. Compartir peticiones o noticias en redes sociales (Twitter, Facebook, blogs).
    c. Asistir a un discurso político, marcha, o manifestación política
    d. Discutir sobre política en las redes sociales (Twitter, Facebook)
    e. Contribuir dinero a un candidato
    f. Contribuir dinero a una organización o a una causa
    g. Servir como voluntario/a para una campaña/causa política
    h. Contactar a un funcionario público, ya sea en persona, por teléfono, correo electrónico, o a través de una carta
    i. Hablar con alguien para demostrarles el significado del voto a favor o en contra de alguna de las iniciativas y/o candidatos
    j. Hacerso socio de a una organización comunitaria local
    k. No quiero responder

Actividades de Involucramiento Cívico

13. Algunas personas participan en grupos y organizaciones, mientras que otras no. ¿Actualmente usted pertenece, o es un voluntario, o asiste a reuniones, o paga una cuota en alguno de los siguientes tipos de grupos? Favor de marcar todos los que le corresponde:
    a. Grupo religioso
    b. Grupo de vecinos u organización comunitaria
    c. Sindicato
    d. Organización profesional
    e. Organización cultural/étnica
    f. Organización política con fines específicos (medio ambiente, inmigración)
    g. Partido político
    h. Asociación cívica (p. ej. Kiwanis)
    i. Otro (favor de explicar)

Asuntos más Importantes

14. Para cada una de las siguientes preguntas, favor de indicar cuánto está de acuerdo con cada declaración. Las opciones de respuesta son:
    a. Totalmente en desacuerdo
    b. Algo en desacuerdo
    c. Ni de acuerdo ni en desacuerdo
    d. Algo de acuerdo
    e. Totalmente de acuerdo

    El cambio climático es una amenaza para la economía de California

    Se deben hacer programas de energía solar baratos y accesibles para los inquilinos y los residentes de bajos ingresos

    Los proyectos y programas locales que se enfrentan al cambio climático y hacen más verde a la ciudad, también deben generar para la gente de la comunidad puestos de trabajo que paguen bien y que ofrezcan beneficios.

    Acceso a actividades recreativas ayudaría a reducir la violencia de su vecindario

    La creación de más centros juveniles y centros recreativos es una solución al problema de las pandillas criminals

    California debería de eliminar el pago de una fianza en el caso de delitos no violentos
15. ¿Ha oído hablar de la Proposición 55?
    a. Definitivamente sí
    b. Probablemente sí
    c. No estoy seguro
    d. Probablemente no
    e. Definitivamente no

Características Demográficas

16. ¿Con qué grupo racial se identifica más fuertemente?
    a. lanco/a
    b. Negro/a, o Afroamericano/a
    c. Indio/a Estadounidense, o native/a de Alaska
    d. Asiático/a

e. Nativo/a de Hawaii o de otra isla del Pacífico.
f. Latino/a o Hispano/a
g. Otro/a

17. ¿Cuál es el último nivel de educación que completó o el título más alto que ha obtenido?
    a. Menos de escuela secundaria
    b. Secundaria incompleta
    c. Graduado de escuela secundaria, diploma de preparatoria o equivalente (por ejemplo: GED)
    d. Universidad incompleta
    e. Título de licenciado (por ejemplo: BA, AB, BS)
    f. Maestría o Título de posgrado
    g. No fue a la escuela en los EE.UU.
18. ¿Qué idioma habla principalmente en su casa con su familia? ¿Solo Inglés, principalmente Inglés, solo Español, principalmente Español o ambos idiomas por igual?
    a. Solo Inglés
    b. Principalmente inglés
    c. Ambos idiomas por igual
    d. Principalmente Español
    e. Solo Español
19. En una escala ideológica, en donde 1 es sumamente liberal, y 7 es sumamente conservador, ¿donde se pondría usted? o, ¿no ha pensado mucho al respeto?
    a. Sumamente liberal
    b. Liberal
    c. Algo liberal
    d. Moderado; a mitad del camino
    e. Algo conservador
    f. Conservador
    g. Sumamente conservador
    h. No he pensado mucho al respeto
    i. No pienso en mí mismo en éstos términos
20. ¿En qué Estado, territorio, o país nació usted?
    a. Un Estado de EE.UU. o Washington, D.C.
    b. Puerto Rico
    c. Otro territorio de EE.UU. (Guam, Samoa Americana, Islas Vírgenes de EE. UU.)
    d. Otro país {ESPECIFIQUE}
21. ¿Dónde nacieron sus padres?
    a. Los dos padres nacieron en EE.UU.
    b. Uno de los padres nació en EE.UU.
    c. Ninguno de los dos nació en EE.UU.
22. ¿En qué año vino a vivir a EE.UU. (continental) por primera vez?

Gracias por su participación en esta encuesta. También nos gustaría invitar a participar los cinco amigos que usted mencionó con quienes habla sobre la política. Favor de indicar las direcciones de correo electrónico de los cinco amigos que enumeró anteriormente.

Email Amigo 1
Email Amigo 2

Email Amigo 3
Email Amigo 4
Email Amigo 5

¿Estaría dispuesto a ser contactado de nuevo? Si es así, favor de darnos el nombre y la dirección de una persona que nos pueda ayudar a contactarlo en caso de que usted cambie de dirección antes del 2018.

1. Nombre de la persona que lo puede contactar
2. Dirección
3. Ciudad, Estado, País, código postal
4. Dirección de correo electrónico
5. Número de teléfono (incluyendo el código de área)

A2.3 Sample Characteristics and Response Rates

Table A2.1. Response Rates in Original Survey

Date	Surveys sent	Surveys bounced	Surveys completed	Response rate
12-1-16	10,122	747	354	4%
12-9-16	10,121	715	367	4%
12-13-16	29,388	2,115	1,003	4%
12-15-16	9,982	607	325	3%
12-19-16	9,654	607	255	3%
12-19-16	29,540	2,131	755	3%
Total	**98,807**	**6,922**	**3,059**	3%

Table A2.2. Response Rates in Latino-Black Oversample Survey

Date	Group	Surveys sent	Surveys bounced	Surveys completed	Response rate
4-27-17	Latino	48,378	3,569	398	0.9%
4-27-17	Black	46,297	4,897	358	0.9%
Total		**95,851**	**8,466**	**756**	**0.9%**

Data for the California population was collected from the U.S. Census Bureau: https://censusreporter.org/profiles/04000US06-california/, and https://www.census.gov/quickfacts/CA. Party registration data for California comes from the California Secretary of State's office, including percentages as of October 24, 2016: http://elections.cdn.sos.ca.gov/ror/ror-pages/15day-gen-16/hist-reg-stats.pdf. Data for the U.S. population was collected from the U.S. Census Bureau: https://www.census.gov/quickfacts/fact/table/

Table A2.3. Evaluating the Sample on Observables

	Sampling frame	Invited to survey	Completed survey	California population	U.S. population
Percent Latino	20.8	21.0	22.8	38.9	17.8
Percent Black	20.8	19.4	17.9	6.5	13.3
Percent Asian	48.6	49.4	51.2	14.8	5.7
Percent White	7.4	7.8	6.3	37.7	61.3
Percent voted in November 2016	78.0	77.7	84.5	75.3 (reg. voters); 58.4 (VEP)	60.2 (VEP)
Percent Democrat	55.5	55.1	61.1	44.9	48
Percent Republican	11.4	11.4	7.7	26.0	44
Percent decline to state	29.3	29.8	27.0	24.3	8
Percent renter	23.6	23.7	28.0	45.7	36.1
Percent female	53.0	52.6	57.2	50.3	50.8
Percent married	11.5	11.3	5.4	49.0	49.0
Age (years)	42.1	41.8	34.5	36.4	37.9
Median income (census block, U.S. dollars)	55,428	56,578	53,717	67,739	57,617

Note: VEP stands for Voting Eligible Population. Reg. voters refers to registered voters.

US/PST045216 and https://censusreporter.org/profiles/01000US-united-states/. Because registration procedures vary between the states, it is difficult to get official party registration data at the national level, so we rely on survey data from Pew Research Center for national level estimates of party registration: http://www.people-press.org/2016/09/13/2-party-affiliation-among-voters-1992-2016/.

A2.4 Interview Protocol

Thank you for taking the time to sit down with me today. I am part of a research study that is trying to understand better how people get involved in canvassing and how those experiences affected them. We want to know about your experiences and opinions–there are no "right" answers. If anything I ask is unclear, please don't hesitate to ask for clarification.
To begin, please describe how you got involved with ______________?
[probe]

- Had you ever done this type of work before?
- Were you invited by a particular person?
- What made you want to spend your time doing this sort of work?

What did you end up doing? (e.g. what type of canvassing, how often, for what type of campaign, for how long?)
What was that experience like for you?
What did you like best?
What did you find the most challenging?
What would you want someone to know about being a canvasser?
What do you think you learned as a result of this work?
Did you learn anything about yourself that you did not know before?
Did you meet people as part of the canvassing team or in the organization that you keep in touch with now?
Have your conversations with friends or family about politics and/or community issues changed since you became involved? If yes, in what ways?
Have the people with whom you talk about politics and/or community issues changed since you became involved? If yes, in what ways?
How do you think your involvement with [organization] has affected your friends' political engagement? Their political opinions?
Have you invited/asked people to participate in canvassing? If yes, how did those conversations go?
Do you think it is important for people in your community to talk about politics? Why or why not? What do you think individuals have to gain by talking about politics?
Think about people you know who don't talk about or are not interested in politics. Why do you think they don't want to think and/or talk about it?
Has your experience as a canvasser changed how you think about your future? What about your political or civic attitudes?
Is there anything about the experience you think was important that we haven't talked about?

Chapter 3 Appendix

Table A3.1. Relationship between Individual-Level Characteristics and Network Size, by Nativity

	Dependent variable: Network size	
	U.S. born (1)	Foreign born (2)
Age	−0.005*	−0.003
	(0.003)	(0.008)
Female	−0.015	0.134
	(0.077)	(0.194)
College	0.141*	0.269
	(0.084)	(0.225)
Renter	0.005	−0.083
	(0.090)	(0.242)
Secular group	0.429***	0.361*
	(0.083)	(0.202)
Religious group	0.170*	−0.041
	(0.088)	(0.219)
Married	−0.040	0.163
	(0.156)	(0.383)
Median income	−0.00000	−0.00000
	(0.00000)	(0.00000)
Pct. Black	−0.004	−0.012
	(0.005)	(0.012)
Pct. White	0.002	−0.012
	(0.005)	(0.011)
Pct. Latino	−0.005	−0.005
	(0.003)	(0.008)
Pct. Asian	0.0004	−0.015
	(0.005)	(0.012)
Pct. high school grad	−0.014**	−0.030**
	(0.006)	(0.015)

Continued

Table A3.1. *Continued*

	Dependent variable: Network size	
	U.S. born (1)	Foreign born (2)
Constant	3.988***	4.854***
	(0.422)	(1.068)
Observations	2,238	397
R^2	0.031	0.038
Adjusted R^2	0.025	0.005
Residual std. err.	1.767 (df = 2224)	1.865 (df = 383)
F statistic	5.460*** (df = 13; 2224)	1.161 (df = 13; 383)

Note: *$p < 0.1$; **$p < 0.05$; ***$p < 0.01$.

Table A3.2. Relationship between Individual-Level Characteristics and Partisan Homogeneity, by Nativity

	Dependent variable: Percentage of copartisans in network	
	U.S. born (1)	Foreign born (2)
Age	−0.039	0.167
	(0.093)	(0.272)
Female	7.728***	8.652
	(2.545)	(6.991)
College	2.006	10.489
	(2.774)	(7.731)
Renter	0.115	−1.892
	(3.046)	(8.980)
Secular group	7.978***	8.231
	(2.926)	(7.317)
Religious group	−6.812***	6.453
	(2.908)	(8.165)
Married	−2.902	−13.472
	(5.104)	(11.697)
Median income	−0.0001	−0.0001
	(0.0001)	(0.0002)

Table A3.2. *Continued*

	Dependent variable: Percentage of copartisans in network	
	U.S. born (1)	Foreign born (2)
Pct. Black	0.092	0.482
	(0.144)	(0.441)
Pct. White	−0.027	0.291
	(0.144)	(0.409)
Pct. Latino	−0.040	0.202
	(0.099)	(0.276)
Pct. Asian	0.052	−0.073
	(0.155)	(0.424)
Pct. high school grad	−0.053	−0.546
	(0.199)	(0.507)
Constant	51.777***	13.457
	(13.532)	(38.158)
Observations	903	135
R^2	0.039	0.127
Adjusted R^2	0.025	0.033
Residual std. err.	36.916 (df = 889)	37.839 (df = 121)
F statistic	2.786*** (df = 13; 889)	1.353 (df = 13; 121)

Note: *$p < 0.1$; **$p < 0.05$; ***$p < 0.01$.

Table A3.3. Relationship between Individual-Level Characteristics and Discussion Frequency, by Nativity

	Dependent variable: Frequency of discussion in network	
	U.S. born (1)	Foreign born (2)
Age	0.007***	−0.002
	(0.002)	(0.007)
Female	0.031	−0.086
	(0.064)	(0.160)

Continued

Table A3.3. *Continued*

	Dependent variable: Frequency of discussion in network	
	U.S. born (1)	Foreign born (2)
College	0.233***	0.289
	(0.068)	(0.182)
Renter	0.198***	−0.214
	(0.074)	(0.198)
Secular group	0.583***	0.671***
	(0.069)	(0.164)
Religious group	0.266***	0.121
	(0.072)	(0.178)
Married	−0.093	0.174
	(0.127)	(0.296)
Median income	−0.00000	0.00000
	(0.00000)	(0.00000)
Pct. Black	0.006	−0.003
	(0.004)	(0.014)
Pct. White	0.005	−0.005
	(0.004)	(0.013)
Pct. Latino	0.001	0.005
	(0.003)	(0.008)
Pct. Asian	0.005	−0.007
	(0.004)	(0.013)
Pct. high school grad	−0.005	−0.016
	(0.005)	(0.012)
Constant	1.807***	2.710**
	(0.379)	(1.234)
Observations	1,792	330
R^2	0.085	0.087
Adjusted R^2	0.079	0.049
Residual std. err.	1.297 (df=1778)	1.382 (df=316)
F statistic	12.764*** (df=13; 1778)	2.309*** (df=13; 316)

Note: *$p < 0.1$; **$p < 0.05$; ***$p < 0.01$.

Table A3.4. Relationship between Individual-Level Characteristics and Network Size, by Ethnorace

	Dependent variable: Network size			
	Asian (1)	Black (2)	Latino (3)	White (4)
Age	−0.020***	0.008	0.002	−0.012
	(0.004)	(0.006)	(0.006)	(0.009)
Female	−0.037	0.094	−0.029	0.078
	(0.102)	(0.172)	(0.161)	(0.254)
College	0.220*	0.137	0.052	0.054
	(0.125)	(0.178)	(0.167)	(0.305)
Renter	0.101	−0.096	−0.105	0.033
	(0.137)	(0.191)	(0.183)	(0.280)
Secular group	0.345***	0.554***	0,238	0.438
	(0.108)	(0.201)	(0.166)	(0.306)
Religious group	0.089	−0.218	0.376*	0.606**
	(0.121)	(0.174)	(0.198)	(0.296)
Married	0.029	0.486*	−0.819**	0.514
	(0.217)	(0.274)	(0.380)	(0.553)
Median income	−0.00000	−0.00001	−0.00000	−0.00001
	(0.00000)	(0.00001)	(0.00000)	(0.00001)
Pct. Black	0.009	−0.011	−0.008	−0.007
	(0.007)	(0.009)	(0.012)	(0.013)
Pct. White	0.001	0.001	−0.007	0.006
	(0.006)	(0.011)	(0.012)	(0.011)
Pct. Latino	−0.002	−0.012*	−0.006	0.004
	(0.004)	(0.007)	(0.008)	(0.009)
Pct. Asian	−0.0004	−0.005	−0.011	0.004
	(0.006)	(0.014)	(0.013)	(0.014)
Pct. high school grad	−0.021***	−0.006	−0.008	−0.020
	(0.008)	(0.013)	(0.013)	(0.024)
Constant	4.254***	4.158***	4.161***	4.128***
	(0.575)	(0.833)	(1.190)	(1.049)
Observations	1,217	496	612	165
R^2	0.040	0.058	0.020	0.068

Continued

Table A3.4. *Continued*

	Dependent variable: Network size			
	Asian (1)	Black (2)	Latino (3)	White (4)
Adjusted R^2	0.030	0.032	−0.001	−0.012
Residual std. err.	1.741 (df=1203)	1.802 (df = 482)	1.896 (df = 598)	1.579 (df = 151)
F statistic	3.885*** (df = 13; 1203)	2.265*** (df = 13; 482)	0.933 (df = 13; 598)	0.849 (df = 13; 151)

Note: *$p < 0.1$; **$p < 0.05$; ***$p < 0.01$.

Table A3.5. Relationship between Individual-Level Characteristics and Partisan Homogeneity, by Ethnorace

	Dependent variable: Percentage of copartisans in network			
	Asian (1)	Black (2)	Latino (3)	White (4)
Age	−0.421***	0.387**	−0.020	0.148
	(0.148)	(0.195)	(0.195)	(0.341)
Female	8.825**	9.705*	2.529	5.798
	(3.482)	(5.722)	(5.276)	(9.306)
College	8.840**	−6.196	7.414	−0.338
	(4.194)	(5.784)	(5.667)	(10.453)
Renter	1.344	−2.410	−5.007	1.863
	(4.770)	(6.429)	(6.458)	(10.414)
Secular group	10.622***	14.872**	−3.160	−3.748
	(3.899)	(7.067)	(5.696)	(12.715)
Religious group	−9.868**	−3.150	2.523	−4.930
	(4.113)	(6.017)	(6.497)	(11.367)
Married	2.466	−8.316	−9.373	−12.248
	(7.628)	(8.155)	(13.630)	(20.632)
Median income	0.00004	−0.0003	−0.0001	−0.0001
	(0.0001)	(0.0002)	(0.0002)	(0.0002)
Pct. Black	0.307	0.387	0.365	−0.348

Table A3.5. *Continued*

	Dependent variable: Percentage of copartisans in network			
	Asian (1)	Black (2)	Latino (3)	White (4)
	(0.250)	(0.299)	(0.318)	(0.531)
Pct. White	−0.078	0.760**	0.419	−0.424
	(0.216)	(0.373)	(0.329)	(0.460)
Pct. Latino	−0.073	−0.0003	0.050	0.014
	(0.152)	(0.223)	(0.213)	(0.370)
Pct. Asian	−0.159	0.322	0.540	−0.388
	(0.224)	(0.422)	(0.357)	(0.534)
Pct. high school grad	0.049	−0.616	−0.218	0.764
	(0.276)	(0.441)	(0.452)	(0.815)
Constant	52.249**	17.827	33.327	71.227
	(21.067)	(28.015)	(28.661)	(43.990)
Observations	462	197	236	76
R^2	0.097	0.097	0.032	0.143
Adjusted R^2	0.071	0.033	−0.024	−0.037
Residual std. err.	36.264 (df = 448)	36.481 (df = 183)	38.905 (df = 222)	37.636 (df = 62)
F statistic	3.717*** (df = 13; 448)	1.517* (df = 13; 183)	0.568 (df = 13; 222)	0.795 (df = 13; 62)

Note: $^{*}p < 0.1$; $^{**}p < 0.05$; $^{***}p < 0.01$.

Table A3.6. Relationship between Individual-Level Characteristics and Discussion Frequency, by Ethnorace

	Dependent variable: Frequency of discussion in network			
	Asian (1)	Black (2)	Latino (3)	White (4)
Age	−0.005	0.013***	0.010*	0,001
	(0.004)	(0.005)	(0.005)	(0.007)
Female	0.007	0.023	0,050	0,156
	(0.084)	(0,146)	(0,128)	(0,217)

Continued

Table A3.6. *Continued*

	Dependent variable: Frequency of discussion in network			
	Asian (1)	Black (2)	Latino (3)	White (4)
College	0,275***	0.038	0,281**	0.388
	(0.102)	(0.150)	(0.132)	(0.253)
Renter	0.054	0.172	0.093	−0.095
	(0,114)	(0.161)	(0.145)	(0.232)
Secular group	0.660***	0.467***	0.558***	0.202
	(0.090)	(0.168)	(0.131)	(0.272)
Religious group	0.242**	0.149	0.382**	−0.059
	(0.100)	(0.147)	(0.154)	(0.256)
Married	0.015	−0.144	−0.008	0.428
	(0.174)	(0.237)	(0.290)	(0.452)
Median income	0.00000	0.00000	0.00000	−0.00000
	(0.00000)	(0.00001)	(0.00000)	(0.000001)
Pct. Black	0.011*	−0.006	0.008	0.003
	(0.006)	(0.010)	(0.009)	(0.015)
Pct. White	0.006	−0.0004	0.002	0.004
	(0.005)	(0.011)	(0.009)	(0.013)
Pct. Latino	0.002	−0.007	0.004	0.008
	(0.004)	(0.007)	(0.006)	(0.010)
Pct. Asian	0.005	−0.007	0.010	0.009
	(0.005)	(0.013)	(0.010)	(0.021)
Pct. high school grad	−0.011*	−0.009	0.002	−0.0005
	(0.007)	(0.011)	(0.010)	(0.021)
Constant	1.979***	2.813***	1.315	2.333*
	(0.502)	(0.964)	(0.895)	(1.281)
Observations	939	409	524	129
R^2	0.086	0.068	0.093	0.073
Adjusted R^2	0.073	0.037	0.070	−0.032
Residual std. err.	1.259 (df = 925)	1.378 (df = 395)	1.382 (df = 510)	1.170 (df = 115)
F statistic	6.654*** (df = 13; 925)	2.200*** (df = 13; 510)	4.010 (df = 13; 510)	0.693 (df = 13; 115)

Note: *$p < 0.1$; **$p < 0.05$; ***$p < 0.01$.

Table A3.7. Relationship between Individual-Level Characteristics and Network Size, by Gender

	Dependent variable: Network size			
	Female (1)	Male (2)	Female (3)	Male (4)
Age	0.0003	−0.013***	−0.01	−0.013***
	(0.004)	(0.004)	(0.004)	(0.004)
College	−0.001	0.351***	0.077	0.391***
	(0.104)	(0.120)	(0.101)	(0.116)
Renter	−0.028	0.014	0.011	0.040
	(0.109)	(0.133)	(0.103)	(0.124)
Secular group	0.544***	0.268**	0.555***	0.286**
	(0.101)	(0.118)	(0.101)	(0.117)
Religious group	0.179*	0.079	0.153	0.089
	(0.108)	(0.126)	(0.108)	(0.125)
Married	0.182	−0.146	0.164	−0.133
	(0.204)	(0.203)	(0.205)	(0.203)
Median income	−0.00000	−0.00000		
	(0.00000)	(0.00000)		
Pct. Black	−0.005	−0.008		
	(0.005)	(0.008)		
Pct. White	0.001	−0.006		
	(0.005)	(0.008)		
Pct. Latino	−0.004	−0.008		
	(0.003)	(0.005)		
Pct. Asian	0.001	−0.009		
	(0.006)	(0.008)		
Pct. high school grad	−0.016**	−0.015*		
	(0.007)	(0.009)		
Constant	3.824***	4.902***	3.171***	3.603***
	(0.458)	(0.739)	(0.144)	(0.171)
Observations	1,541	1,095	1,541	1,095
R^2	0.037	0.032	0.023	0.025
Adjusted R^2	0.029	0.022	0.020	0.019

Continued

Table A3.7. *Continued*

	Dependent variable: Network size			
	Female (1)	Male (2)	Female (3)	Male (4)
Residual std. err.	1.796 (df = 1528)	1.759 (df = 1082)	1.805 (df = 1534)	1.761 (df = 1088)
F statistic	4.878*** (df = 12; 1528)	3.012*** (df = 12; 1082)	6.152*** (df = 6; 1534)	4.611*** (df = 6; 1088)

Note: *p < 0.1; **p < 0.05; ***p < 0.01.

Table A3.8. Relationship between Individual-Level Characteristics and Partisan Homogeneity, by Gender

	Dependent variable: Percent copartisan			
	Female (1)	Male (2)	Female (3)	Male (4)
Age	0.127	−0.269**	0.156	−0.252*
	(0.114)	(0.135)	(0.111)	(0.136)
College	−0.044	7.532*	−0.303	4.636
	(3.334)	(4.161)	(3.236)	(4.026)
Renter	−1.131	−0.072	−0.083	2.445
	(3.580)	(4.896)	(3.377)	(4.421)
Secular group	8.674**	7.184*	9.043***	8.275*
	(3.476)	(4.318)	(3.451)	(4.357)
Religious group	−4.755	−6.085	−4.668	−4.596
	(3.396)	(4.578)	(3.383)	(4.569)
Married	−6.317	−6.842	−6.066	−4.596
	(6.128)	(7.267)	(6.096)	(7.271)
Median income	−0.0001	−0.0001		
	(0.0001)	(0.0001)		
Pct. Black	0.225	−0.638*		
	(0.151)	(0.358)		
Pct. White	0.151	−0.754**		
	(0.152)	(0.348)		

Table A3.8. *Continued*

	Dependent variable: Percent copartisan			
	Female (1)	Male (2)	Female (3)	Male (4)
Pct. Latino	0.087	−0.520**		
	(0.105)	(0.229)		
Pct. Asian	0.171	−0.824**		
	(0.167)	(0.361)		
Pct. high school grad	−0.288	0.331		
	(0.231)	(0.308)		
Constant	41.424***	126.506***	47.676***	50.698***
	(13.591)	(34.921)	(4.650)	(6.101)
Observations	636	403	636	403
R^2	0.027	0.070	0.020	0.030
Adjusted R^2	0.008	0.041	0.010	0.015
Residual std. err.	36.950 (df = 623)	37.142 (df = 390)	36.906 (df = 629)	37.649 (df = 396)
F statistic	1.433 (df = 12; 623)	2.439*** (df = 12; 390)	2.122** (df = 6; 629)	2.009* (df = 6; 396)

Note: $^{*}p < 0.1$; $^{**}p < 0.05$; $^{***}p < 0.01$.

Table A3.9. Relationship between Individual-Level Characteristics and Discussion Frequency, by Gender

	Dependent variable: Discussion frequency			
	Female (1)	Male (2)	Female (3)	Male (4)
Age	0.010***	0.001	0.011***	0.001
	(0.003)	(0.003)	(0.003)	(0.003)
College	0.156*	0.335***	0.174**	0.308***
	(0.085)	(0.097)	(0.083)	(0.093)
Renter	0.070	0.271**	0.037	0.281***
	(0.090)	(0.108)	(0.086)	(0.101)

Continued

Table A3.9. *Continued*

	Dependent variable: Discussion frequency			
	Female (1)	Male (2)	Female (3)	Male (4)
Secular group	0.644***	0.563***	0.659***	0.579***
	(0.084)	(0.098)	(0.083)	(0.097)
Religious group	0.292***	0.195*	0.294***	0.215**
	(0.088)	(0.103)	(0.087)	(0.102)
Married	−0.036	−0.023	−0.029	−0.030
	(0.167)	(0.162)	(0.167)	(0.161)
Median income	0.00000	−0.00000		
	(0.0000)	(0.0000)		
Pct. Black	0.003	0.009		
	(0.004)	(0.010)		
Pct. White	0.002	0.005		
	(0.004)	(0.010)		
Pct. Latino	−0.0003	0.005		
	(0.003)	(0.006)		
Pct. Asian	−0.0001	0.007		
	(0.005)	(0.010)		
Pct. high school grad	−0.004	−0.009		
	(0.006)	(0.007)		
Constant	1.888***	1.773*	2.011***	2.278***
	(0.395)	(0.960)	(0.118)	(0.141)
Observations	1,261	862	1,261	862
R^2	0.093	0.077	0.088	0.070
Adjusted R^2	0.084	0.064	0.084	0.064
Residual std. err.	1.334 (df = 1248)	1.277 (df = 849)	1.334 (df = 1254)	1.277 (df = 855)
F statistic	10.619*** (df = 12; 1248)	5.881*** (df = 12; 849)	20.260*** (df = 6; 1254)	10.807*** (df = 6; 855)

Note: *$p < 0.1$; **$p < 0.05$; ***$p < 0.01$.

Chapter 5 Appendix

A5.1 Descriptive Statistics

Table A5.1. Policy Preferences by Ethnorace, Nativity, and Gender

	Asian	Black	Latino	White	US born	Foreign born	Male	Female
Environmental issues								
Local projects and programs should address climate change.	4.29	4.45	4.42	4.31	4.38	4.26	4.26	4.43
Solar programs should be made available to low-income and renters.	4.22	4.45	4.46	4.29	4.36	4.19	4.21	4.41
Climate change is a threat to CA economy.	4.27	4.19	4.21	4.29	4.27	4.17	4.22	4.28
Social justice issues								
Increased access to recreation activities would help reduce gang violence.	4.01	4.13	4.22	3.87	4.08	4.02	4.01	4.13
Creating more youth centers and recreation centers is a solution to gang activity.	3.93	4.09	4.12	3.84	4.01	3.91	3.91	4.06
California should eliminate bail fees for nonviolent offenses.	3.19	3.61	3.32	3.34	3.37	3.08	3.29	3.34

A5.2 Environmental Policy Preferences by Nativity

Table A5.2. Relationship between Network Characteristics and Belief that Local Projects that Address Climate Change Should Create Jobs, by Ethnorace

	Dependent variable: Local projects that address climate change should create jobs (strongly disagree to strongly agree)			
	Asian (1)	Black (2)	Latino (3)	White (4)
Percent of Democrats	0.003***	0.003**	0.001	0.008***
	(0.001)	(0.001)	(0.001)	(0.002)
Network size	0.020	0.036	0.049**	0.140***
	(0.016)	(0.027)	(0.021)	(0.048)
Discussion frequency	0.102***	0.015	0.116***	0.054
	(0.028)	(0.050)	(0.040)	(0.086)
Constant	3.992***	4.033***	3.972***	3.207***
	(0.145)	(0.239)	(0.200)	(0.390)
Observations	982	357	470	137
R^2	0.139	0.119	0.072	0.300
Adjusted R^2	0.132	0.099	0.056	0.257
Residual std. err.	0.724 (df=973)	0.768 (df=348)	0.733 (df=461)	0.695 (df=128)
F statistic	19.699*** (df=8; 973)	5.866*** (df=8; 348)	4.487*** (df=8; 461)	6.873*** (df=8; 128)

Note: Models control for political knowledge, education (college degree or not), party identification (Republican or not), age, and gender (female or not). $^{*}p < 0.10$; $^{**}p < 0.05$; $^{***}p < 0.01$.

Table A5.3. Relationship between Network Characteristics and Belief that Climate Change Threatens California's Economy, by Ethnorace

	Dependent variable: Climate change threatens CA's economy (strongly disagree to strongly agree)			
	Asian (1)	Black (2)	Latino (3)	White (4)
Percent of Democrats	0.005***	0.003*	0.001	0.010***
	(0.001)	(0.001)	(0.001)	(0.002)
Network size	0.062***	0.078**	0.038	0.036
	(0.019)	(0.032)	(0.028)	(0.064)
Discussion frequency	0.103***	0.090	0.110**	0.164
	(0.034)	(0.059)	(0.054)	(0.115)
Constant	3.687***	3.078***	3.880***	3.529***
	(0.179)	(0.280)	(0.267)	(0.518)
Observations	981	361	474	139
R^2	0.138	0.266	0.075	0.290
Adjusted R^2	0.131	0.249	0.059	0.247
Residual std. err.	0.893 (df=972)	0.910 (df=352)	0.979 (df=465)	0.933 (df=130)
F statistic	19.433*** (df=8; 972)	15.923*** (df=8; 352)	4.724*** (df=8; 465)	6.647*** (df=8; 130)

Note: Models control for political knowledge, education (college degree or not), party identification (Republican or not), age, and gender (female or not). *$p < 0.10$; **$p < 0.05$; ***$p < 0.01$.

Table A5.4. Relationship between Network Characteristics and Belief that Solar Energy Programs Should Be Available to Low-Income Residents and Renters, by Ethnorace

	Dependent variable: Solar energy programs should be available (strongly disagree to strongly agree)			
	Asian (1)	Black (2)	Latino (3)	White (4)
Percent of Democrats	0.003***	0.002	0.001	0.004**
	(0.001)	(0.001)	(0.001)	(0.002)
Network size	0.025	0.044	0.030	0.100**
	(0.019)	(0.029)	(0.022)	(0.050)
Discussion frequency	0.109***	0.035	0.089**	0.183**
	(0.034)	(0.053)	(0.041)	(0.090)
Constant	4.084***	4.228***	4.093***	3.891***
	(0.178)	(0.256)	(0.206)	(0.405)
Observations	981	360	467	139
R^2	0.147	0.152	0.060	0.346
Adjusted R^2	0.140	0.133	0.043	0.305
Residual std. err.	0.888 (df=972)	0.826 (df=351)	0.756 (df=458)	0.728 (df=130)
F statistic	20.898*** (df=8; 972)	7.875*** (df=8; 351)	3.640*** (df=8; 458)	8.581*** (df=8; 130)

Note: Models control for political knowledge, education (college degree or not), party identification (Republican or not), age, and gender (female or not). $^{*}p < 0.10$; $^{**}p < 0.05$; $^{***}p < 0.01$.

A5.3 Environmental Policy Preferences by Gender

Table A5.5. Relationship between Network Characteristics and Belief that Local Projects that Address Climate Change Should Create Jobs, by Nativity

	Dependent variable: Local projects that address climate change should create jobs (strongly disagree to strongly agree)	
	U.S. born (1)	Foreign born (2)
Percent of Democrats	0.0003	0.002
	(0.001)	(0.002)
Network size	0.049	0.190*
	(0.038)	(0.101)
Discussion frequency	0.137***	0.198**
	(0.027)	(0.076)
Political knowledge	0.007	−0.103
	(0.036)	(0.103)
College	−0.081*	−0.031
	(0.049)	(0.137)
Republican	−0.847***	−0.734***
	(0.090)	(0.202)
Age	−0.006***	−0.007
	(0.002)	(0.005)
Female	0.048	0.156
	(0.046)	(0.123)
Constant	4.027***	3.213***
	(0.208)	(0.602)
Observations	1,004	149
R^2	0.129	0.202
Adjusted R^2	0.122	0.156
Residual std err.	0.698 (df = 995)	0.727 (df = 140)
F statistic	18.389*** (df = 8; 995)	4.421*** (df = 8; 140)

Note: $^{*}p < 0.10$; $^{**}p < 0.05$; $^{***}p < 0.01$.

Table A5.6. Relationship between Network Characteristics and Belief that Solar Energy Programs Should Be Available to Low-Income Residents and Renters, by Nativity

	Dependent variable: Solar energy programs should be available (strongly disagree to strongly agree)	
	U.S. born (1)	Foreign born (2)
Percent of Democrats	0.002**	0.001
	(0.001)	(0.002)
Network size	0.040	−0.041
	(0.043)	(0.119)
Discussion frequency	0.159***	0.161*
	(0.031)	(0.089)
Political knowledge	−0.045	0.006
	(0.042)	(0.121)
College	−0.127**	−0.985***
	(0.057)	(0.161)
Republican	−1.073***	−0.985***
	(0.104)	(0.237)
Age	−0.005***	0.003
	(0.002)	(0.005)
Female	0.141***	0.172
	(0.053)	(0.144)
Constant	3.945***	3.850***
	(0.237)	(0.707)
Observations	1,006	149
R^2	0.156	0.172
Adjusted R^2	0.149	0.125
Residual std. err.	0.809 (df = 997)	0.854 (df = 140)
F statistic	23.075*** (df = 8; 997)	3.646*** (df = 8; 140)

Note: $^{*}p < 0.10$; $^{**}p < 0.05$; $^{***}p < 0.01$.

Table A5.7. Relationship between Network Characteristics and Belief that Climate Change Threatens California's Economy, by Nativity

	Dependent variable: Climate change threatens CA's economy (strongly disagree to strongly agree)	
	U.S. born (1)	Foreign born (2)
Percent of Democrats	0.001*	0.0002
	(0.001)	(0.003)
Network size	0.118**	0.067
	(0.047)	(0.157)
Discussion frequency	0.139***	0.223*
	(0.034)	(0.117)
Political knowledge	0.015	0.150
	(0.045)	(0.159)
College	0.087	−0.143
	(0.062)	(0.212)
Republican	−1.458***	−0.357
	(0.113)	(0.311)
Age	−0.003	−0.008
	(0.002)	(0.007)
Female	−0.030	0.062
	(0.058)	(0.189)
Constant	3.370***	3.170***
	(0.259)	(0.930)
Observations	1,009	149
R^2	0.179	0.072
Adjusted R^2	0.173	0.019
Residual std. err.	0.881 (df = 1000)	1.122 (df = 140)
F statistic	27.345*** (df = 8; 1000)	1.365 (df = 8; 140)

A5.4 Criminal Justice Policy Preferences by Nativity

Table A5.8. Relationship between Network Characteristics and Belief that Local Projects that Address Climate Change Should Create Jobs, by Gender

	Dependent variable: Local projects that address climate change should create jobs (strongly disagree to strongly agree)	
	Female (1)	**Male** (2)
Percentage of Democrats	0.001	0.001
	(0.001)	(0.001)
Network size	0.132***	0.008
	(0.047)	(0.054)
Discussion frequency	0.119***	0.169***
	(0.030)	(0.045)
Political knowledge	−0.003	−0.004
	(0.040)	(0.060)
College	−0.062	−0.103
	(0.055)	(0.080)
Republican	−0.871***	−0.786***
	(0.125)	(0.114)
Age	−0.004**	−0.011***
	(0.002)	(0.003)
Constant	3.637***	4.282***
	(0.254)	(0.313)
Observations	694	460
R^2	0.110	0.159
Adjusted R^2	0.101	0.146
Residual std. err.	0.652 (df = 686)	0.775 (df = 452)
F statistic	12.116*** (df = 7; 686)	12.207*** (df=7; 452)

Note: *$p < 0.1$; **$p < 0.05$; ***$p < 0.01$.

Table A5.9. Relationship between Network Characteristics and Belief that Solar Energy Programs Should Be Available to Low-Income Residents and Renters

	Dependent variable: Solar energy programs should be available (strongly disagree to strongly agree)	
	Female (1)	Male (2)
Percentage of Democrats	0.002**	0.002
	(0.001)	(0.001)
Network size	0.053	0.011
	(0.052)	(0.065)
Discussion frequency	0.146***	0.173***
	(0.033)	(0.055)
Political knowledge	−0.010	−0.092
	(0.044)	(0.073)
College	−0.089	−0.174*
	(0.060)	(0.098)
Republican	−1.067***	−1.037***
	(0.134)	(0.140)
Age	−0.006***	−0.003
	(0.002)	(0.003)
Constant	3.965***	4.089***
	(0.277)	(0.378)
Observations	696	460
R^2	0.136	0.147
Adjusted R^2	0.127	0.134
Residual std. err.	0.712 (df = 688)	0.951 (df = 452)
F statistic	15.453*** (df = 7; 688)	11.138*** (df = 7; 452)

Note: *$p < 0.1$; **$p < 0.05$; ***$p < 0.01$.

Table A5.10. Relationship between Network Characteristics and Belief that Climate Change Threatens California's Economy, by Gender

	Dependent variable: Climate change threatens CA's economy (strongly disagree to strongly agree)	
	Female (1)	Male (2)
Percentage of Democrats	0.001	0.001
	(0.001)	(0.001)
Network size	0.140**	0.082
	(0.064)	(0.067)
Discussion frequency	0.126***	0.179***
	(0.041)	(0.057)
Political knowledge	0.030	0.065
	(0.055)	(0.075)
College	0.054	0.082
	(0.075)	(0.101)
Republican	−1.027***	−1.421***
	(0.167)	(0.145)
Age	−0.005**	−0.004
	(0.002)	(0.003)
Constant	3.299***	3.317***
	(0.344)	(0.390)
Observations	698	461
R^2	0.090	0.213
Adjusted R^2	0.081	0.201
Residual std. err.	0.887 (df = 690)	0.981 (df = 453)
F statistic	9.719*** (df = 7; 690)	17.494*** (df = 7; 453)

Note: *$p < 0.1$; **$p < 0.05$; ***$p < 0.01$.

A5.5 Criminal Justice Policy Preferences by Gender

Table A5.11. Relationship between Network Characteristics and Belief that California Should Eliminate Bail Fees for Nonviolent Offenses, by Ethnorace

	Dependent variable: CA should eliminate bail fees for Nonviolent offenses (strongly disagree to strongly agree)			
	Asian (1)	Black (2)	Latino (3)	White (4)
Percent of Democrats	0.002*	0.0002	0.001	0.011***
	(0.001)	(0.002)	(0.002)	(0.003)
Network size	−0.009	0.037	0.065*	0.074
	(0.024)	(0.043)	(0.036)	(0.080)
Discussion frequency	0.082*	0.054	0.211***	0.206
	(0.043)	(0.080)	(0.067)	(0.147)
Constant	3.016***	3.682***	2.130***	1.937***
	(0.223)	(0.380)	(0.335)	(0.676)
Observations	972	356	467	137
R^2	0.083	0.025	0.054	0.275
Adjusted R^2	0.076	0.002	0.038	0.229
Residual std. err.	1.104 (df=963)	1.222 (df=347)	1.217 (df=458)	1.170 (df=128)
F statistic	10.916*** (df=8; 963)	1.105 (df=8; 347)	3.279*** (df=8; 458)	6.058*** (df=8; 128)

Note: Models control for political knowledge, education (college degree or not), party identification (Republican or not), age, and gender (female or not). $^{*}p < 0.10$; $^{**}p < 0.05$; $^{***}p < 0.01$.

Table A5.12. Relationship between Network Characteristics and Belief that Increased Access to Recreational Activities Will Reduce Gang Violence in Your Neighborhood, by Ethnorace

	Dependent variable: Increased access to recreational activities will reduce gang violence (strongly disagree to strongly agree)			
	Asian (1)	Black (2)	Latino (3)	White (4)
Percent of Democrats	0.003***	−0.002	0.002**	0.003
	(0.001)	(0.002)	(0.001)	(0.002)
Network size	0.002	−0.051	0.042	0.063
	(0.018)	(0.034)	(0.027)	(0.057)
Discussion frequency	0.082**	0.163***	0.075	0.169
	(0.033)	(0.061)	(0.050)	(0.102)
Constant	3.752***	4.479***	3.807***	3.674***
	(0.171)	(0.293)	(0.250)	(0.461)
Observations	980	362	474	139
R^2	0.038	0.081	0.057	0.203
Adjusted R^2	0.030	0.061	0.041	0.154
Residual std. err.	0.850 (df=971)	0.954 (df=353)	0.918 (df=465)	0.829 (df=130)
F statistic	4.834*** (df=8; 971)	3.910*** (df=8; 353)	3.543*** (df=8; 465)	4.132*** (df=8; 130)

Note: Models control for political knowledge, education (college degree or not), party identification (Republican or not), age, and gender (female or not). *$p < 0.10$; **$p < 0.05$; ***$p < 0.01$.

Table A5.13. Relationship between Network Characteristics and Belief that Creating More Youth Centers and Recreational Centers Is a Solution to Gang Activity

	Dependent variable: Creating youth centers is a solution to gang activity (strongly disagree to strongly agree)			
	Asian (1)	Black (2)	Latino (3)	White (4)
Percent of Democrats	0.003***	−0.001	0.003***	0.007***
	(0.001)	(0.002)	(0.001)	(0.002)
Network size	0.012	0.010	0.022	0.072
	(0.018)	(0.034)	(0.028)	(0.061)
Discussion frequency	0.082**	0.133**	0.070	0.033
	(0.033)	(0.062)	(0.053)	(0.110)
Constant	3.776***	4.162***	3.666***	3.416***
	(0.172)	(0.297)	(0.262)	(0.495)
Observations	981	361	471	139
R^2	0.067	0.064	0.068	0.151
Adjusted R^2	0.059	0.043	0.051	0.098
Residual std. err.	0.854 (df=972)	0.960 (df=352)	0.962 (df=462)	0.891 (df=130)
F statistic	8.735*** (df=8; 972)	3.009*** (df=8; 352)	4.183*** (df=8; 462)	2.881*** (df=8; 130)

Note: Models control for political knowledge, education (college degree or not), party identification (Republican or not), age, and gender (female or not). $^{*}p < 0.10$; $^{**}p < 0.05$; $^{***}p < 0.01$.

Table A5.14. Relationship between Network Characteristics and Belief that California Should Eliminate Bail Fees for Nonviolent Offenses, by Nativity

	Dependent variable: CA should eliminate bail fees for Nonviolent offenses (strongly disagree to strongly agree)	
	U.S. born (1)	Foreign born (2)
Percent of Democrats	0.001	0.007**
	(0.001)	(0.003)
Network size	−0.036	−0.152
	(0.064)	(0.160)
Discussion frequency	0.225***	0.038
	(0.046)	(0.120)
Political knowledge	0.190***	0.252
	(0.060)	(0.163)
College	0.001	0.329
	(0.082)	(0.217)
Republican	−1.403***	−0.946***
	(0.150)	(0.319)
Age	−0.006**	0.008
	(0.003)	(0.007)
Female	−0.018	−0.188
	(0.077)	(0.194)
Constant	2.599***	3.162***
	(0.355)	(0.952)
Observations	998	149
R^2	0.123	0.160
Adjusted R^2	1.167 (df = 989)	1.149 (df = 140)
Residual std err.	1.167 (df = 989_	1.149 (df = 140)
F statistic	17.302*** (df = 8; 989)	3.329*** (df = 8; 140)

Note: *$p < 0.10$; **$p < 0.05$; ***$p < 0.01$.

Table A5.15. Relationship between Network Characteristics and Belief that Increased Access to Recreational Activities Will Reduce Gang Violence in Your Neighborhood, by Nativity

	Dependent variable: Increased access to recreational activities will reduce gang violence in your neighborhood (strongly disagree to strongly agree)	
	U.S. born (1)	Foreign born (2)
Percent of Democrats	−0.0001	0.003
	(0.001)	(0.002)
Network size	0.024	−0.188
	(0.047)	(0.122)
Discussion frequency	0.137***	0.273***
	(0.034)	(0.091)
Political knowledge	−0.115**	−0.283**
	(0.046)	(0.124)
College	0.009	−0.102
	(0.062)	(0.165)
Republican	−0.562***	−0.402*
	(0.113)	(0.242)
Age	−0.006***	−0.004
	(0.002)	(0.005)
Female	0.077	−0.063
	(0.058)	(0.147)
Constant	3.967***	4.978***
	(0.261)	(0.723)
Observations	1,007	149
R^2	0.058	0.146
Adjusted R^2	0.051	0.098
Residual std. err.	0.881 (df = 998)	0.872 (df = 140)
F statistic	7.691*** (df = 8; 998)	3.001*** (df = 8; 140)

Note: *$p < 0.10$; **$p < 0.05$; ***$p < 0.01$.

Table A5.16. Relationship between Network Characteristics and Belief that Creating More Youth Centers and Recreational Centers Is a Solution to Gang Activity, by Nativity

	Dependent variable: Creating youth centers is a solution to gang activity (strongly disagree to strongly agree)	
	U.S. born (1)	Foreign born (2)
Percent of Democrats	0.001	0.002
	(0.001)	(0.002)
Network size	0.009	−0.123
	(0.048)	(0.129)
Discussion frequency	0.113***	0.163*
	(0.035)	(0.096)
Political knowledge	−0.087*	−0.104
	(0.046)	(0.131)
College	0.002	−0.096
	(0.063)	(0.174)
Republican	−0.736***	−0.566**
	(0.115)	(0.256)
Age	−0.006***	0.002
	(0.002)	(0.006)
Female	0.063	−0.095
	(0.059)	(0.156)
Constant	3.992***	4.350***
	(0.266)	(0.764)
Observations	1,008	149
R^2	0.072	0.082
Adjusted R^2	0.065	0.030
Residual std. err.	0.896 (df = 999)	0.922 (df = 140)
F statistic	9.719*** (df = 8; 999)	1.569 (df = 8; 140)

Note: *$p < 0.10$; **$p < 0.05$; ***$p < 0.01$.

Table A5.17. Relationship between Network Characteristics and Belief that California Should Eliminate Bail Fees for Nonviolent Offenses, by Gender

	Dependent variable: CA should eliminate bail fees for nonviolent offenses (strongly disagree to strongly agree)	
	Female (1)	**Male** (2)
Percentage of Democrats	0.001	0.003
	(0.001)	(0.002)
Network size	0.002	−0.091
	(0.085)	(0.084)
Discussion frequency	0.246***	0.128*
	(0.054)	(0.069)
Political knowledge	0.207***	0.170*
	(0.072)	(0.091)
College	0.031	0.096
	(0.098)	(0.123)
Republican	−1.310***	−1.311***
	(0.218)	(0.175)
Age	−0.005	−0.008*
	(0.003)	(0.004)
Constant	2.201***	3.153***
	(0.458)	(0.489)
Observations	691	457
R^2	0.107	0.147
Adjusted R^2	0.098	0.134
Residual std. err.	1.155 (df = 683)	1.187 (df = 449)
F statistic	11.673*** (df = 7; 683)	11.050*** (df = 7; 449)

Note: $^{*}p < 0.1$; $^{**}p < 0.05$; $^{***}p < 0.01$.

Table A5.18. Relationship between Network Characteristics and Belief that Increased Recreational Activities Will Reduce Gang Violence in Your Neighborhood

	Dependent variable: Increased access to recreational activities will reduce gang violence (strongly disagree to strongly agree)	
	Female (1)	Male (2)
Percentage of Democrats	0.0001	0.001
	(0.001)	(0.001)
Network size	−0.020	0.008
	(0.063)	(0.062)
Discussion frequency	0.155***	0.150***
	(0.041)	(0.052)
Political knowledge	−0.111**	−0.177**
	(0.054)	(0.069)
College	0.044	−0.082
	(0.074)	(0.092)
Republican	−0.631***	−0.466***
	(0.165)	(0.132)
Age	−0.004*	−0.006**
	(0.002)	(0.003)
Constant	4.112***	4.212***
	(0.340)	(0.363)
Observations	697	460
R^2	0.049	0.072
Adjusted R^2	0.039	0.058
Residual std. err.	0.876 (df = 689)	0.897 (df = 452)
F statistic	5.054*** (df = 7; 689)	5.006*** (df = 7; 452)

Note: *$p < 0.1$; **$p < 0.05$; ***$p < 0.01$.

Table A5.19. Relationship between Percentage of Democrats in Network and Belief that Creating More Youth Centers and Recreational Centers Is a Solution to Gang Activity, by Gender

	Dependent variable: Creating youth centers is a solution to gang activity (strongly disagree to strongly agree)	
	Female (1)	**Male** (2)
Percentage of Democrats	0.0002	0.003**
	(0.001)	(0.001)
Network size	−0.034	0.003
	(0.064)	(0.063)
Discussion frequency	0.107***	0.138***
	(0.041)	(0.053)
Political knowledge	−0.101*	−0.070
	(0.055)	(0.071)
College	0.051	−0.098
	(0.075)	(0.095)
Republican	−0.453***	−0.840***
	(0.167)	(0.136)
Age	−0.005**	−0.006*
	(0.002)	(0.003)
Constant	4.282***	3.880***
	(0.344)	(0.373)
Observations	698	460
R^2	0.031	0.123
Adjusted R^2	0.022	0.110
Residual std. err.	0.885 (df = 690)	0.921 (df = 452)
F statistic	3.189*** (df = 7; 690)	9.077*** (df = 7; 452)

Note: *$p < 0.1$; **$p < 0.05$; ***$p < 0.01$.

Chapter 6 Appendix

A6.1 Turnout in the June 2016 Primary Election

Table A6.1. Relationship between Network Characteristics and Voting in June 2016 by Ethnorace

	Dependent variable: Voted in June 2016			
	Asian (1)	Black (2)	Latino (3)	White (4)
Percent copartisan	0.002***	0.001	0.001	0.003*
	(0.001)	(0.001)	(0.001)	(0.001)
Network size	−0.031	0.058	−0.029	−0.096
	(0.037)	(0.063)	(0.037)	(0.130)
Discussion frequency	0.078***	0.041	0.097***	0.106
	(0.026)	(0.039)	(0.036)	(0.080)
Political knowledge	0.093***	0.093*	0.091*	0.013
	(0.034)	(0.050)	(0.050)	(0.096)
Female	−0.024	0071	0.006	−0.018
	(0.042)	(0.064)	(0.063)	(0.114)
Age	0.001	0.006***	−0.0004	−0.004
	(0.002)	(0.002)	(0.002)	(0.004)
College	−0.121**	0.063	0.081	0.018
	(0.051)	(0.066)	(0.065)	(0.130)
Constant	0.237	−0.386	0.073	0.642
	(0.205)	(0.309)	(0.245)	(0.750)
Observations	536	213	258	93
R^2	0.084	0.128	0.078	0.086
Adjusted R^2	0.072	0.098	0.052	0.010
Residual std. err.	0.470 (df = 528)	0.440 (df = 205)	0.487 (df = 250)	0.494 (df = 85)
F statistic	6.919*** (df = 7; 528)	4.306*** (df = 7; 205)	3.001*** (df = 7; 250)	1.137 (df = 7; 85)

Note: *$p < 0.10$; **$p < 0.05$; ***$p < 0.01$.

Table A6.2. Relationship between Network Characteristics and Voting in June 2016 by Nativity

	Dependent variable: Voted in June 2016	
	U.S. born (1)	Foreign born (2)
Percent copartisan	0.002***	0.002**
	(0.0004)	(0.001)
Network size	−0.016	0.007
	(0.025)	(0.068)
Discussion frequency	0.071***	0.078
	(0.018)	(0.051)
Political knowledge	0.095***	0.140**
	(0.024)	(0.069)
Female	0.003	0.049
	(0.030)	(0.081)
Age	0.001	0.005*
	(0.001)	(0.003)
College	−0.007	−0.010
	(0.033)	(0.091)
Constant	0.094	−0.457
	(0.137)	(0.403)
Observations	1,031	149
R^2	0.063	0.102
Adjusted R^2	0.056	0.057
Residual std. err.	0.472 (df = 1023)	0.486 (df = 141)
F statistic	9.748*** (df = 7; 1023)	2.282** (df = 7; 141)

Note: *$p < 0.1$; **$p < 0.05$; ***$p < 0.01$.

Table A6.3. Relationship between Network Characteristics and Voting in June 2016 by Gender

	Dependent variable: Voted in June 2016	
	Female (1)	Male (2)
Percent copartisan	0.002***	0.001**
	(0.001)	(0.001)
Network size	−0.070**	0.036
	(0.034)	(0.032)
Discussion frequency	0.046**	0.120***
	(0.022)	(0.027)
Political knowledge	0.102***	0.096***
	(0.029)	(0.036)
Age	0.003**	0.0002
	(0,001)	(0.002)
College	−0.036	0.026
	(0.040)	(0.048)
Constant	0.375**	−0.305
	(0.180)	(0.188)
Observations	710	471
R^2	0.068	0.092
Adjusted R^2	0.060	0.080
Residual std. err.	0.473 (df = 703)	0.473 (df = 464)
F statistic	8.512*** (df = 6; 703)	7.822*** (df = 6; 464)

Note: $^{*}p < 0.1$; $^{**}p < 0.05$; $^{***}p < 0.01$.

A6.2 Turnout in the November 2016 General Election

Table A6.4. Relationship between Network Characteristics and Voting in November 2016 by Ethnorace

	Dependent variable: Voted in November 2016			
	Asian (1)	Black (2)	Latino (3)	White (4)
Percent copartisan	0.0001	−0.0002	−0.0003	−0.0004
	(0.0004)	(0.001)	(0.001)	(0.001)
Network size	−0.016	−0.033	0.023	−0.046
	(0.026)	(0.041)	(0.026)	(0.097)
Discussion frequency	0.024	0.050*	0.003	−0.039
	(0.018)	(0.025)	(0.025)	(0.060)
Political knowledge	0.068***	0.056*	0.012	−0.008
	(0.024)	(0.033)	(0.035)	(0.072)
Female	0.013	0.041	0.006	0.027
	(0.029)	(0.042)	(0.045)	(0.085)
Age	0.002*	0.006***	0.002	0.001
	(0.001)	(0.001)	(0.002)	(0.003)
College	0.011	0.101**	0.095**	0.088
	(0.036)	(0.043)	(0.046)	(0.097)
Constant	0.624***	0.401**	0.607***	1.135**
	(0.143)	(0.202)	(0.174)	(0.562)
Observations	536	213	258	93
R^2	0.029	0.178	0.035	0.020
Adjusted R^2	0.017	0.150	0.008	−0.060
Residual std. err.	0.328 (df = 528)	0.287 (df = 205)	0.346 (df = 250)	0.370 (df = 85)
F statistic	2.291** (df = 7; 528)	6.351*** (df = 7; 206)	1.308 (df = 7; 250)	0.253 (df = 7; 85)

Note: $^{*}p < 0.10$; $^{**}p < 0.05$; $^{***}p < 0.01$.

Table A6.5. Relationship between Network Characteristics and Voting in November 2016 by Nativity

	Dependent variable: Voted in November 2016	
	U.S. born (1)	Foreign born (2)
Percent copartisan	−0.0002	0.0004
	(0.0003)	(0.001)
Network size	0.001	0.019
	(0.017)	(0.048)
Discussion frequency	0.017	0.032
	(0.012)	(0.036)
Political knowledge	0.035**	0.104**
	(0.017)	(0.049)
Female	0.018	0.009
	(0.021)	(0.058)
Age	0.002***	0.003
	(0.001)	(0.002)
College	0.072***	−0.106
	(0.022)	(0.064)
Constant	0.596***	0.339
	(0.094)	(0.286)
Observations	1,031	149
R^2	0.040	0.070
Adjusted R^2	0.033	0.024
Residual std. err.	0.324 (df = 1023)	0.345 (df = 141)
F statistic	6.081*** (df = 7; 1023)	1.525 (df = 7; 141)

Note: *$p < 0.1$; **$p < 0.05$; ***$p < 0.01$.

Table A6.6. Relationship between Network Characteristics and Voting in November 2016 by Gender

	Dependent variable: Voted in November 2016	
	Female (1)	**Male** (2)
Percent copartisan	0.0002	−0.001
	(0.0003)	(0.0004)
Network size	0.003	0.003
	(0.023)	(0.023)
Discussion frequency	0.013	0.034*
	(0.015)	(0.019)
Political knowledge	0.033*	0.061**
	(0.020)	(0.026)
Age	0.002**	0.003***
	(0.001)	(0.001)
College	0.080***	0.004
	(0.027)	(0.034)
Constant	0.615***	0.501***
	(0.122)	(0.134)
Observations	710	471
R^2	0.035	0.049
Adjusted R^2	0.027	0.036
Residual std. err.	0.320 (df = 703)	0.337 (df = 464)
F statistic	4.243*** (df = 6; 703)	

Note: $^{*}p < 0.1$; $^{**}p < 0.05$; $^{***}p < 0.01$.

Notes

Chapter 1

1. We use the term *ethnoracial* to describe groups in order to capture the intersection between race and ethnicity. Scholars have long debated which is the more appropriate term to describe group experiences. The word *race* presupposes a common biological or genealogical ancestry among people. Ethnicity places more of an emphasis on cultural practices than on common genetic traits. Many scholars use the terms *race/ethnicity* or *ethnorace* to describe the ways in which factors often attributed to culture, such as language, can be racialized. In other words, ascriptive attributions can be based on linguistic or cultural practices that are not "racial" but still can have racialized consequences. Because we believe the lived experiences of the populations discussed in this book include racialized ethnic and/or cultural traits, we describe them as ethnoracial groups.
2. Those biases can also affect the interpretation of information about different ethnoracial groups. Shoda et al. (2014) find that individuals with more negative evaluations of African Americans engaged in motivated reasoning that resulted in bias against Blacks. These biases affect individuals' ability to absorb facts that contradict their preconceived notions (Kunda 1990; Redlawsk 2002; Nyhan and Reifler 2010), which can affect their interpretation of current events.
3. To be clear, we are not suggesting that previous researchers have made this assumption. Rather, we are emphasizing the importance of exploring the extent to which the seminal findings from White samples can be generalized to other, less privileged groups. As we discuss further in Chapter 2, there are empirical limitations making it challenging to study discussion networks among non-whites.
4. These community organizers are from the following three organizations: Community Coalition (CoCo), Strategic Concepts in Organizing and Policy Education (SCOPE), and Asian Pacific Environmental Network (APEN). We discuss these groups and our interview methodology in more detail in Chapter 2.
5. Leighley and Matsubayahi's study (2009) is limited to looking at the relationship between political discussion networks and policy preferences, specifically attitudes toward affirmative action and assistance for Blacks.
6. We appreciate that gender is not a binary category. For our sample, we used Political Data Inc. (PDI), a data vendor, to provide the gender information. Their gender options include only male and female. Therefore, when we use the terms "women/female" or "men/male," in the text, we are referring to female-identified and male-identified respondents, as determined by PDI.

7. https://www.migrationpolicy.org/programs/data-hub/charts/immigrant-population-over-time?width=900&height=850&iframe=true (last accessed 24 June 2019).

Chapter 2

1. See Lacy and Stamm (2015) for a review of the importance of this work.
2. Huckfeldt, Robert, and Sprague, John. Presidential Election Campaign Study, 1984: [South Bend, Indiana]. Ann Arbor, MI: Inter-university Consortium for Political and Social Research [distributor], 2006-01-12. https://doi.org/10.3886/ICPSR06522.v1
3. Huckfeldt, Robert, and Sprague, John. Indianapolis-St. Louis Election Study, 1996–1997. Ann Arbor, MI: Inter-university Consortium for Political and Social Research [distributor], 2007-05-07. https://doi.org/10.3886/ICPSR02962.v2
4. While there were Black survey respondents, they were intentionally excluded from the study analysis.
5. We acknowledge that our sampling could have been improved had we used stratified listing or density quota sampling and multilingual surveys, as advocated by Barreto et al. (2018). We did seek to collect large samples of ethnoracial group members as the authors suggest, but our surveys were only available in English and Spanish.
6. The full invitation email and survey instrument are available in the Appendix. We started by only inviting about 10,000 respondents to participate in the survey because we did not know exactly what our response rate would be and we did not want to go over budget. We were also limited to sending only about 50,000 emails per week from our Qualtrics account, including reminder emails, so we had to start with a smaller sample. Once we got a better sense for our response rate, we started inviting larger numbers of individuals to participate.
7. See the Appendix for a detailed analysis showing these differences.
8. Because this survey was fielded farther away from the election than the first survey, some survey questions were omitted or modified. A list detailing differences between the two surveys is available in the Appendix (A2.2), as well as the full survey instruments. Reminder emails were sent on May 2, 2017 and May 8, 2017. Latino respondents had the option of taking the survey in English or Spanish.
9. The total number of responses was 761; the response rate for both Latinos and Blacks is ~0.9 percent. More details are available in the Appendix.
10. In this snowball sample, the response rate was ~13 percent.
11. 78.3 percent reported being born in a U.S. state, 0.14 percent reported being born in Puerto Rico, 0.4 percent reported being born another U.S. territory, 16.6 percent reported being born in another country, and 4.5 percent refused to answer the question.
12. Our income information is based on PDI data. Using a person's registration address, PDI imputes income information for individuals based on the median household income of the person's census block. They do not provide individual-level income

information. Because self-reported income information is often inaccurate, we did not ask respondents to report their income on our survey.

13. We only present comparisons across ethnorace, since nativity was not asked in the ANES and only asked in the Los Angeles sample of the MSCUI. We conduct an analysis by nativity in GSS as well as an analysis by gender in the GSS and ANES; they are available in the online Appendix.
14. Bobo, Lawrence, James Johnson, Barry Bluestone, Irene Browne, Sheldon Danziger, Philip Moss, Chris Tilly. *Multi-City Study of Urban Inequality, 1992–1994: [Atlanta, Boston, Detroit, and Los Angeles]*. Ann Arbor, MI: Inter-university Consortium for Political and Social Research [distributor], 2008-04-23. https://doi.org/10.3886/ICPSR02535.v3
15. Davis, James Allan, and Tom W. Smith: *General Social Survey(s), year(s)*. (Machine-readable data file). Principal Investigator, James A. Davis; Director and Co-Principal Investigator, Tom W. Smith; Co-Principal Investigator, Peter V. Marsden, NORC ed. Chicago: National Opinion Research Center, producer, 2002; Storrs, CT: The Roper Center for Public Opinion Research, University of Connecticut, distributor. Microcomputer format and codebook prepared and distributed by MicroCase Corporation.
16. The American National Election Studies (www.electionstudies.org). These materials are based on work supported by the National Science Foundation under grant numbers SES 1444721, 2014-2017, the University of Michigan, and Stanford University.
17. Using party registration to estimate party identification offers an advantage over self-reported party identification. We can avoid any social desirability bias that individuals might experience reporting their partisanship on a survey.
18. For those interested in exploring the results with alternative model specifications, the online Appendix includes many analyses using models more complex than the OLS estimates that we present in the book. For the sake of parsimony and statistical power, we chose to use the simplest models possible so long as they were roughly consistent with the results from the more expansive models.
19. As a test of robustness, we do control for these characteristics in a standard ordinary least squares regression, but we reserve these analyses for the online Appendix since these variables are not measured at the individual level.
20. The hierarchical linear models in this analysis were estimated using the lme4 package for the R statistical software language. These zip code effects were modeled as random effects.
21. The interview protocol is available in the Appendix (A2.4). Interviews were conducted by an experienced interviewer, and the interviews lasted anywhere from 30 to 45 minutes.
22. We acknowledge that this approach does not necessarily capture political discussion among the "average" person of color. We follow outstanding qualitative work on discussion networks by Walsh (2004) by interviewing those actively engaged in discussion. In our case, we focus on those deliberately tasked with trying to inform and mobilize others in their community to understand how their role, as likely opinion leaders, has affected others in their networks.

Chapter 3

1. See Christakis and Fowler (2011) for a more in-depth discussion of this subject matter, as well as Huckfeldt and Sprague (1995).
2. Specifically, 18.9 percent of Latino dyads were between other relatives, whereas only 12.9 percent of Asian Americans dyads ($p < .001$), 15.4 percent of Black dyads ($p < .05$), and 13.8 percent of White dyads ($p < .01$) were other relatives.
3. 4.2 percent of Black dyads were between a parent ego and child discussant (alter), compared with 2.6 percent of Latino dyads ($p < .05$), 1.6 percent of Asian Americans dyads ($p < .001$), and 2.5 percent of White dyads ($p < .10$).
4. 15.5 percent of White dyads were between adult children (respondents) and their parents, compared with 10 percent of Latino dyads ($p < .001$), 9.8 percent of Asian Americans dyads ($p < .001$), and 12.4 percent of Black dyads ($p < .10$).
5. This difference is not statistically significant between Black and White dyads. 10.3 percent of White dyads were between coworkers, compared with 13.6 percent of Asian Americans dyads ($p < .05$), and 14.4 percent of Latino dyads ($p < .05$).
6. Family members were the most common political discussants regardless of immigrant generation status, with 38.2 percent of dyads among first-generation respondents being between family members, 36.8 percent of second-generation respondents, and 42.9 percent of 2.5-generation respondents. The biggest difference based on generation is that 39.9 percent of dyads among second-generation respondents was among close friends, whereas 31.9 percent of 2.5-generation respondent dyads was among close friends.
7. Unfortunately, our data only contains ethnoracial information on respondents who completed our initial survey or the snowball sample survey. As such, the number of dyads in which ethnoracial information for both the initial respondent (the ego) and their discussants (alters) is limited. We also estimated ethnicity using discussants' first and last names (e.g., see Ye et al. 2017) to try to increase our sample size. However, this method seems to underestimate Black discussants, and the results using these estimates are different from those in our snowball sample. For example, we find that 72.0 percent of our dyads are coethnic using the self reported snowball sample data, but we only find that 34.3 percent of our dyads are coethnic using the name estimates. Even if we restrict our name estimates to only those for whom the probability a name matches an ethnicity is very high (over .90), we still only find that about 35 percent of the dyads are between coethnics. It is possible that the snowball sample is biased toward coethnicity if we believe that coethnic discussants would be more likely to participate in the survey in the snowball sample than non-coethnic discussants. However, we did not inform the discussants invited to the snowball survey of the person who listed them, which should make this less likely. Because the probabilistic estimates are likely less reliable than our self-reported ethnicity from the snowball sample, we choose to present the snowball sample results, but we acknowledge the serious limitations in sample size.
8. This includes those who responded as *other* and *refused*.

9. The difference did not reach statistical significance at the $p < .05$ level.
10. http://www.ppic.org/publication/california-voter-and-party-profiles/
11. Unfortunately, our data does not allow us to break out this analysis by nativity and country of origin; our samples are simply too small. We would hypothesize, given past research, that both affect social network composition. That is an important area for future research (Abrajano and Alvarez 2010; Wong et al. 2011; Hajnal and Lee 2011; García Bedolla 2014).
12. See Verba et al. 1995; Rosentsone and Hanson 1993; and Leighley and Matsubayashi 2009 for a more in-depth discussion.
13. The secular group variable is coded as 1 if respondents are members of any of these groups, and 0 otherwise (no secular group membership). The religious group variable is coded as 1 if respondents are members of a religious group, and 0 otherwise.
14. Knowing that self-reported income data is notoriously unreliable, we instead rely on information provided by our data vendor, Political Data, Inc., which geocoded each registered voter's physical registration address from the voter file and then imputed these variables for each registered voter based on the census information for that individual's census tract.

Chapter 4

1. Full details on how we operationalize these variables is available in Chapter 2.
2. These differences are statistically significant at ($p < .001$) level.
3. The dependent variable is the average level of (dis)agreement across the six efficacy items described in Table 3.1, rescaled to range between 0 and 1, just as shown in Figure 3.1. Thus, efficacy scores closer to 1 are the most efficacious and scores closer to 0 are least efficacious.

Chapter 5

1. We could imagine these effects being even more problematic in cases in which information gets translated from one language to another. Among immigrant communities, for example, children are sometimes responsible for translating political information for their parents and other family members. Given the complexity of the political system, it is possible that information can get lost depending on the quality of the translation or the age and experience of the translator. This is an interesting topic for future researchers to explore.
2. Another way to measure political knowledge is what Eveland and Hively (2009) refer to as the knowledge structure density (KSD), which is defined as the extent to which individuals see connections or relationships among various concepts within the political domain—issues, individuals, or networks. The survey items asked respondents to assess how interconnected certain issues were (e.g., heathcare, energy costs, education, unemployment, etc.). They also use a measure capturing knowledge of candidates' issue stances about the two major presidential candidates. Network size

predicts political knowledge (measured as KSD) as does discussion frequency. This suggests that those with larger networks tend to see politics as more closely related to one another.

3. https://www.americanprogress.org/issues/race/news/2016/04/25/136361/5-things-to-know-about-communities-of-color-and-environmental-justice/
4. The responses to each of these statements was based on a 5-point scale ranging from strongly disagree to strongly agree.
5. Refer to Chapter 2 for a detailed explanation on how these variables were measured.
6. These variables are coded in the same manner as in earlier analyses. Please see discussion in Chapter 2.
7. Note that the coefficient on discussion frequency is statistically significant at the $p < .01$ level in the U.S.-born sample, and $p < .10$ level in the foreign-born sample. This difference is likely due to the sample size.
8. These distributions are available in Table A5.1 of the Appendix.
9. Each question is measured on a scale of 1 to 5, and the average difference is .105.

Chapter 6

1. The survey question was "Some people participate in groups and organizations while others do not. Do you currently belong to, volunteer with, attend meetings of, or pay dues for any of the following types of groups? Please check all that apply. Religious group, neighborhood or community organization, labor union, professional organization, ethnic/cultural organization, issue-oriented political organization (e.g. environment, immigration, etc.), political party, civic association (e.g. Rotary club, Lyons club), other (please explain), refused."
2. The specific activities were: signed a paper or online petition; shared, reblogged, or retweeted news articles or petitions on social media; attended a political speech, march, rally, or demonstration; talked about politics on social media, given money to a political candidate; given money to an organization or cause; volunteered for a political campaign or political cause; contacted a government official either in person, by phone, email, social media, or with a letter; talked to anyone and try to show them why they would vote for or against one of the ballot initiatives or candidates; or joined a local community organization.
3. Because statewide elections have the highest turnout levels, we believe this is the most appropriate way to measure vote propensity among our respondents. It also is a common parameter used by our partner groups to determine which voters to target for outreach, making it the best measure to use in our analysis.
4. Please see the Appendix for results analyzing the two most recent single elections (Tables A6.1–A6.6). Looking specifically at the November 2016 election, it appears that none of the political discussion network characteristics was significantly associated with turnout, regardless of nativity or ethnorace. Network characteristics were significantly associated with turnout in the June 2016 primaries, however. Specifically, there is a positive association between partisan homogeneity and turnout among

the U.S. born and foreign born. Network size was not associated with turnout. In the 2016 primary, discussion frequency was positively associated with turnout among the U.S. born but not the foreign born. Partisan homogeneity was positively associated with turnout in the June 2016 primary among Asian Americans and White respondents, but not Black or Latino respondents.

Chapter 7

1. https://www.census.gov/content/dam/Census/library/working-papers/2009/demo/us-pop-proj-2000-2050/analytical-document09.pdf
2. Leighley and Matsubayahi's study (2009) is limited to looking at the relationship of political discussion networks and policy preferences, specifically attitudes toward affirmative action and assistance for Blacks.
3. Although our analyses do not include class, we encourage future researchers to do so.

References

Aarøe, Lene, and Michael Bang Petersen. 2018. "Cognitive Biases and Communication Strength in Social Networks: The Case of Episodic Frames." *British Journal of Political Science* 1–21.

Abraído-Lanza, Ana F., Sandra E. Echeverría, and Karen R. Flórez. 2016. "Latino Immigrants, Acculturation, and Health: Promising New Directions in Research." *Annual Review of Public Health* 37: 219–236.

Abrajano, Marisa. 2010. *Campaigning to the New American Electorate: Advertising to Latino Voters*. Palo Alto, CA: Stanford University Press.

Abrajano, Marisa. 2015. "Re-Examining the Racial Gap in Political Knowledge." *Journal of Politics* 65: 31–49.

Abrajano, Marisa, and R. Michael Alvarez. 2010. "Assessing the Causes and Effects of Political Trust Amongst U.S. Latinos." *American Politics Research* 38 (1): 110–141.

Abrajano, Marisa A., and R. Michael Alvarez. 2012. *New Faces, New Voices: The Hispanic Electorate in America*. Princeton, NJ: Princeton University Press.

Abrams, Samuel, Torben Iversen, and David Soskice. 2010. "Informal Social Networks and Rational Voting." *British Journal of Political Science* 41: 229–257.

Abramson, Paul.1983. *Political Attitudes in America: Formation and Change*. San Francisco: W. H. Freeman.

Ahn, T. K., Robert Huckfeldt, and John Barry Ryan. 2014. "Experts, Activists, and Democratic Politics: Are Electorates Self-Educating?" In *Experts, Activists, and Democratic Politics: Are Electorates Self-Educating?*, Cambridge Studies in Public Opinion and Political Psychology. Cambridge: Cambridge University Press, 2014.

Alexander, Michelle. 2010. *The New Jim Crow: Mass Incarceration in the Age of Colorblindness*. New York: The Free Press.

Almeida, J., S. V. Subramanian, I. Kawachi, and B. E. Molnar. 2011. "Is Blood Thicker than Water? Social Support, Depression, and the Modifying Role of Ethnicity/Nativity Status." *Journal of Epidemiology and Community Health* 65: 51–56.

Almond, Gabriel, and Sydney Verba. 1963. *The Civic Culture*. Princeton, NJ: Princeton University Press.

Alvarez, R. Michael, and Lisa Garcia Bedolla. 2003. "The Foundations of Latino Partisanship: Evidence from the 2000 Election." *Journal of Politics* 65: 31–49.

Applegate, Brandon K., Francis T. Cullen, and Bonnie Sue Fisher. 2002. "Public Views toward Crime and Correctional Policies: Is There a Gender Gap?" *Journal of Criminal Justice* 30 (2): 89–100.

Atkeson, Lonna Rae, Lisa A. Bryant, Thad E. Hall, Kyle L. Saunders, and R. Michael Alvarez. 2010. "A New Barrier to Participation: Heterogeneous Application of Voter Identification Policies." *Electoral Studies* 29 (1): 66–73.

Baldassari, Delia, and Mario Diani. 2007. "The Integrative Power of Civic Networks." *American Journal of Sociology* 113 (3): 735–780.

Balogun, Oluwakemi M. 2011. "No Necessary Tradeoff: Context, Life Course, and Social Networks in the Identity Formation of Second-Generation Nigerians in the USA." *Ethnicities* 11 (4): 436–466.

Barreto, Matt A., Mara Cohen-Marks, and Nathan D. Woods. 2009. "Are All Precincts Created Equal? The Prevalence of Low-Quality Precincts in Low-Income and Minority Communities." *Political Research Quarterly* 62 (3): 445–458.

Barreto, Matt A., Lorrie Frasure-Yokley, Edward D. Vargas, and Janelle Wong. 2018. "Best Practices in Collecting Online Data with Asian, Black, Latino, and White Respondents: Evidence from the 2016 Collaborative Multiracial Post-Election Survey." *Politics, Groups, and Identities* 6 (1): 171–180.

Bello, Jason, and Meredith Rolfe. 2014. "Is Influence Mightier Than Selection? Forging Agreement in Political Discussion Networks During a Campaign." *Social Networks* 36: 134–56.

Beltrán, Cristina. 2013. "Crossings and Correspondences: Rethinking Intersectionality and the Category Latino." *Politics and Gender* 9 (4): 479–483.

Bennett, Stephen, Stacie Rhine, and Richard Flickinger. 2000. Reading's Impact on Democratic Citizenship in America. *Political Behavior* 22 (3): 167–195.

Berelson, Bernard, Paul F. Lazarsfeld, and William McPhee. 1944. *Voting: A Study of Opinion Formation in a Presidential Campaign*. Chicago: University of Chicago Press.

Birch, Tracy. 2013. *Trading Democracy for Justice: Criminal Convictions and the Decline of Neighborhood Political Participation*. Chicago: University of Chicago Press.

Bisgin, Halil, Nitin Agarwal, and Xiaowei Xu. 2010. "Investigating Homophily in Online Social Networks," *2010 IEEE/WIC/ACM International Conference on Web Intelligence and Intelligent Agent Technology*, Toronto, ON, 533–536.

Bobo, Lawrence D., and Frank Gilliam. 1990. "Race, Sociopolitical Participation and Empowerment." *American Political Science Review* 84 (2): 377–393.

Bobo, Lawrence, James Johnson, Barry Bluestone, Irene Browne, Sheldon Danziger, Philip Moss, . . . Chris Tilly. *Multi-City Study of Urban Inequality, 1992–1994: [Atlanta, Boston, Detroit, and Los Angeles]*. Ann Arbor, MI: Inter-university Consortium for Political and Social Research [distributor], 2008-04-23. https://doi.org/10.3886/ICPSR02535.v3

Bolsen, Toby, James N. Druckman, and Fay Lomax Cook. 2014. "The Influence of Partisan Motivated Reasoning on Public Opinion." *Political Behavior* 36 (2): 235–262.

Bond, Robert M., Christopher J. Fariss, Jason J. Jones, Adam DI Kramer, Cameron Marlow, Jaime E. Settle, and James H. Fowler. 2012. "A 61-million-person experiment in social influence and political mobilization." *Nature* 489 (7415): 295.

Bullard, Robert, and Benjamin Chavis, Jr. 1999. *Environmental Racism: Voices from the Grassroots*. Boston: South End Press.

Burns, Nancy, Kay Lehman Schlozman, and Sidney Verba. 2001. *The Private Roots of Public Action: Gender, Equality, and Political Participation*. Cambridge, MA: Harvard University Press.

Bursztyn, Leonardo, and Robert Jensen. 2017. "Social Image and Economic Behavior in the Field: Identifying, Understanding, and Shaping Social Pressure." *Annual Review of Economics* 9: 131–153.

Carll, Erin. 2017. "Disparate Vantage Points: Race, Gender, County Context, and Attitudes About Harsh Punishments in the US." *Social Science Research* 64: 137–153.

Carlson, Taylor. 2018. "Modeling Political Information Transmission as a Game of Telephone." *Journal of Politics* 80 (1): 348–352.

Carlson, Taylor N. 2019. "Through the Grapevine: Informational Consequences of Interpersonal Political Communication." *American Political Science Review* 113 (2): 325–339.

Carlson, Taylor N., Marisa Abrajano, and Lisa García Bedolla. 2019. "Political Discussion Networks and Political Engagement among Voters of Color." *Political Research Quarterly*.

Carroll, Susan J., and Richard L. Fox. 2018. *Gender and Elections: Shaping the Future of American Politics*, 4th ed. Cambridge, MA: Cambridge University Press.

Castañeda, Heide, Seth M. Holmes, Daniel S. Madrigal, Maria-Elena DeTrinidad Young, Naomi Beyeler, and James Quesada. 2015. "Immigration as a Social Determinant of Health." *Annual Review of Public Health* 36: 375–392.

Cattenberg, Gabriela, and Alejandro Moreno.2006. "The Individual Bases of Political Trust: Trends in New and Established Democracies." *International Journal of Public Opinion Research* 18 (1): 31–48.

Centola, Damon, and Michael Macy. 2007. "Complex Contagions and the Weakness of Long Ties." *American Journal of Sociology* 113 (3): 702–734.

Chan, Sophia. "Effects of attention to campaign coverage on political trust." International Journal of Public Opinion Research 9.3 (1997): 286–296.

Chiang, Yen-Sheng. 2007. "Birds of Moderately Different Feathers: Bandwagon Dynamics and the Threshold Heterogeneity of Network Neighbors." *Journal of Mathematical Sociology* 31: 47–69.

Cho, Wendy K. Tam. 1999. "Naturalization, Socialization, Participation: Immigrants and (Non-) Voting." *The Journal of Politics* 61 (4): 1140–1155.

Christakis, Nicholas A., and James H. Fowler. 2009. *Connected: The surprising power of our social networks and how they shape our lives.* Little, Brown and Company. Hachette Book Group. New York, NY.

Chwe, Michael S. 1999. "Structure and Strategy in Collective Action." *American Journal of Sociology* 105 (1): 128–156.

Coffé, H., and C. Bolzendahl. 2010. "Same Game, Different Rules? Gender Differences in Political Participation." *Sex Roles* 62 (5–6): 318–333. doi:10.1007/s11199-009-9729-y

Cohen, Jean L. 1999. "Changing Paradigms of Citizenship and the Exclusiveness of the Demos." *International Sociology* 14 (3): 245–268.

Cole, Elizabeth, and Abigail J. Stewart. 1996. "Meanings of Political Participation among Black and White Women: Political Identity and Social Responsibility." *Journal of Personality and Social Psychology* 71: 130–140.

Conover, Pamela Johnston, Donald D. Searing, and Ivor M. Crewe. 2002. "The Deliberative Potential of Political Discussion." *British Journal of Political Science* 32 (1): 21–62.

Curran, Sara R., and Estela Rivero-Fuentes. 2003. "Engendering Migrant Networks: The Case of Mexican Migration." *Demography* 40 (2): 289–307.

Davis, Benjamin, Guy Stecklov, and Paul Winters. 2002. "Domestic and International Migration from Rural Mexico: Disaggregating the Effects of Network Structure and Composition." *Population Studies* 56: 291–309.

Davis, James Allan, and Tom W. Smith: *General Social Survey(s), year(s).* (Machine-readable data file). Principal Investigator, James A. Davis; Director and Co-Principal Investigator, Tom W. Smith; Co-Principal Investigator, Peter V. Marsden, NORC ed. Chicago: National Opinion Research Center, producer, 2002; Storrs, CT: The Roper Center for Public Opinion Research, University of Connecticut, distributor. Microcomputer format and codebook prepared and distributed by MicroCase Corporation.

Dawson, Michael C. 1994. *Behind the Mule. Race and Class in African American Politics* Chicago: University of Chicago Press.

Dawson, Michael C. 2001. *Black Visions: The Roots of Contemporary African-American Ideologies*. Chicago: University of Chicago Press.

Delli Carpini, Michael X., and Scott Keeter. 1996. *What Americans Know about Politics and Why It Matters*. New Haven: Yale University Press.

DeSipio, Louis. 1996. *Counting on the Latino Vote: Latinos as a New Electorate*. Charlottesville, VA: University of Virginia Press.

DiMaggio, Paul, and Filiz Garip. 2012. "Network Effects and Social Inequality." *Annual Review of Sociology* 38: 93–118.

Dittmar, Kelly, Kira Sanbonmatsu, and Susan J. Carroll. 2018. *A Seat at the Table: Congresswomen's Perspectives on Why Their Presence Matters*. New York: Oxford University Press.

Djupe, Paul A., and Anand Edward Sokhey. 2014. "The distribution and determinants of socially supplied political expertise." *American Politics Research* 42 (2): 199–225.

Dobard, John, Leila Forouzan, and Alejandra Ramirez-Zarate. 2017. "Making Public Participation Equitable: Recommendations for an Office of Civic Engagement in Los Angeles." https://www.advancementprojectca.org/wp-content/uploads/2018/11/OCE-Report_Final_.pdf

Donato, Katharine, and Ebony M. Duncan. 2011. "Migration, Social Networks, and Child Health in Mexican Families." *Journal of Marriage and Family* 73: 713–728.

Downs, Anthony. 1957. *An Economic Theory of Democracy*. New York: Harper & Row.

Ebert, Kim, and Dina G. Okamoto. 2013. "Social Citizenship, Integration, and Collective Action: Immigrant Civic Engagement in the United States." *Social Forces* 91 (4): 1267–1292.

Erel, Umut. 2010. "Migrating Cultural Capital: Bourdieu in Migration Studies." *Sociology* 44 (4): 642–660.

Erickson, Emily, and Nicholos Occhiuto. 2017. "Social Networks and Macrosocial Change." *Annual Review of Sociology* 43: 229–248.

Eveland, William P. 2004. "The Effect of Political Discussion in Producing Informed Citizens: The Roles of Information, Motivation, and Elaboration. *Political Communciation* 21 (4): 177–193.

Eveland, William P., and Osei Appiah. 2019. "A National Conversation About Race? Political Discussion Across Lines of Racial and Partisan Difference." *Journal of Race, Ethnicity and Politics* 1–27.

Eveland, William P., and M. H. Hively. 2009. "Political Discussion Frequency, Network Size, and "Heterogeneity" of Discussion as Predictors of Political Knowledge and Participation." *Journal of Communication* 59: 205–224.

Eveland, William P., and Steven B. Kleinman. 2013. "Comparing General and Political Discussion Networks Within Voluntary Organizations Using Social Network Analysis". *Political Behavior* 35 (1): 65–87.

Feldman, Stanley. 1983. "The Measurement and Meaning of Political Trust." *Political Methodologist* 9: 341–354.

Fraga, Luis R., John A. Garcia, Rodney E. Hero, Michael Jones-Correa, Valerie Martinez-Ebers, and Gary M. Segura. 2006. "Su Casa Es Nuestra Casa: Latino Politics Research and the Development of American Political Science." *The American Political Science Review* 100 (4): 515–521.

Frey, William H. 2015. "Census Shows Modest Declines in Black-White Segregation." Brookings Institute. https://www.brookings.edu/blog/the-avenue/2015/12/08/census-shows-modest-declines-in-black-white-segregation.

Frymer, Paul. 2010. *Uneasy Alliances: Race and Party Competition in America*. Princeton, NJ: Princeton University Press.

Fu, Hongyun, and Mark J. VanLandingham. 2012. "Mental Health Consequences of International Migration for Vietnamese Americans and Mediating Effects of Physical Health and Social Networks: Results from a Natural Experiment Approach." *Demography* 49: 393–424.

García Bedolla, Lisa. 2005. *Fluid Borders: Latino Power, Identity, and Politics in Los Angeles*. Berkeley, CA: University of California Press.

García Bedolla, Lisa. 2007. "Intersections of Inequality: Understanding Marginalization and Privilege in the Post-Civil Rights Era." *Politics & Gender* 3 (2): 232–248.

García Bedolla, Lisa. 2009. "Latino Migration and US Foreign Policy." *Spring Berkeley Review of Latin American Studies* 50.

García Bedolla, Lisa. 2014. *Latino Politics*, 2nd ed. Cambridge, UK: Polity.

García Bedolla, Lisa, and Melissa Michelson. 2012. *Mobilizing Inclusion: Transforming the Electorate Through Get-Out-the-Vote Campaigns*. New Haven, CT: Yale University Press.

Gardner, Martha. 2005. *The Qualities of a Citizen: Women, Immigration, and Citizenship, 1870–1965*. Princeton, NJ: Princeton University Press.

Garrett, R. Kelly. 2009a. "Echo Chambers Online?: Politically Motivated Selective Exposure among Internet News Users." *Journal of Computer-Mediated Communication* (14): 265–285.

Garrett, R. Kelly. 2009b. "Politically Motivated Reinforcement Seeking: Reframing the Selective Exposure Debate." *Journal of Communication* 59 (4): 676–699.

Gastil, John, and James P Dillard. 1999. "Increasing Political Sophistication through Public Deliberation." *Political Communication* 16 (1): 3–23.

Gerber, Alan S., Donald P. Green, and Christopher W. Larimer. 2008. "Social pressure and voter turnout: Evidence from a large-scale field experiment." *American Political Science Review* 102 (1): 33–48.

Gidengil, Elisabeth, and Dietlind Stolle. 2009. "The Role of Social Networks in Immigrant Women's Political Incorporation." *International Migration Review* 43 (4): 727–763.

Goldberg, David T. 2002. *The Racial State*. Cambridge, MA: Blackwell Publisher.

Gurin, Patricia. 1985. "Women's Gender Consciousness." *Public Opinion Quarterly* 49 (2): 143–163.

Gutierrez, David. 1995. *Walls and Mirrors: Mexicans Americans, Mexican Immigrants and the Politics of Ethnicity*. Berkeley, CA: University of California Press.

Hajnal, Zoltan, and Mark Baldassare. 2001. *Finding Common Ground: Racial and Ethnic Attitudes in California*. San Francisco: Public Policy Institute of California.

Hajnal, Zoltan, Nazita Lajaverdi, and Lindsay Nielsen. 2017. "Voter Identification Laws and the Suppression of Minority Votes." *The Journal of Politics* 79 (2): 363–379.

Hajnal, Zoltan, and Taeku Lee. 2011. *Why Americans Don't Join the Party: Race, Immigration, and the Failure (of Political Parties) to Engage the Electorate*. Princeton, NJ: Princeton University Press.

Hall, Peter, and Michèle Lamont. 2013. "Why Social Relations Matter for Politics and Successful Societies." *Annual Review of Political Science* 16: 49–71.

Hancock, Ange-Marie. 2016. *Intersectionality: An Intellectual History*. New York: Oxford University Press.

Haney López, Ian. 1996. *White by Law: The Legal Construction of Race*. New York: New York University Press.

Hardin, Russell. 2002. *Trust and Trustworthiness*. New York: Russell Sage.

Hardy-Fanta, Carol, Pei-Te Lien, Diane Pinderhughes, and Christine Sierra. 2016. *Contested Transformations: Race, Gender and Leadership in 21st Century America*. New York: Cambridge University Press.

Hellerstein, Judith K., Melissa McInerney, and David Neumark. 2010. "Spatial Mismatch, Immigrant Networks, and Hispanic Employment in the United States." *Annals of Economics and Statistics* 99/100: 141–167.

Hero, Rodney. 2000. *Faces of Inequality: Social Diversity in American Politics*. New York: Oxford University Press.

Huckfeldt, Robert, Paul E. Johnson, and John Sprague. 2004. *Political Disagreement: The Survival of Diverse Opinions Within Communication Networks*. New York: Cambridge University Press.

Huckfeldt, Robert, and John Sprague. 1988. "Choice, Social Structure, and Political Information: The Information Coercion of Minorities." *American Journal of Political Science* 32 (2): 467–482.

Huckfeldt, Robert R., and John Sprague. 1995. *Citizens, Politics, and Social Communication: Information and Influence in an Election Campaign*. New York: Cambridge University Press.

Huckfeldt, Robert, and John Sprague. 2006. *Presidential Election Campaign Study, 1984: [South Bend, Indiana]*. Ann Arbor, MI: Inter-university Consortium for Political and Social Research [distributor], 2006-01-12. https://doi.org/10.3886/ICPSR06522.v1

Huckfeldt, Robert, and John Sprague. 2007. *Indianapolis-St. Louis Election Study, 1996–1997*. Ann Arbor, MI: Inter-university Consortium for Political and Social Research [distributor], 2007-05-07. https://doi.org/10.3886/ICPSR02962.v2

Hunter, Lori M., Jessie K. Luna, and Rachel M. Norton. 2015. "Environmental Dimensions of Migration." *Annual Review of Sociology* 41: 377–397.

Ihme, T., and M. Tausendpfund. 2018. "Gender Differences in Political Knowledge: Bringing Situation Back in." *Journal of Experimental Political Science* 5 (1): 39–55. doi:10.1017/XPS.2017.21

Jacobson, Matthew Frye. 1998. *Whiteness of a Different Color: European Immigrants and the Alchemy of Race*. Cambridge, MA: Harvard University Press.

Jardina, Ashley. 2019. *White Identity Politics*. New York: Cambridge University Press.

Jewell, R. Todd, and David J. Molina. 2009. "Mexican Migration to the U.S.: A Comparison of Income and Network Effects." *Eastern Economic Journal* 35: 144–159.

Jones-Correa, Michael. 1998. *Between Two Nations: The Political Predicament of Latinos in New York City*. Ithaca, NY: Cornell University Press.

Karpowitz, Christopher F., Tali Mendelberg, and Lee Shaker. 2012. "Gender Inequality in Deliberative Participation." *American Political Science Review* 106 (3): 533–547.

Karpowitz, Christopher F., and Tali Mendelberg. 2014. *The Silent Sex: Gender, Deliberation, and Institutions*. Princeton, NJ: Princeton University Press.

Kim, Claire Jean. 2000. *Bitter Fruit: The Politics of Black-Korean Conflict in New York City*. New Haven, CT: Yale University Press.

King, Desmond. 2000. *Making Americans: Immigration, Race, and the Origins of the Diverse Democracy*. Cambridge, MA: Harvard University Press.

Klofstad, Casey A. 2011. *Civic Talk: Peers, Politics and the Future of Democracy.* Philadelphia: Temple University Press.

Klofstad, Casey, and Benjamin Bishin. 2014. "Do Social Ties Encourage Immigrant Voters to Participate in Other Campaign Activities?" *Social Science Quarterly* 95: 295–310.

Klofstad, Casey A., Scott D. McClurg, and Meredith Rolfe. 2009. "Measurement of Political Discussion Networks." *Public Opinion Quarterly* 73 (3): 462–483.

Klofstad, Casey A., Anand Edward Sokhey, and Scott D. McClurg. 2013. "Disagreeing about Disagreement: How Conflict in Social Networks Affects Political Behavior." *American Journal of Political Science* 57 (1): 120–134.

Knoke, David. 1990. "Networks of Political Action: Toward Theory Construction." *Social Forces* 68 (4): 1041–1063.

Kraft, Patrick W. n.d. "Let's Talk Politics: A Naive Approach for Measuring Political Sophistication." Paper presented at the 33rd Annual Meeting of the Society for Political Methodology. July 2016. Houston, TX.

Krissman, Fred. 2005. "Sin Coyote ni Patrón: Why the 'Migrant Network' Fails to Explain International Migration." *International Migration Review* 39 (1): 4–44.

Kunda, Ziva. 1990. "The Case for Motivated Reasoning." *Psychological Bulletin* 8 (3): 480–498.

Lacy, Stephen and Michael Stamm. 2016. "Reassessing the People's Choice: Revisiting a Classic and Excavating Lessons for Research About Media and Voting." *Mass Communication and Society* 19 (2): 105–126.

Lake, Ronald La Due, and Robert Huckfeldt. 1998. "Social Capital, Social Networks, and Political Participation." *Political Psychology* 19 (3): 567–584.

Lee, Jennifer, and Min Zhou. 2015. *The Asian American Achievement Paradox.* New York: Russell Sage Foundation.

Leighley, Jan E. 2001. *Strength in numbers?: The political mobilization of racial and ethnic minorities.* Princeton University Press.

Leighley, Jan E., and Tetsuya Matsubayashi. 2009. "The Implications of Class, Race, and Ethnicity for Political Networks." *American Politics Research 37* (5): 824–855.

Levi, Margaret, and Laura Stoker. 2000. "Political Trust and Trustworthiness." *Annual Review of Political Science* 3: 475–507.

Levitan, L. C., and P. S. Visser. 2009. Social Network Composition and Attitude Strength: Exploring the Dynamics within Newly Formed Social Networks. *Journal of Experimental Social Psychology* 45 (5): 1057–1067.

Lewis, Kevin. 2013. "The Limits of Racial Prejudice." *PNAS* 110 (47): 18814–18819.

Lin, Nan. 1999. "Social Networks and Status Attainment." *Annual Review of Sociology* 25: 467–487.

Liu, Mao-Mei. 2013. "Migrant Networks and International Migration: Testing Weak Ties." *Demography* 50: 1243–1277.

Logan, John R., Jennifer Darrah, and Sookhee Oh. 2012. "The Impact of Race and Ethnicity, Immigration and Political Context on Participation in American Electoral Politics." *Social Forces* 90 (3): 993–1022.

Lyons, Jeffrey, Anand E. Sokhey, Scott D. McClurg, and Drew Seib. 2016. "Personality, Interpersonal Disagreement, and Electoral Information." *The Journal of Politics* 78 (3): 806–821.

Markus, G. B. 1979. The Political Environment and the Dynamics of Public Attitudes: A Panel Study. *American Journal of Political Science* 23: 338–359.

Masuoka, Natalie, and Jane Junn. 2013. *The Politics of Belonging: Race, Public Opinion, and Immigration.* Chicago: University of Chicago Press.

McDevitt, Michael, and Steven H. Chaffee. 2002. "From Top-Down to Trickle-Up Influence: Revisiting Assumptions about the Family in Political Socialization." *Political Communication* 19: 281–301.

McKenzie, David, and Hillel Rapoport. 2010. "Self-Selection Patterns in Mexico-U.S. Migration: The Role of Migration Networks." *Review of Economics and Statistics* 92 (4): 811–821.

McLeod, J. M., and L. Becker. 1981. "The Uses and Gratifications Approach." In *Handbook of Political Communication,* edited by D. Nimmo and K. Sanders, 67–100. Thousand Oaks, CA: Sage.

McPherson, Miller, Lynn Smith-Lovin, and James M. Cook. 2001. "Birds of a Feather: Homophily in Social Networks." *Annual Review of Sociology* 27 (1): 415–444.

Mendelberg, Tali, and Christopher Karpowitz. 2007. "How People Deliberate about Justice: Groups, Gender, and Decision Rules." In *Deliberation, Participation and Democracy*, edited by Shawn Rosenberg, 101–129. London: Palgrave Macmillan.

Mendelberg, Tali, Christopher F. Karpowitz, and Nicholas Goedert. 2014. "Does descriptive representation facilitate women's distinctive voice? How gender composition and decision rules affect deliberation." *American Journal of Political Science* 58 (2): 291–306.

Mendelberg, Tali, Christopher F. Karpowitz, and J. Baxter Oliphant. 2014. "Gender inequality in deliberation: Unpacking the black box of interaction." *Perspectives on Politics* 12 (1): 18–44.

Meyer, David S., and Debra C. Minkoff. 2004. "Conceptualizing Political Opportunity." *Social Forces* 82 (4): 1457–1492.

Michelson, Melissa R. 2001. "Trust in Chicago Latinos". Journal of Urban Affairs 23: 323–334.

Michelson, Melissa R. 2003. "The Corrosive Effect of Acculturation: How Mexican Americans Lose Political Trust." *Social Science Quarterly* 84: 919–933.

Miller, Arthur. 1974. "Political Issues and Trust in Government: 1964–1970." *American Political Science Review* 68: 951–972.

Morehouse Mendez, Jeanette, and Tracy Osborn. 2010. "Gender and the Perception of Knowledge in Political Discussion." *Political Research Quarterly* 63 (2): 269–279.

Mouw, Ted. 2006. "Estimating the Causal Effect of Social Capital: A Review of Recent Research." *Annual Review of Sociology* 32: 79–102.

Mouw, Ted, Sergio Chavez, Heather Edelblute, and Ashton Verdery. 2014. "Binational Social Networks and Assimilation: A Test of the Importance of Transnationalism." *Social Problems* 61 (3): 329–359.

Mutz, Diana C. 2002. "The Consequences of Cross-Cutting Networks for Political Participation." *American Journal of Political Science* 46: 838–855.

Mutz, Diana C. 2006. *Hearing the Other Side: Deliberative versus Participatory Democracy.* New York: Cambridge University Press.

Neville, Stephen, Jeffery Adams, Jed Montayre, Peter Larmer, Nick Garrett, Christine Stephens, and Fiona Alpass. 2018. "Loneliness in Men 60 Years and Over: The Association With Purpose in Life." *American Journal of Men's Health* 12 (4): 730–739.

Ngai, Mae. 2004. *Impossible Subjects: Illegal Aliens and the Making of Modern America.* Princeton, NJ: Princeton University Press.

Nyhan, Brendan, and Jason Reifler. 2010. "When Corrections Fail: The Persistence of Political Misperceptions." *Political Behavior* 32 (2): 303–330.

Omi, Michael and Howard Winant. 1994. *Racial Formation in the United States*. New York, NY: Routledge.

Pantoja, Adrian D., Ricardo Ramirez, and Gary M. Segura. 2001. "Citizens by Choice, Voters by Necessity: Patterns in Political Mobilization by Naturalized Latinos." *Political Research Quarterly* 54 (4): 729–750.

Parker, Christopher. 2009. *Fighting for Democracy: Black Veterans and the Struggle against White Supremacy in the Postwar South*. Princeton, NJ: Princeton University Press.

Pask, Gordon. 1980. "Developments in Conversation Theory - Part 1." *International Journal of Man-Machine Studies* 13: 357–411.

Patterson, Thomas E. 1994. *Out of Order*. New York: Knopf.

Pearson, Adam, Matthew Ballew, Sarah Naiman, and Jonathon Schuldt. 2017. "Race, Class, Gender and Climate Change Communication." In *Oxford Research Encyclopedia, Climate Science* 10.1093/acrefore/9780190228620.013.412.

Perez, Efren. 2015. "Mind the Gap: Why Large Group Deficits in Political Knowledge Emerge and What to Do About Them". *Political Behavior* 37 (4): 933–954.

Pinderhughes, Diane. 1990. "The Articulation of Black Interests by Black Civil Rights, Professional and Religious Organizations." In *The Social and Political Implications of the 1984 Jesse Jackson Presidential Campaign*, edited by Lorenzo Morris, 125–134. New York: Praeger.

Portes, Alejandro, and Ruben Rumbaut. 2014. 4th Edition. *Immigrant America: A Portrait*. Berkeley, CA: University of California Press.

Presser, Stanley. 1990. "Can Changes in Context Reduce Vote Overreporting in Surveys?" *Public Opinion Quarterly* 54 (4): 586–593.

Putnam, Robert D. 2000. "Bowling Alone: America's Declining Social Capital." In *Culture and Politics*, edited by Lane Crothers and Charles Lockhart, 223–234. New York: Palgrave Macmillan.

Ramakrishnan, S. Karthick. 2005. *Democracy in Immigrant America: Changing Demographics and Political Participation*. Palo Alto, CA: Stanford University Press.

Ramakrishnan, S. Karthick, and Irene Bloemraad, eds. 2008. *Civic Hopes and Political Realities: Immigrants, Community Organizations, and Political Engagement*. New York: Russell Sage Foundation.

Ramakrishnan, S. Karthick, and Thomas J. Espenshade. 2001. "Immigrant Incorporation and Political Participation in the United States." *International Migration Review* 35 (3): 870–909.

Reardon, Sean F., Joseph Townsend, and Lindsay Fox. 2015. "Characteristics of the Joint Distribution of Race and Income Among Neighborhoods." (CEPA Working Paper No.15-01). Retrieved from Stanford Center for Education Policy Analysis: http://cepa.stanford.edu/wp15-01 [last accessed 20 Dec 2019].

Redlawsk, David P. 2002. "Hot Cognition or Cool Consideration? Testing the Effects of Motivated Reasoning on Political Decision Making." *The Journal of Politics* 64 (4): 1021–1044.

Ryan, John Barry. 2011. "Accuracy and bias in perceptions of political knowledge." *Political Behavior* 33 (2): 335–356.

Sapiro, Virginia. 2004. "Not Your Parents' Political Socialization: Introduction for a New Generation." *Annual Review of Political Science* 7: 1–23.

Sapiro, Virginia, and Pamela Johnston Conover. 1997. "The Variable Gender Basis of Electoral Politics: Gender and Context in the 1992 US Election." *British Journal of Political Science* 27 (4): 497–523.

Scheufele, Dietram A., Matthew Nisbet, Dominique Brossard, and Eric Nisbet. 2004. "Social Structure and Citizenship: Examining the Impacts of Social Setting, Network Heterogeneity, and Informational Variables on Political Participation." *Political Communication* 21 (3): 315–338.

Settle, Jaime E. 2018. *Frenemies: How Social Media Polarizes America*. Cambridge, UK: Cambridge University Press.

Settle, Jaime, Robert Bond, and Justin Levitt. 2011. "The Social Origins of Political Behavior." *American Politics Research* 39 (2): 239–263.

Settle, Jaime E., and Taylor N. Carlson n.d. "Disinclined and Disengaged: How Our Brains, Bodies, and Biases Lead Us to Avoid Politics." *American Politics Research* 39 (2): 239–263.

Shaw, Daron, Rodolfo O. De La Garza, and Jongho Lee. 2000. "Examining Latino turnout in 1996: A three-state, validated survey approach." *American Journal of Political Science* 44 (2): 338–346.

Shingles, R. D. 1981. "Black Consciousness and Political Participation: The Missing Link." *American Political Science Review* 75: 76–91.

Shoda, Tonya M., Allen R. McConnell, and Robert J. Rydell. 2014. "Having Explicit-Implicit Evaluation Discrepancies Triggers Race-Based Motivated Reasoning." *Social Cognition* 32 (2): 190–202.

Silver, Brian D., Paul R. Abramson, and Barbara A. Anderson. 1986. "The Presence of Others and Overreporting of Voting in American National Elections." *Public Opinion Quarterly* 50 (2): 228–239.

Sinclair, Betsy. 2012. *The Social Citizen: Peer Networks and Political Behavior*. Chicago: University of Chicago Press.

Smith, Rogers. 1997. *Civil Ideals: Conflicting Visions of Citizenship in US History*. New Haven, CT: Yale University Press.

Smith, Rogers. 2003. *Stories of Peoplehood: The Politics and Morals of Political Membership*. New York: Cambridge University Press.

Smith, Sandra. 2010. "Race and Trust." *Annual Review of Sociology* 36: 453–475.

Song, H., Minozzi, W., Lazer, D., Neblo, M. A., and Ognyanova, K. The Accidental Pundit: Intention and Opportunity in Political Discussion. Paper presented at the 9th Annual Political Networks Workshops & Conference (PolNet 2016), June 2016. Retrieved from SSRN: https://ssrn.com/ abstract=2796448.

Soss, Joe, and Vesla Weaver. 2017. Police Are Our Government: Politics, Political Science, and the Policing of Race–Class Subjugated Communities *Annual Review of Political Science* 20 (1): 565–591

Stoker, Laura, and M. Kent Jennings. 2005. "Political Similarity and Influence between Husbands and Wives." In *The Social Logic of Politics*, edited by Alan Zuckerman, 51–74. Philadelphia: Temple University Press.

Stokes, Donald E. 1962. Popular Evaluation of Government: An Empirical Assessment. In *Ethics and Bigness: Scientific, Academic, Religious, Political and Military* edited by H. Cleveland and H. D. Lasswell, 61–72. New York: Harper.

Stoll, Michael A., and Janelle S. Wong. 2007. "Immigration and Civic Participation in a Multiracial and Multiethnic Context." *International Migration Review* 41 (4) 880–908.

Stroud, Natalie Jomini. 2008. "Media Use and Political Predispositions: Revisiting the Concept of Selective Exposure." *Political Behavior* 30 (3): 341–366.

Tannen, D. 1991. "Teachers' Classroom Strategies Should Recognize that Men and Women Use Language Differently." *The Chronicle of Higher Education* 37 (40): Bl, B3.

Tate, Katherine. 1993. *From Protest to Politics: The New Black Voters in American Elections*. Cambridge, MA: Harvard University Press.
Thornbury, Scott, and Diana Slade. 2006. *Conversation: From Description to Pedagogy*. New York: Cambridge University Press.
Tseng, Vivian, and Janelle Wong. 2008. "Political Socialisation in Immigrant Families: Challenging Top-Down Parental Socialisation Models." *Journal of Ethnic and Migration Studies* 34 (1): 151–168.
Verba, Sidney, Kay Lehman Schlozman, and Henry E. Brady. 1995. *Voice and equality: Civic voluntarism in American politics*. Harvard University Press.
Walsh, Katherine Cramer. 2004. *Talking about Politics: Informal Groups and Social Identity in American Life*. Chicago: University of Chicago Press.
Walsh, Katherine Cramer. 2007. *Talking About Race: Community Dialogues and the Politics of Difference*. Chicago: University of Chicago Press.
Weisberg, Yanna, Colin DeYoung, and Jacob Hirsh. 2011. "Gender Differences in Personality across the Ten Aspects of the Big Five." *Frontiers in Psychology* 2: 178
Williams, J. T. 1985. Systematic Influences on Political Trust: The Importance of Perceived Institutional Performance. *Political Methodologist* 11: 125–142.
Wolfinger. Raymond. 1980. *Who Votes?* New Haven, CT: Yale University Press.
Wong, Janelle. 2006. *Democracy's Promise: Immigrants and American Civic Institutions*. Ann Arbor, MI: University of Michigan Press.
Wong, Janelle, S. Karthick Ramakrishnan, Taeku Lee, and Jane Junn. 2011. *Asian American Political Participation: Emerging Constituents and Their Political Identities*. New York: Russell Sage Foundation Press.
Wyattt, Robert, Elihu Katz, and Joohan Kim. 2000. "Bridging the Spheres: Political and Personal Conversation in Public and Private Spaces." *Journal of Communication* 50: 71–92
Ye, Junting, Shuchu Han, Yifan Hu, Baris Coskun, Meizhu Liu, Hong Qin, and Steven Skiena. 2017. "Nationality classification using name embeddings." In *Proceedings of the 2017 ACM on Conference on Information and Knowledge Management*, pp. 1897–1906. ACM.
Young, Iris Marion. 1990. *Justice and the Politics of Difference*. Princeton, NJ: Princeton University Press.
Young, Iris Marion. 2005. "Modernity, Emancipatory Values, and Power: A Rejoinder to Adams and Orloff." *Politics & Gender* 1 (3): 492–500.
Zuckerman, Alan S. (Ed.). 2005. *The Social Logic of Politics: Personal Networks as Contexts for Political Behavior*. Philadelphia, PA: Temple University Press.

Index

Tables and figures are indicated by *t* and *f* following the page number

www.ingramcontent.com/pod-product-compliance
Ingram Content Group UK Ltd.
Pitfield, Milton Keynes, MK11 3LW, UK
UKHW051020210726
13857UKWH00006B/619